THE RELUCTANT ROCKETMAN

A Curious Journey in World Record Breaking

BY

Sarah Kasprowicz

Ray D.

Pete Farnsworth 3/2016
President: Reac. Dyn., Inc.
Manager of Vehicle Engineering
Leah M. Farnsworth
Secretary - Treasurer

M000240332

GreenBean Creative Solutions LLC

www.greenbeancreativesolutions.com

707 West Moreland Blvd., Suite 6

Waukesha, WI 53188

Copyright 2013 by Sarah Kasprowicz

All rights reserved.

ISBN: 0988199475

ISBN 13:   9780988199477

Cover Design: "LandSpeed" Louise Ann Noeth
www.landspeedproductions.biz

CONTENTS

To my parents, Ray and Phyllis,
for your unflappable belief that we could do this and for instilling
a certain confidence and independence in me that fuels my ambition.

To my husband, Paul,
for your support and tireless editing efforts, which made this book
so much better. Your intelligence and thirst for knowledge
amazes me every single day.

To my son, Paul Junior,
for being my constant inspiration.
You have the power to design your dreams and live them.
Believe.

Author's Purpose

The earliest memory I have of The Blue Flame is boasting about it on the school bus. In second grade I would corner my seatmate to inform him or her that my dad was famous. Then I would flash a grainy black and white photo of the rocket car from my prized *Guinness Book of World Records* which I had borrowed (stolen) from my older sister's bookshelf. I had spent hours reading those thin, slippery pages, fascinated with Masuriya Din's 102 inch long mustache, agape at the photo of the tallest man, Robert Wadlow, standing next to his brothers at almost nine feet tall, and horrified by the photo of Murari Mohan Aditya's record breaking fingernails twisting and twirling in bizarre curlicues.

My dad, Ray Dausman, designed and closely managed the fabrication of the rocket engine for The Blue Flame, the fastest American-built car to date. In 1970 The Blue Flame broke the world land speed record and streaked across the Bonneville Salt Flats at 622.407 mph.

The Blue Flame was never talked about in my house when I was growing up. My dad had a framed photo of the rocket car in his office, but he never mentioned it. It wasn't until he saw me reading the *Guinness Book of World Records* that he ever claimed connection with the car.

He simply said, "Did you know that I'm in that book?"

"This book?" I was confused. Was there some gross picture of him with the longest beard or an entry about my dad holding the world record for coin swallowing?

Dad took the book from me and flipped around until he found it. On page 296 was the entry for fastest cars. In the Rocket-Engined category was a picture of the same car Dad had framed in his office.

"Huh," was all I could say.

"That's my rocket engine in The Blue Flame. It's the fastest car in the world," he told me with a smirk.

I didn't believe him right away. My dad loved to pull my leg and was quite adept at doing so with a straight face. But Mom confirmed his story and I've been fascinated ever since. I was full of questions. Why didn't he ever tell us about the world record? How come he never told us that he built the rocket for The Blue Flame? How could it be that he flunked out of Purdue because he couldn't pass a math class, but he was fluent in rocketry formulas? Why is The Blue Flame on permanent display in a German museum?

So come, sit next to me on the bus. This time I have much more than a black and white photo from my *Guinness Book* to share with you.

PROLOGUE

Sarah's Journal Entry-Sinsheim, Germany: 1998

The museum was huge. It was like an airplane hangar with wall to wall horsepower. The shining tile aisles were dotted with gleaming cars of every make, model and year worthy of display. I figured a true auto fan could lapse into a violent seizure with so many classics to choose from. Which spectacular specimen would they approach first? The Mercedes collection? The armored vehicle section? The low-slung sports cars? Too many choices. Too many dreams come true. Luckily, I was immune to such perils. I was interested in just one car, a car I had wondered about most of my life. As we walked down a short flight of stairs, butterflies cartwheeled in the confines of my stomach. Hans Jurgen, Director of Marketing for the Auto & Technik Museum Sinsheim, led the way.

I saw it. The car was parked on a platform in the center of the vast room. I could see a bright blue fuselage with a giant hypodermic needle extending from the glossy cigar-shaped body. I knew the needle was really a metal pitot tube which displayed the airspeed to the oxygen-masked, flame retardant-clad driver riding this rocket the wrong way.

My eyes slid over the Flame, left to right, and took in the impressive blue, silver and gray length. I was surprised how skinny it was. It seemed like I could hug the body at its widest place and have my hands touch on either side. I admit I really felt like doing that. Give it a hug. For my dad. He should be here. After all, it was because of him that the car was built. The Blue Flame was so much a part of his life.

An organ played "The Entertainer" and echoes of clipped conversations of comical disbelief mingled with the laughter of delighted children. "…shau am dieser Corvette…" "Wow! Prima!" "Is that really a…?" "…waren gemacht." "A Bugatti! I can't believe it!" "Schoen, sehr schoen." German and English slid off my ears like raindrops on car wax.

I glanced at Hans Jurgen and he nodded at my unspoken request. Slowly, I climbed onto the platform. Two very large aluminum wheels with custom-made Goodyear tires were planted on either side at the rear of the car. The rocket fired from the back of the car, but it was covered by the fuselage and a Plexiglas window, so I couldn't inspect it further. A tailfin rose above the engine compartment and sloped down to the driver's cockpit and then lower still as it extended a full 38 feet to the sharpened, piercing blue tip. Two small wheels near the front of the car spun very close together, almost looking like one wheel on a three-wheeled car. I knew the official land speed record rules defined a car as having four wheels so this bit of design ingenuity impressed me.

It truly looked like a rocket at rest, waiting for its next launch. I imagined the scream of the rocket and the hiss of the tires as it leapt off the platform with renewed thrust and flame, reborn to take the record again.

The cockpit was compact. The driver, Gary Gabelich, must have been a small guy because I knew I would have had a hell of a time stuffing myself inside. A few gauges and levers marked the black dashboard and I wondered where the parachute pull was located. The windshield was only a few inches high and wrapped around the driver's seat. I couldn't imagine flying across the Bonneville Salt Flats crammed in that tiny compartment. I shivered at the thought.

I ran my hands over the rivets in the body and remembered that they were all snapped into place at the Reaction Dynamics shop in Milwaukee. The metal was smooth and cool. Hans Jurgen smiled awkwardly and jotted something on his clipboard, probably "Rewax immediately. Buff fingerprints." I wondered who painted the car because they did an amazing job blending the dark blue at the tip with lighter shades of blue and then finally silver blue at the rear. "The Blue Flame" was painted in all capital black and blue letters *slanting back as if from g-force alone. Much smaller black and silver capital letters spelled out "Driver Gary Gabelich", "Designed and Built by Reaction Dynamics and IGT Institute of Gas Technology" and "Goodyear." I took pictures of the car from every angle, careful to wipe away my tears between shots for fear I would return from Germany with nothing but photos of the ceiling or Hans Jurgen's shoes to show my dad. My throat was stretched and strangely thick with pride. One of the few times in my life I was stripped of words. I simply stared at the display of photos of this great car.*

My eyes rested on a mannequin on the other side of the car. I could only see the back of a fake head and a white racing helmet slung across a fake wrist. I glanced around the room at the other exhibits and didn't see any other mannequins. Evidently the museum thought someone deserved to accompany The Blue Flame in triumphant celebration. I hopped down from the platform and hurried around to the other side. I think Hans Jurgen was somewhat alarmed at my behavior, but he didn't try to interfere. I gazed up at Gary Gabelich the mannequin. He was smiling in a vaguely confident way, as if no further explanation was necessary. He was clad in a blue Goodyear jacket with yellow and white vertical racing stripes and a Blue Flame patch bragging across his back, white pants and white tennis shoes. I must have contemplated Gary for too long, because Hans Jurgen felt the need to check in.

"Oh! Such a young woman to have a father who built The Blue Flame! He must have been very young when he built the rocket."

I swiveled toward Hans Jurgen and smiled, "He wasn't even thirty years old."

"Such talent! To do this he is truly a great talent!"

Yes, I thought to myself. We must tell his story.

Ray

CHAPTER 1

BOTTLE ROCKETS AND BUSINESS DEALS

1944: Age 5

I liked to blow things up, I guess. Actually, I liked explosive reactions. That sounds more politically correct and less like I am reading from a terrorist handbook. As a young child I was free to run loose in my neighborhood in Harvey, Illinois to find my own adventures. One of my favorite things to do was sit still, listen and use my imagination. I loved to sit on my front porch and listen to the Illinois Central Railroad switchyards. The clanging and the shoving of cars mixed with the jostling of the tracks and whooshing of steam erupting from pressure relief valves on the train engines kept me fascinated for hours at a time.

My friend Eddie Davidson lived right next door and he introduced me to rockets. Since he was several years older than I, he knew about such things and loved to show me what he could do. He was about fifteen years old and I was probably five years old when I started going next door to his house to check out his antics and adventures. Eddie was a patient guy and didn't mind that I was so much younger. Maybe

1

watching Eddie was my first attempt at surrounding myself with people who were smarter and had more answers than I did.

Eddie was a licensed HAM radio operator. He had built his own short-wave radio transmitter and receiver. He had it set up in his bedroom and let me come upstairs and listen in. I would sit real quietly and listen to Eddie's conversations with people all over the world. I hoped to build my own unit when I grew up.

One day I watched Eddie emerge from his house and head toward the alley with an armload of strange supplies. It looked like he was going to cook up a recipe or something because it looked like he had raided his mother's kitchen. I jumped up and followed him.

"Eddie! Eddie what are you doing with your mom's stuff?" I asked.

"What?" He stopped and spun around. He was carrying a glass Coca-Cola bottle and what looked like ingredients for a cake. Eddie had short dark hair and intense blue eyes. He was a skinny kid with dirty fingernails and the required boyhood scrapes and scratches along his freckly arms. He wasn't wearing any shoes and I could see his dirty feet were planted in the dry, wispy grass in his backyard.

"Whatcha going to do?" I tried again. Sometimes Eddie was secretive, maybe he just wanted to keep me interested in his adventures. Once or twice he told me was training to be a spy and would probably be sent to Germany. The year *was* 1944, so he had me living on the edge with his stories of soldiers and undercover missions.

"I'm going to practice exploding things. That's what I'm going to do. Are you volunteering to be blown up? I could use the practice before they send me to fight the Nazis," he said, carefully scanning me, up and down. Was he wondering how much cake ingredients he needed to blow me up?

"No. I'll just watch," I told him.

"Ya sure?" he asked, giving me one more chance to be blown up.

"I'm sure. I have to be home by supper."

"Just watch then, but don't tell anyone. This is top secret, Ray." He looked at me with his best undercover spy scowl, drawing one eyebrow down and glancing around the alley to make sure no one was there.

Eddie placed the glass Coca-Cola bottle in the middle of the gravel alley, right behind our garage. I hoped my dad wouldn't be home until we were done blowing things up and I also hoped the blown up things wouldn't include his garage. When Eddie was sure the bottle wouldn't tip over, he placed a plastic funnel into the bottle and poured white powder from a yellow cardboard box into it until the bottom was covered with a pile two inches high. He carefully wiped off the powder that spilled down the outside of the bottle with his grubby, dirt-smeared hands, and looked at me.

"The white explosive powder is bicarbonate of soda. If you spill some you have to wipe it up or you'll blow up too much stuff. When I add vinegar it will explode, so get back, Ray," he instructed me, waving the funnel in the air for emphasis.

I backed up to the edge of the gravel and he picked up a glass bottle filled with a clear liquid. He waved his hand impatiently, motioning to me that I should back up even more so I ended up on the grass in our backyard. I thought I was too far away to see anything and started to feel restless. He wasn't a spy. Anyone knew that.

Eddie put the funnel back into the bottle and stood up. He crouched down next to the bottle, but kept his right leg sticking straight out to give him a quick getaway. For a moment he struggled with keeping the funnel in place and lifting the large glass vinegar bottle to the lip of the funnel. He splashed vinegar into the funnel and all over his blue jeans. Eddie scooted backwards and fell, gravel grinding into his palms as his bare feet scraped for purchase so he could escape.

The acid and vinegar combined in a violent reaction, releasing carbon dioxide at a rapid rate. A whooshing blast of gas and vinegar came shooting out of the top of the bottle, which tipped over, shooting vinegar and gas right at Eddie. His jeans and white t-shirt were covered in foamy vinegar sludge and he lay there, squeezing his eyes shut against the blast.

"Whoa! Eddie!" I shouted. "What happened?"

"Ah, Ray," he said, "ya know rockets don't always shoot off the right way. That's why I gotta practice this some more." Eddie wiped his eyes with the back of his hand and squinted at me.

"Okay, Eddie," I said. "Next time it will probably work."

Eddie's spy explosion reminded me of the sounds of the nearby switchyards. The chemical reaction produced the same whooshing sound as the steam engines. I decided to try this experiment on my own. I asked my mother if I could borrow the same ingredients Eddie had used and she agreed. As a matter of fact, Mother and Dad never resisted when I asked to do my experiments. They just sort of humored me and kept providing me with a little bit of vinegar and every once in a while a box of bicarbonate of soda. Everything was just fine as long as I kept myself busy without blowing up the garage and just asked for a few common kitchen items from time to time.

I must have gone through several boxes of bicarbonate of soda and a couple bottles of vinegar in my spare time just doing this chemical reaction over and over again. Sometimes I'd let it shoot up in the air and sometimes I'd put the Coca-Cola bottle on the sidewalk on its side and let it shoot down the sidewalk like a little jet-powered car. Eddie went on to other spying adventures and pretty much left me alone to blow things up. As far as I know he wasn't sent to Germany.

BICARBONATE OF SODA AND VINEGAR ROCKET

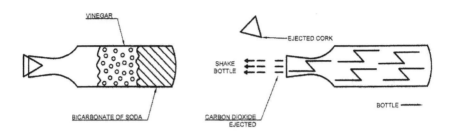

Rocket design I used when I was five years old

■　■　■

1969: Age 30

Twenty-five years later I was sitting on the edge of the bed holding my hands over my face. It felt like my head was going to blow up. My customary airplane migraine had accompanied me from Milwaukee to Buffalo, New York the night before and I could barely function by the time I reached the Tonawanda Holiday Inn. Before attempting to sleep, I popped two APC tablets and hoped to be rid of the headache by morning.

Sleep escaped me and the headache persisted, pounding away the hours until I was unaware of anything but the pain. It was worse than the night before. When the phone rang I squinted at the bedside clock. It read 11:30 a. m. I was supposed to be in the business office of Galaxy Manufacturing Company at 9:00 to check on the progress of the rework on the alternate rocket nozzle insert. It had to be remade due to faulty welding we hadn't noticed before shipment to Milwaukee the previous August.

I answered the phone, wondering if it was Don Magro, the machine shop manager calling to see if I was still alive and planning to show up as promised.

"Hello."

"Good morning, Ray." It was Dick Keller, one of my two my business partners at our company, Reaction Dynamics. He was calling from Milwaukee.

"I called Galaxy and they suggested I try the motel," he said.

As soon as I heard the tone of Dick's voice I knew there was a problem. I knew him well.

"What's up?" I asked, hoping it wouldn't be too bad.

"We need to make a decision," said Dick.

"What kind of decision?" I asked.

"Pete and I were called down to The Institute of Gas Technology yesterday to meet with the project sponsor's reps. We were told that the American Gas Association is requiring us to sign over the ownership of the Flame to IGT or they'll cut off further funding for the project," Dick explained in a rush.

"What the hell for?" I barked.

The Blue Flame land speed record car we were building was sponsored by the American Gas Association (AGA), a massive consortium of companies selling and distributing methane, commonly known as natural gas. The Institute of Gas Technology (IGT) in Chicago was the research and development arm of AGA. IGT also handled the sale and distribution of industry hardware such as valves, piping and storage tanks. IGT was overseeing the land speed record project for AGA, although the sponsorship contract gave full control of the car's development to our company, Reaction Dynamics.

"Well, they think we're mishandling the project and they have concerns that we're over budget and behind schedule. They believe it is time they took control," he said.

"What did you and Pete say to them?" I demanded.

"We told them we wanted to discuss it with you before we made a final decision," said Dick.

"The car is ours, Dick." I told him, wincing.

The pain was getting even worse. I was feeling nauseated and light-headed, maybe from the sickening thought of signing away The Blue Flame and any future business prospects for our new company. If we were successful at setting the world land speed record the sponsor would be allowed six months to exhibit and promote The Blue Flame. However, our company retained full ownership.

"I know. Pete knows. We told them we wanted to talk to you first."

"Did you try to negotiate a compromise or change their minds?" I asked him, my voice hoarse and urgent.

"Pete and I think we should do what they want so they don't drop us altogether. It would be better to get a chance to set the record doing it their way than not doing it at all," he said quietly.

"Dick! The American Gas Association is not going to drop us. They can't just forget about the project at this point! They have too much money in it now." I was incredulous he was talking this way.

He didn't respond.

"We are almost done," I continued. "The rocket engine is built and ready for testing. They're just bluffing, hoping to get the record *and* the car by threatening us with cancellation. You can't believe they would pull out now!"

Silence stretched from Milwaukee to Tonawanda. Would Dick and Pete really cave in to IGT? The future of Reaction Dynamics depended on the company retaining ownership of The Blue Flame. Maybe this phone call was just a formality and they had already signed over the car. If two signed and one didn't, majority would rule in this corporation of three.

"Don't do anything until I get back. I have to be here until Galaxy finishes the insert on Friday and I'll fly back that night," I told Dick.

"Okay. We'll wait until next week to settle this," he said.

We exchanged terse goodbyes. I hung up the phone with sweaty hands. Perspiration broke out all over my body in prickly protests to my conversation with Dick. My migraine had just rocketed from bad to severe. I hoped some fresh air would help. I grabbed a glass from the bathroom counter, filled it with water and snatched three more APC tablets from the plastic pill bottle on the cheap laminate nightstand. I gulped down the tablets. As I walked out the motel room door and into the parking lot I could still taste the flat tap water, rusty and obstinate as iron city pipes.

The motel was located in a commercial district of Tonawanda. There were no trees, just a bleak landscape of small commercial buildings, a couple of gas stations and a lone McDonald's restaurant about a half block down the street. All of the buildings were a shade of dirty gray, brown and black. The scene was hardly one to help relieve a troubled body and mind.

Still, I knew at that moment that I would not sign my name to a new deal that would ensure the demise of my company. We were in business for ourselves. There was no way I would deliberately put Reaction Dynamics out of business after only one and a half years of effort. The Flame project was our big opportunity to get a business reputation as a high tech company with space age skills. If we became only a footnote in The Blue Flame story as builders of the car, our opportunity would be lost. After the speed record was set, only the Flame's driver and IGT would get any publicity if we left it up to IGT to publicize the role of Reaction Dynamics in the land speed record.

Worried, I gazed blankly at the McDonald's yellow arches. My stomach was churning at the likelihood that Pete and Dick had already made up their minds. A worn out Chevy Bel Air, gray with neglect and red with rust, turned into the parking lot of the restaurant with a raspy rattle as its rear end scraped along the concrete. That bumper and I had both seen better days.

CHAPTER 2

KANKAKEE CHILDHOOD AND LILY DALE PSYCHICS

1949: age 10

I had the time of my life messing around in Kankakee, Illinois. Life for a Kankakee kid in the late forties and early fifties was one big possibility and endless afternoon. My father's job required him to move frequently, so I got to know many Illinois towns, but Kankakee was my favorite.

My father's name is Ray, too. He was Raymond Haney and I am Raymond Joseph. I don't know why my parents chose not to make me a Junior, but they didn't. Dad was an electrical engineer and worked for the Public Service Company of Northern Illinois. He was the manager of the electrical distribution department and was in charge of laying out the electrical power lines in the proper place and getting permission from the landowners to allow the service company to put telephone poles on their property. He was from a very small town called Milford Junction, Indiana, and was the first person in his family to attend college. He earned a degree in electrical engineering from Purdue University in 1928. My father was a hard worker, but an easygoing man. He went to work, came home in time to eat supper, read the paper and work around the house. He was always fixing or building something in the garage. I would stand around and watch him tinker with his tools and sometimes he let me help. One time he taught me how to paint the house and I helped him carefully brush in the paint and clean the brushes when we were done.

My mother, Dorothy, was from Indianapolis, and graduated from a hospital school of nursing in the 1930s. She was a very strong, intelligent woman who made no bones about the fact that education was extremely important. Each of her six children were expected go to college and my father agreed with her on that. She was the teaching type of mother, always available to show us how to do something. If she didn't know how she would make sure Dad taught us. She made sure her boys knew how to cook, and my brothers claim they were sometimes required to cook supper. I just remember she taught me how to bake cakes and sew buttons on my shirts. I guess that's all my sweet tooth will recall.

My parents, Ray and Dorothy, with my sister Nola (1931)

If my mother wanted to do something there was nothing my father or anyone else could do to change her mind. She ran an extremely tight ship and made all of the major financial decisions regarding the household. If my father disagreed, they would argue about it until he eventually deferred to her. She was not restrictive in what her kids could do as long as we didn't get hurt or do the wrong thing. If Mother would frown in disapproval, we didn't do it. Mother was the enforcer and disciplinarian in our house. Her idea of punishment was either a spanking or the suspension of a coveted childhood privilege such as a bike, fishing pole or precious summertime freedom to roam. My mother was proud of the fact that our neighbors would compliment her on our good behavior.

Every four years our family moved to a new town. This was part of Public Service Company's policy. We lived in Harvey, Streater, Kankakee and in 1951 my father was transferred back to Harvey. The frequent moves didn't bother me because it was the way it had to be, I guess. Change was good, so I learned.

We lived on the corner of Greenwood Avenue and Bourbonnais Street in Kankakee, which was in the middle of town. Our house was a white clapboard, two-story that once upon a time was a farmhouse. The living room, bathroom, kitchen and my parents' bedroom were on the first floor. The three girls shared a bedroom upstairs to the left and the three boys' room was to the right. My father wanted to buy a house outside of town on the Kankakee River, but my mother prevailed in order to be closer to St. Patrick's School and the center of town. There was a tall evergreen tree in our front yard on Greenwood Avenue and a cherry tree in the back with all of the other old trees lining Bourbonnais Avenue. The backyard was flat and led to our garage which faced the gravel alley running behind Greenwood Avenue.

I have five siblings, but I don't remember much about their lives in Kankakee. The oldest is Nola, then Marilyn, me, Roger, Dorothy and Harold. All I know for sure is that we all had to be home for supper by 5:30 when Dad got home and I always sat in the southwest corner chair at the kitchen table. Everybody had to be home for the evening when it got dark outside. I remember the girls would spend most of their time in their room reading *Seventeen* magazines or listening to "The Hit Parade" on their radio. If they ever left the house I didn't pay attention to where they went. My brothers, I assume, found their own lives in the alleys and backyards of Kankakee just like I did.

One afternoon I pedaled my way through Cobb Park looking for something to do. I was an average-sized kid, but wiry and strong. I had brown, curly hair, green eyes and freckles all over my body. As usual I was wearing a plain white t-shirt, blue jeans and no shoes because we never wore shoes in the summer except to go to church.

My tires made that special hiss like running water as I sped along the fine gravel path. My bike was nothing special. It was covered in chipped green and black paint with no particular design or racing stripes. It didn't have any gears or handbrakes. The handlebars were the typical sort found in those days, straight across but curved toward the rider at the very ends, like a stretched out parentheses. Tiny stones sprayed to each side of my tires and I grasped my fishing pole against the white rubber handgrip on my right side. I spotted my best friend, Art Yonke, near the baseball diamond.

Cobb Park was one of our favorite places to mess around. Most days you could find enough neighborhood kids to play baseball or football. It depended on who showed up with what kind of ball. The park was littered with towering oak trees and had a carpet of lush green grass. There was a brick bathroom building on the east side of the park, a swing set in the middle and a baseball diamond near the river on the south side. The ball never went into the water because we always batted away from the river, toward the swing set. Large green metal trash cans were plopped down every twenty yards or so and the fine gravel bike path meandered across the park with no specific attention to reason.

Art was facing the river so he didn't see me approach. I sped up and was careening toward him with a wild smile on my face. Just in the nick of time I slammed my right pedal backward and my bike went into a controlled skid, slanting sideways and kicking up gravel. He turned around with a startled expression and jumped back, but not in time to avoid the gravel showering him from his bare feet to his waist.

"Whaddya escape from over *there*?" he asked, pointing across the river. The imposing limestone clock tower that poked up from the opposite tree line belonged to the insane asylum. It was the Kankakee State Hospital aka Illinois Eastern Hospital for the Insane and the root of many a Kankakee-kid legend. Sometimes we rode our bikes across the bridge in town and went up there. We would pedal through the grounds and look at what we called "the crazy people" sitting around on the lawn.

"Yeah, I was visiting your relatives. Hey! What do you want to do?" I laughed at him because he was still brushing gravel off of his jeans.

"I've still got some M-80's. Do you have any matches?" he asked. Art was my height and build with straight blonde hair and slate gray eyes. He had fewer freckles than I did, but, then again, so did most kids. Art had a small gap between his two front teeth, long skinny arms and legs, bony fingers and a perpetual grin.

Art and I had chipped in to buy a gross of firecrackers from the Army Surplus Store in Kankakee. The M-80s were used for basic training during World War II to simulate battle explosions. The army had billions of these things left over after the war and I bought a box whenever I could spare the paper route money.

I dug in my jeans pocket and pulled out a tin of matches. There were certain things a kid needed to carry with him. A fishing pole and tin of matches could come in handy at any time.

"Yeah, I've got 'em. Let's throw them in the river!" I suggested. One of the advantages of the M-80's versus regular bottle rockets and fire-crackers was that they were waterproof and would explode under water.

I left my bike leaning against the closest oak tree and we trotted down to the river. We looked left and right along the bank to see if any hobos were camped out or carp fishermen were around because they might tell us to scram. The coast was clear.

Art pulled two M-80's from his front jeans pocket and held out his hand for the matches. He lit the fuse and tossed it into the river. A couple of seconds ticked by. Suddenly a huge geyser of water shot into the air and we had to hop backwards to avoid getting wet. As best friends do, he immediately handed over the remaining M-80 and tin of matches. I repeated the process, but threw it as far as I could. Maybe I could make it land on other side and send the mental patients running for cover. It landed less than half way across the river and sent up a sparkling geyser as we stood hooting and hollering in appreciation.

"Got any more?" I asked.

"Nope, left the box at home," he answered.

We stood on the bank of the river in companionable silence, watching the brownish-greenish water drift by. The current was calm and quiet along this stretch. Art and I could watch the river glide by all day, and sometimes we did.

"Well, let's get a root beer," Art said. We often contemplated our next move on the corner of Indiana and River Streets, leaning against the orange walls of the A & W Root beer stand. Art and I had determined that a five cent root beer helped us decide what to do next.

I am on the left and my best friend, Art Yonke, is on the right (1949)

■ ■ ■

1969

I had neither five cents nor a root beer, so I decided to walk to the McDonald's and get some black coffee. Maybe the extra caffeine would help my migraine. The fresh air and stiff breeze of the November morning was invigorating after my stale night in the motel. I contemplated my partners' priorities and how that would affect what they might do in this situation.

All parties involved in The Blue Flame project had different and sometimes conflicting priorities. Was this now a contest between team members? Who would prevail? Who would have to sacrifice their dream in order to break the world land speed record?

Dick Keller was the person who sold the American Gas Association and The Institute of Gas Technology on the prospect of sponsoring The Blue Flame project in the first place. Dick worked for IGT and used his connections to approach the AGA for funding. He would probably be under pressure to go along with AGA's demands to turn over control of the project since he had proposed the project to them in the first place. I believe Dick's priority was to cooperate with the sponsor and make sure The Blue Flame had a chance to break the world record.

Pete Farnsworth, on the other hand, would be much less concerned with IGT's position on the project. He was a trained truck mechanic. However, in his spare time he was also a race car builder and successful drag racer. He loved to do it and I believe he was most concerned with his status in the racing community. The Blue Flame was his opportunity to get international recognition. I believe Pete's priority was to get his car to the salt flats with a shot at the world record. He would not want to risk being uncooperative with IGT. Most of his peers already knew he was building the Flame. I figured Pete would rather keep his chance at the land speed record than fight for the big picture. It seemed like we were two votes toward caving in.

I was not concerned with IGT's future. My short-term interest was rocket propulsion and engineering, but my long-term interest had always been starting my own business. This was my chance to make a business of engineering design.

Pete, Dick and I had combined goals of world records, international recognition and building a successful business. IGT was promoting natural gas as the fuel of the future. I believe IGT wanted The Blue Flame to break the world record so they could develop a compelling ad campaign.

In fact, I was unhappy with IGT. A project like this was being held to unprecedented budget and time constraints. Since a project of this nature had never been attempted, the restrictions were basically pulled out of a hat. Professionals in the engineering and design field knew that these kinds of projects were budget busters and rarely finished in the time originally predicted. Reaction Dynamics was conducting research and development, not just building another car. The propulsion system for The Blue Flame was of a type that NASA hadn't even perfected yet. It was similar to the propulsion design for the Lunar Landing Module destined to transport astronauts to the moon's surface.

The sponsor's efforts to adhere to such a strict and unrealistic budget and timeline caused the project to unravel, Reaction Dynamics to falter and ultimately risked our chance at setting the world record. The three owners of our fledgling company had separate roles and responsibilities. The pressure to deliver the world record caused Pete, Dick and me to develop resentment towards each other. Tension and blame were brewing amongst the three of us and I believe we all thought the other two were falling short.

Dick and Pete were responsible for the design and construction of the car. They were the ones who wisely brought in Professors Dr. Paul Torda and Dr. Carl Uzgiris from the Department of Mechanical and Aerospace Engineering at the Illinois Institute of Technology (IIT) to consult about the vehicle's design and aerodynamics. The Blue Flame's design was groundbreaking, so there were no blueprints to copy. Dr. Torda and Dr. Uzgiris embraced the challenge to consult on this project of world record proportions. Dick networked and arranged the connections between IGT, IIT, AGA and Reaction Dynamics. Pete built the car according to the specifications provided by Dr. Torda and Dr. Uzgiris.

I was responsible for the design, construction and testing of the propulsion system. It was completed under the $32,078 budget and before the projected deadline of September, 1969. The rocket was sitting at Reaction Dynamics in Milwaukee waiting for testing.

But the car was far from finished. A steelworkers' strike put the timeline behind schedule making it difficult to obtain the metal needed to fabricate the car. When the steelworkers went back to work, a truckers' strike immediately followed. The metal was finally available, but there were no truckers to transport it.

I walked into Galaxy Manufacturing holding my second large cup of coffee. I felt a little better after drinking a massive dose of caffeine. Don Magro took one look at me and asked, "Are you okay?"

"I think so. I had a bad night. How is the machining of the insert coming?" I answered, sipping my lukewarm drink as we went into his office.

Don replied with his usual response to a customer who had inquired repeatedly about the status of their overdue order, "It is almost finished. We hope to have it for you tomorrow."

Jerry Muhs, Don's business partner, walked out of the shop area to greet me. He was Galaxy's chief and only machinist.

"Hi, Ray. Good to see you," he said with a nod.

"Hi, Jerry. Is the insert done yet?" I asked.

"Oh we've got a couple of days work left on that. We've run into a snag with the nozzle bell. There's an eighteen inch diameter on that, and I've got to be slow about it or it could end up as scrap," he explained.

I had experience machining stainless steel and was aware of this problem. If Jerry rushed with the cutting tool, the insert would be wrenched out of the lathe chuck's grip and ruined. Stainless could be tricky and had to be well lubricated during machining to prevent galling, which led to the cutting tool binding up on the surface of the metal.

I looked at Don. "I'm not going anywhere until the insert is finished. I can't make another trip. There are some problems in Milwaukee and I have to leave by Friday night. If you want your final payment on the rocket engine work, the insert had better be done by then."

Jerry grimaced and walked back into the shop.

The insert wasn't a necessary part of the engine. Its only purpose was to provide a means of boosting the rocket engine thrust from 11,000 pounds to 13,500 pounds when operated in the monopropellant mode (one fuel) using 90% hydrogen peroxide. We probably would not put it to use unless the bipropellant system (two fuels) using liquefied natural gas (LNG) became inoperative due to mechanical failure of one or more parts in the engine. The bipropellant system relied on the flow control orifice and heat exchanger, so if either part malfunctioned the rocket would only use the hydrogen peroxide as fuel, thereby staying in the monopropellant mode. Hopefully, that would not happen. If the rocket engine only used hydrogen peroxide then we would set a record of 700 mph with one fuel (hydrogen peroxide) instead of achieving the 1,000 mph the engine was perfectly capable of at the full thrust of 22,000 pounds and two fuels (hydrogen peroxide plus the liquid natural gas.)

The rocket engine had been delivered to Reaction Dynamics several weeks ago. I was pleased with its appearance and felt it was a fine piece of workmanship by Galaxy Manufacturing and Avins Fabricating Company. Dick agreed with me. On the other hand, Pete was not so pleased. He pointed out that the rocket nozzle insert was not well made. He saw that the bell of the insert was slightly out of round. I measured the bell and confirmed this to be the case. Pete was right.

I said, "This won't be a significant problem even if we have to use this component. The rocket engine will have enough power to break the record with just the peroxide."

Pete replied, "This insert is a piece of shit."

Dick said nothing, which was unusual.

I was angered by Pete's comment. What did he know about rockets? I didn't say anything because we didn't plan to use the insert anyway. I believed Pete was just interested in aesthetics and didn't want any parts looking less than perfect.

A few days later I decided to call Galaxy and tell them I was bringing the nozzle insert back and would stay there until the problem was corrected. This turned out to take about ten days. The trip was a big waste of valuable time and project money. I felt that I was the only one concerned about spending project money. I had finished my end of the contract on time and on budget with the arrival of the engine at Reaction Dynamics. The construction of the car was still far behind schedule.

In retrospect I can see that fixing the insert was a mistake. The insert was like a sleeve slipped into the rocket nozzle, which made the opening of the rocket nozzle more narrow. The more narrow the opening, the more pressure that built up as the exhaust was trying to escape the nozzle. The higher the pressure, the higher the "push" or thrust of the rocket.

Reaction Dynamics did try to use the insert during their world record attempts in 1970 because The Blue Flame wasn't getting enough thrust. The crew installed the insert, but all the extra machining to make the insert perfect for Pete weakened the sides. The remaining metal proved too thin to withstand the force of the rocket engine. I believe the weakened insert was ripped off of its bolts during a record attempt, therefore, not helping to increase the thrust of the rocket. If we had left the insert alone, it would have been strong enough to provide extra thrust because the slightly imperfect shape would not have affected its performance.

Pete and I didn't speak about any of this. It was tense between us. Dick acted as middle man between the two "departments" of Reaction Dynamics. The vehicle construction department (Pete) and the propulsion department (me) had ceased to see eye to eye. We kept our distance. I was leery of spending so much time away from the shop, but I had to go to Buffalo and get a new nozzle insert.

At Galaxy, Don was on the phone, apparently with another impatient customer. "We should have it ready for you tomorrow. Yes, certainly. You can pick it up tomorrow. Okay, goodbye."

He turned toward me and smiled. "We should take the afternoon off. A trip to Lily Dale will make you feel much better."

Take the afternoon off? Didn't he realize I was impatient? I hesitated, speculating that afternoons off could be affecting their productivity. That would certainly explain why Don constantly assured their customers their parts would be done "tomorrow." I was about to repeat my demands, but quickly realized Don might be right. He didn't want me to be a distraction to Jerry by hovering over his shoulder and lurking about the shop, glancing at my watch.

"It can't hurt," I said. Maybe it would actually save time by leaving Jerry alone so he could focus.

Lily Dale was a summer retreat and study center for the local ministers of the Spiritualist religion. It was situated on Lily Dale Lake near Lily Dale, New York. Each minister lived in a small cottage on campus during the summer months. The ministers professed to be able to communicate with the souls of the dead. Visitors merely had to knock on any cottage door and ask for a reading. If the minister was so inclined, a reading could be had for a small donation. Don took me there once before while I was visiting Galaxy and I suspect he had been there more than once on his own. Maybe he and his new wife Andrea were followers of the Spiritualist faith. I did not ask. The trip to Lily Dale seemed like a good diversion from my vigil at Galaxy. I could use the entertainment.

It was about 1:30 when Don and I jumped in his car and headed for Lily Dale. The drive took about one hour. Autumn was about over, so there weren't too many residents with the advent of cool weather. There were ten or twelve ministers still ensconced at the campus. Don brought along a tape recorder so I could record a reading. I wasn't sure any ministers would allow their reading to be recorded, but it was worth a try. My migraine was gone by the time we arrived so the trip was already worth the effort.

I knocked on a door at random. The lady minister who answered was very young and pretty. I was surprised that such a young woman could attain the status of a reader. I was not averse to getting a reading from a good-looking woman, so I requested one.

"Sure. My name is Emily. That will be a five dollar donation, please." I assumed the donations were going to the religion, but now I was not so sure.

"Do you mind if I tape record my reading?" I asked, holding out the tape recorder.

"No problem," she replied.

I set the recorder on a small table near my chair. There was a fan running on the table to keep the air circulating. Emily contacted her medium who seemed to be a Native American because she assumed the voice and tone of some sort of American Indian language when talking to him. She had a short conversation with her medium which, of course, I could not understand.

"Did you know someone who died a very painful death related to a problem in the stomach region?" Emily asked.

I looked at her and didn't say anything because she went right back to her spiritual conversation, ignoring me.

"Do you know a young girl who died of appendicitis?" she asked.

I paused and waited for her to ignore me again. When she didn't, I responded, "My Aunt Mildred died of appendicitis when she was sixteen. She was my mother's sister."

"Mildred says hello to you and your family," Emily informed me.

I paid my five dollars and went looking for Don.

We went into the town of Lily Dale and had a spaghetti lunch, complete with greasy garlic bread and small tossed salads. Don suggested we return to the campus for a free group reading session. Since I had nothing else to do while Jerry finished the insert, I agreed again.

Students and visitors assembled in a large tent in the center of the campus. Anyone from the crowd could ask for a reading from the floor. A stage was set up at one end of the tent and the ministers were standing on the stage, ready for questions. They would take one question at a time.

We observed for about half an hour. Most people wanted to know about dead friends or relatives. Did these deceased souls have a message for them, things like that.

"You should ask about The Blue Flame project, Ray!" Don prodded me.

I raised my hand and asked a female minister, "What can you tell me about The Blue Flame project I am working on? My company is building a rocket car to set a new land speed record. Will it be a success?"

She thought about it for about ten seconds. "There will be some kind of problem with the fuel system. Does that sound possible?"

"I don't think so," I answered.

She contemplated the matter again. "I do not understand the details of the car, but I am sure the fuel system will not work."

I decided I had gone far enough.

"Thank you," I replied.

I sensed that maybe my migraine would soon be back.

As we walked back to the car I asked Don, "How could a woman minister know anything about a rocket engine? Do you think she could be on to something?"

He just looked at me and shrugged his shoulders.

The plot had thickened. First the distressing call from Dick about losing the car, and now this puzzling prediction about the fuel system. A fresh wave of frustration followed me back to Don's car. I didn't have any interest in solving mysteries. Not since I was a boy. Back then, mysteries were just a light diversion if I had a few minutes between dinner and bedtime. I would stretch out in front of the radio in our living room and wait for the story to start.

CHAPTER 3

SUMMER FUN AND SINKING FEELING

1949

My school picture when I was about 10 years old

"Who knows…what evil…Illlurks… in the hearts of men? The Shadow knows!" The telltale creepy music and maniacal laughter announced the beginning of one of my favorite radio shows. I plunked myself down in front of the radio to listen while Lamont Cranston, amateur criminologist, used his "hypnotic power to cloud men's minds so that they cannot see him." I waited patiently while the announcer urged me to go right out and get Wildroot Cream Oil and something called a Perfect-O-Lite. If the A & W didn't sell it, I didn't need it.

My parents were on the front porch talking quietly and I had the living room all to myself, a rare treat. There was no sign of any siblings who would threaten to change the station. I could hear music from my sisters' radio leak down the stairs so I turned up the volume for "The Shadow." I was tired from four consecutive games of baseball at Riverview Park. A nasty scrape burned the entire length of my left calf from a slide at third base that seemed like a good idea at the time. I stretched out on the floor and drifted off to sleep before Lamont Cranston brought The Red Menace to justice.

The next day my mother caught me while I was headed out the back door, hoping to find my friend Joe Romery in the alley. Joe lived three doors down and had a basketball hoop attached to his garage. Sometimes we got together with some other kids on our block to play a game of horse.

"Raymond, help me with the groceries," my mother said, smiling. The kitchen smelled faintly of coffee, blueberry waffles and Armor's Lighthouse cleanser. I glanced out the window, searching the alley. If my friends started without me I'd have to stand around and watch until they were done with a game.

"Okay, sure." I said, because there was no other answer. Unfortunately, I was passing through at the same moment Mother returned from Kroger's. We unpacked what seemed like enough provisions to last us until I was shipped off to college. Since Kroger's and my mother agreed that you should "Live better for less," she was a faithful customer.

I unpacked and she put away. It was endless. Sweetheart soap, Epsom salt, Kroger pork & beans, Spry shortening, Swift's premium, skinless wieners, Mott's applesauce, Heinz pickles, Carnation milk, Sunshine Hi-Lo crackers, Pillsbury flour and pan-ready frying chicken. I stopped looking at the labels and watched the alley. Bobby Larigi and Terry Supernant were headed toward Joe's garage.

"So, Raymond, what are you up to today?" she asked, Oxydol soap powder in one hand and Dreft in the other. I wondered if I had let a swear word slip and she was planning on washing my mouth out. Some of my friends actually had their mouths washed out with soap for uttering foul language but it had never happened to me. My mother always threatened she'd do it if she had to, so one day I decided to see what it would be like. In our bathroom we always had a cake of Ivory Snow soap "for daintier washing." I made sure no one was around and I licked the soap to see if it was really that bad. My face screwed up and my tongue recoiled. I stood at the sink spitting like a fiend and rinsing my mouth with scoops of tap water. I decided I should try and avoid that punishment at all costs.

"Not much, just messing around. Looks like Joe's got a gang out back ready to play horse," I said casually.

"Why don't you take Roger and Harold with you?" she suggested.

"I'm pretty sure they're already out there," I said. I had no idea where they were, but the alley was a possibility.

"Good," she said, "go ahead. We're having fried chicken tonight so make sure you're back in time to get a leg."

One of the disadvantages of having five siblings was there was always a limited number of legs on a fried chicken.

I ran out the back door and jumped off the top of the wooden steps. I flew across the grass and grabbed the corner of our garage as I spun myself into the alley. My friends were gathered near the basketball hoop, watching Terry Supernant attempt his next shot. Terry was tall with very curly blonde hair. He was wearing blue jeans and a black t-shirt. Terry squinted at the basket and bounced the ball. It was around 80 degrees and sunny so the gravel was warm on my feet.

I watched him square up about twelve feet from the basket at a forty-five degree angle. He bounced the ball five times, picked it up and bent his knees. He bounced the ball three more times and then released it smoothly. As soon as it sailed through the metal hoop, I saw Bobby Larigi's shoulders droop. He had a running bet with Terry and I think he owed him close to eight thousand dollars in lost games of horse. I picked up the pace.

"Hey, guys!" I asked, "Who's got what?" My bare feet skidded across the gravel alley. Most houses in Kankakee had detached garages that faced the alley, but some houses didn't, so that gave us more room to play. There was an empty lot across from the Romery's basketball hoop which we used for football and assorted messing around.

Alleys were the domain of the neighborhood kids. Adults didn't use the alley except when our fathers worked in their garages in the evening while listening to a WGN broadcast of a White Sox game. Our mothers generally had other places to be, except when they had to park a car. A walk down an alley on a summer day would get you a basketball game, one or two marbles tournaments, several bike riders, a couple of walkers and maybe a rag picker if you were lucky. Rag pickers were gypsy-type men that rode through the alleys in horse-drawn carts. If you had a bunch of rags you could take them out to the rag picker and he would give you a little money for them. Rag pickers made money by sharpening scissors and knives so if he bought your rags he would invariably ask if you needed sharper knives.

"Terry's got nothin', Billy's got H-O-R and I've got H," Bobby answered. Bobby was a short, thin kid with very dark curly hair. His eyes were light brown, almost amber. He was wearing blue jeans, no shirt and no shoes. Joe Romery looked a lot like Bobby with dark curly hair and a thin frame, but he had one blue eye and one brown eye. My mother always mixed up their names since she usually didn't see them up close or together. Then again she called me "RogerHaroldRaymond" half the time so maybe she just wasn't good with names.

I joined in when they were finished. My free throws were improving, but my lay ups on both sides needed practice. I always picked a straight-on jump shot when it was my turn. Side shots and angle shots were not my best, probably because the only time I touched a basketball was for a game of horse.

Terry beat the pants off of us four games in a row. I decided that the public schools must have better basketball equipment. I waved so long and walked home to get my bike. My dark blue t-shirt was sticking to my skin like slime on a rock.

Long hot days filled with Kroger's fried chicken and back alley games were some of the best times of my life. Why can't things always be as easy as when you're ten years old?

■　■　■

1969

It wasn't easy to sort out issues with Reaction Dynamics when I was several states away. Don and I drove back to Galaxy Manufacturing and parted company for the day. I went back to the Holiday Inn. After taking a shower, I went outside and sat next to the small pool behind the motel. There were a few families splashing around and a drooling black lab pressed his nose against the chain link fence, hoping to be invited. A blonde woman with red sunglasses walked by, patted him on the head and said, "There you go, Bruce. Good boy. Good boy."

I reclined in a metal and plastic chaise lounge out of drool range and closed my eyes so I could think. The steady sound of traffic blended in with the yelps and splashes of the pool activity. My thoughts wandered over my predicament until my stomach started to rumble.

That night I ate in the motel restaurant. As I worked my way through meat loaf, mashed potatoes and a creamy chocolate milkshake, I thought about what might happen with the AGA and Reaction Dynamics.

My partners would assume that they already knew all they had to know about rockets from their experience with our prototype for The Blue Flame. The prototype, the X-1, was a low-powered and safe drag race car. It had a monopropellant 90% hydrogen peroxide engine, and we never had a bad experience with it. The driver merely opened a ball valve allowing the peroxide to rush into the decomposition chamber, passing through the treated pure-silver mesh screens. This created instant superheated steam and oxygen gas which shot out of the rocket nozzle at 3,200 feet per second, generating a forward thrust of 2,500 pounds. This was equivalent to 2,000 horsepower at the car's top speed. The propulsion system of the X-1 did not require burning fuel at high temperatures. The exhaust gas velocity was very low compared to The Blue Flame.

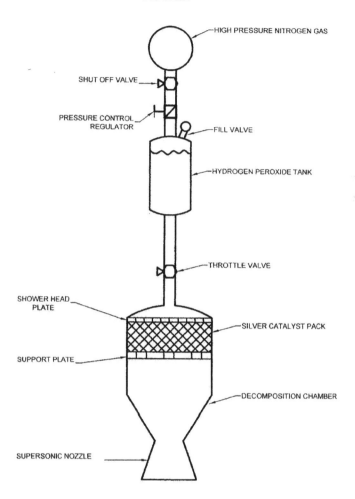

Sketch of the X-1 rocket propulsion system

In contrast, The Blue Flame engine operated a bipropellant system using hydrogen peroxide and liquefied natural gas. It was a high-powered and potentially very dangerous. It was imperative that we run tests at a real test facility operated by experienced professionals.

The pool area was quiet and deserted. I must have been ruminating longer than I thought. The sun had set and the light by the pool was dim and dreary. The other motel guests had gathered their belongings by the pool and retired for the night. Even Bruce the dog had turned in. I allowed myself one more thought about my predicament. I could only control myself. I decided that people have been doing stupid things since the start of time and people will continue to do stupid things no matter what I did or said. I could only control myself and my reaction. I needed to move forward and hope that logic and reason would prevail.

Don Magro and I shook hands the following morning and I walked out of Galaxy Manufacturing with the finished insert. I thanked his partner Jerry and everyone for their effort and drove to the airport to catch my flight to Milwaukee. As I flew west over Michigan I wondered what the future held for the project and for me. The horizon dipped and bobbed in time with the turbulence. I leaned my forehead against the smudged oval window. No matter how hard I pressed, the line in the sky remained elusive.

■ ■ ■

1949

I knew what I was after. Fish. Today was a great day to snag some small mouth bass out of the Kankakee River. I pedaled through the side yard next to our house and turned right. I coasted halfway down Greenwood Avenue, happy for a breeze against my sweaty face. The river was four blocks straight ahead at Cobb Park, but I turned on River Street to see if Art was home yet. He had gone hunting with his father that morning. Art's family supplemented their diet with local wildlife cuisine from time to time. His father took him rabbit and squirrel hunting all over Kankakee County. For Art's eleventh birthday, his dad gave him an over-and-under shotgun and a .22 rifle. After that, Art counted on me to be his squirrel-hunting sidekick.

We'd ride our bikes two miles north of town and Art would quietly patrol the area for varmints. As a sidekick, I just followed along trying not to scrape up my bare feet on the uneven rocks and scratchy weeds. I carried a green canvas tote bag with a long shoulder strap. Whenever Art killed a rabbit or squirrel I would twist its head off, let it bleed out on the ground and then toss it in the canvas bag. I didn't like the killing, head twisting or the mess. After a couple of times I decided to retire and spend some time being thankful my father wasn't a hunter.

Art was singing something and carrying his fishing pole toward the garage. I pulled up to the curb and shouted, "So! Rabbit soup tonight? How about some squirrels?"

He looked at me and grinned. I realized he wasn't singing, he was chanting his favorite ditty. Art called out, "Gene, Gene made a machine! Frank, Frank turned the crank! Joe, Joe made it go! Art, Art let a fart and blew the whole damn thing apart!"

I never figured out if he thought this was a compliment. It looked like he was ready for the river so I said, "How about some fishing? It's a good day to mess around in the river."

Art looked around and when he didn't see any parents to object he went over to his garage and wheeled out his bike.

"Yeah. Got a couple hours, anyway," he said.

Art lived in a prime location because his house was less than a block from the A & W root beer stand. We took a right on River Street and passed the Shell station and several small businesses. It only took a few minutes to get to our fishing spot. We left our bikes on the sidewalk and prepared to climb down to the river bank. The road was much higher than the river at this point, so we held our fishing poles in our mouths and used a wall of an old brewery building next to the river as our ladder. This old crumbling wall had large pieces of limestone jutting out of the ruins of the brewery that served as our rungs as we scrambled down to the river.

I went first and Art started singing his farting song again. Since his rear end was just a couple of feet above me I hoped he wouldn't make good on his promise. As soon as my feet touched the stones below I hopped away from the wall and started looking for bait.

Massive glaciers really did a number on Kankakee County during the last ice age 10,000 years ago. The ice advanced and receded several times and ground up the landscape. The glaciers would pick up huge amounts of earth and reform the countryside by leaving gaping holes and spitting large piles of rocks and soil across the region. This glacial till of limestone, granite and sandstone was scattered along the river and in surrounding fields.

We found our bait under rocks along the shore. I started lifting medium sized rocks to find some crayfish or hellgrammites. After four tries I had success when I spotted a crayfish wedged between two rocks. I grabbed it and tossed it on the shore. Art's job was to find some good sticks for fishing pole props. Several overgrown bushes grew near the embankment and he tore off a couple branches and started walking toward me.

After a couple more tries I found a crayfish for Art so we spent a few moments piercing the crayfish and making sure our bobbers were attached near the end of the line. We both had steel casting rods about three feet long. In order to make a good cast you had to hold one thumb on the line, bring the rod back and flick your wrist while letting go of the line. Since we had bobbers we could set our poles on the riverbank and explore or wade in the water while we waited for a bite. Art cast first and I followed soon after. One time he didn't wait for me to get out of the way and his fishing hook landed in my hair and almost ripped my ear off. Ever since then I let him go first and made sure I was out of the line of fire.

Art handed me a branch and I snapped off the ends until I was left with one fork about two feet long. I pushed it into the riverbank about ten feet from the water and put my fishing pole in the convenient notch at the top. The pole needed to stay put, so I picked up a big rock and put it on top of the line about halfway between the water and my nifty homemade fishing pole holder.

I smelled hot dogs. I looked up at the river. To our left was a railroad bridge and on the right was an automobile bridge. The river was about a hundred yards across and the current was a little faster than at Cobb Park. There was a cement dam running the entire width of the river about halfway between the two bridges. Directly across the river was a factory and I could hear the water pounding over the dam and car tires humming across the bridge to my right. I saw smoke underneath the automobile bridge and realized where the hot dog smell was coming from.

Two hobos were sitting under the bridge with a small campfire between them. They saw me looking at them and waved so I waved back. Sometimes we ran into vagrants in our fishing spot because the hobos would hop off the train at the railroad bridge, head into town to buy some food and cook it up under the bridge. Most of them were very friendly and told us interesting stories about riding the rails. Mother always told me not to go near the hobos. They might not be nice people. We did it anyway.

We sat on the bank watching our bobbers in silence. Art and I could spend hour upon hour staring at nothing and just picking our noses. It was amazing. Once in a while one of us would pipe up, "Terry Supernant hasn't lost a game of horse since Easter." Or "We got twelve rabbits today. I had to twist the heads off every one of them. Lots of rabbit heads laying around out there now."

I was getting too hot in the summer sun, so I decided to wade across the river. Most of the time we just leaned up against the dam and let the water cascade over our backs and shoulders. If we wanted to swim we could either go the city pool or the YMCA. My mother didn't encourage us to go to the YMCA because it was run by a Protestant group. My family was Catholic, and Mother was leery of Protestant activities. I didn't encourage us to go to the YMCA because I didn't like their rules. Kids had to swim naked.

Art and I set off across the river, side by side. The water was just a couple of feet deep, so it came up to my waist at its deepest point. I wondered how long it would take us to make it to the opposite bank, which was approximately a football-field's length away. The rocks were not sharp, so we didn't have to worry about cutting our feet. The edges had been polished by the constant pull of the water and a coat of spongy algae turned the stones into slippery marbles under our feet. My jeans immediately doubled in weight with rushing water. The current pressed against my left leg so I put most of my weight on that side to make sure I didn't get swept away. I felt around with my right foot for a stable place to advance. My arms felt light and free as I waved them up and down then back and forth to keep my footing.

I heard a splash and looked to my right. Art was down. He was trying to stand up again while the current was sending him straight for the bridge. I could see his arms slapping the water, trying to push himself out of the water and back on his feet.

"Ah rats, Ray! Holy crap! What the…" he sputtered between bobs. He looked at the bridge and tried to turn to get back to shore before he was pulled up against the cement bridge support. We tried to keep away from the bridge supports because the water tended to churn like a washing machine around the base of each support. One time Art had banged up against the center support six or seven times before he was able to push himself away from it and coast downstream.

"Art! Just pick up your knees and ride it! You're right in the middle of the supports---you're clear! You're clear!" I shouted. He ignored me and went down face first. He managed to get a hand on the riverbed and steady himself enough to squat. He slowly stood up and kept his hands straight out in front of him. His head was bent forward and he was facing the bridge. I could see rivulets of water stream down his back. After a couple seconds he started to shuffle to his right, carefully stepping on to the bank where we started.

I looked across the river and figured since I was almost halfway across I should keep going. It took me almost half an hour to pick my way across the river and back, but I was glad I took the time to see if I could do it. Art was sitting on the rocky shore with his fishing pole in his hand, yawning.

"Ray, it's almost five o'clock so I'll see ya later," he said.

"Me, too. Hey, that was fun! Next time we can switch places and I'll grab ya if you start to swim by," I assured him.

"Maybe. Yeah. Or I'll push you under if you get in my way," he grinned.

Art and I walked across the river several times that summer. Each time we tried to do it faster than before. Adults passing by never gave us any trouble or called the police when they would see us pulling this stunt. No one seemed concerned in the least. If a boy tried to cross that same river today, I think five or six witnesses would call 911 before the boy got his knees wet.

■ ■ ■

In 1949 we had more freedom to find adventures. One of the biggest around town that year was Sherb's Banana Split Challenge. One day I decided to go for it.

Art was waiting at the corner of Hickory Street and Chicago Avenue. My paper route money jangled in my right jeans pocket in greedy anticipation of an ice cream feast. I swerved and punched him in the shoulder as I sped past him on my bike. I pumped my legs to gain speed and avoid his revenge.

"Ray, ya jerk!" he stood on his pedals and jammed his feet up and down in his best effort to catch me before I reached Court Street. We raced north along Chicago Avenue. I gave a swift glance left then right before I barreled through the intersection at Station Street. Art was half a block behind me and chanting his fart poem, "Mark Mark made it start!" The houses blurred together as my bike cut a close tunnel through the dense scent of newly mown grass.

Art and I arrived at the corner of Court Street neck and neck. His front tire grazed my right foot as he tried to take the lead. We tilted into a sharp left turn and headed into the main commercial district of Kankakee. The sidewalk was nearly empty, but one old woman in a yellow dress and matching hat scowled at me as she hurried into Watland Brothers Camera Shop. Art's left pedal scraped the sidewalk and he overcorrected his bike and almost smashed into a light pole. Kankakee had replaced the old ornamental street lights with modern mercury vapor lamps earlier in the month. They were brighter than the old lights but we weren't used to them yet so he didn't even see it until it was almost too late. I kept pedaling.

We walked into Sherb's Ice Cream-Odette with eager faces and loose change. They had a "Lights On Special" this week in honor of the new streetlights. Businesses all over town were capitalizing on the new street lights by having "Lights On Days" with special discounts. The "Her" shop was selling dresses for $2.49, and at Kroehler's Furniture you could get a new davenport for $198. I had my sights set on Sherb's Banana Split Challenge.

Art slapped me on the back of the head and said, "Beat ya!" and slid into a booth. Sherb's was a typical ice cream parlor with a long, curving counter and short stools upholstered in black. The floor was tiled in a black and white checkerboard pattern and a line of booths with wooden tables and seats lined the wall on the left side. The walls were plastered with advertisements painted in bright colors on pieces of metal. Wrigley's "Chewing gum aids digestion" was nailed to the wall just above our table.

"Hello, boys, what will you have?" our waitress appeared at our table. She was a high school girl with straight blonde hair pulled up in a high ponytail. Her uniform was a pink dress with a round white collar and white plastic buttons down the front. She didn't look too happy to be wearing that or taking our order.

"I'll have the Banana Split Challenge!" I informed her with a confident smile. If you ordered two banana splits and ate them both they didn't charge you for the second one.

"You can't share, you know," she warned me.

"No, he's having his own," I assured her.

She looked at Art.

"I'll have two scoops of chocolate," he said.

"Ice cream aids digestion!" I told her. Art laughed and slapped the wooden table with both hands.

She spun on her heels and walked away.

A few minutes later she brought us our ice cream and we dug in with great enthusiasm. I heard Art's spoon clinking against his glass dish, the high pitched giggling of two waitresses behind the counter, metal lids clanking and cooler doors dropping. As I kept eating, those sounds faded away and all I could hear was the roar of the ice cream tidal wave coursing between my ears. I gulped down hunks of vanilla draped in warm, gooey fudge mixed with bites of creamy chocolate. The flavors blended nicely with the firm texture of banana slices and feathery sweetness of the whipped cream topping.

Art finished first. He watched me pop the cherry into my mouth and shove the empty dish into the chrome napkins dispenser. I noticed he had chocolate ice cream on the end of his nose and smeared above his satisfied smile. He shoved the second banana split in front of me. I wasn't worried because I was a professional.

The second banana split was still good, but my taste buds were a little numb by then and it took me twice as long to eat it. Art kept making gagging noises like he was throwing up. He clutched his throat and pretended to keel over on his bench, clunking his head on the wooden seat.

"Very funny. You'll see. I'm almost done," I said.

"I don't think you'll be able to fit on your bike after that. Want me to go get my wagon? I can wheel ya home," he laughed.

I patrolled the bottom of the glass dish with my spoon to see if there were any more globs of fudge hiding in the beige puddle of melted ice cream. My hand felt heavy as I lifted the second cherry to my lips. It crunched quietly between my teeth.

I looked at Art. "I did it."

"Why?" he asked.

"Figured I could," I replied.

The challenge in 1969 was not so sweet.

CHAPTER 4

CRUCIAL MEETING

1969

The bitter November air whistled through a crack in Dick's windshield as he drove along Highway 41 towards Chicago. I was riding shotgun and Pete was in the backseat. Our appointment at IGT was set for 9:00 A.M. and the lanes were clogged with cranky commuters. No one spoke.

We were passing the last adult toy store just south of Racine when someone finally broke the silence. Dick punched the accelerator and asked, "So what happened at Galaxy?"

"Jerry finished it. We're covered if the bipropellant system fails," I answered.

"Good," said Pete. I doubted he much cared. He was a stocky man with brown hair and his palms were stained with a thin coat of motor oil that had seeped into the cracks of his hands and stayed there. Pete was a blue-collar type, but very talented, and extremely intelligent.

Bolts of blame ricocheted between the seats and bounced against the glass. Pete might have been concerned he was going to be in the hot seat with IGT for a lack of progress on the car. He had wanted to be in charge of building the car, so his shoulders were loaded with responsibility. In the end he did a good job. However, I believe the project suffered from his lack of time management skills.

I thought Pete should have enlisted more help with the tedious job of welding the thin aluminum panels and superstructure into the shape of the vehicle airframe. There were hundreds of pieces of aluminum to be welded into a precise shape. Some panels were as small as two to three square inches.

Pete had been doing nothing but welding for weeks. I had asked him why he didn't hire more welders. He told me that would cost too much money and he wanted to make sure the job was done right. He never said he did not want to share credit with building the car with anyone else, but I am entitled to my opinion.

Pete built the Flame single-handedly with the exception of ten to twelve part-time friends working on a part-time schedule with part-time commitment. His friends worked a few hours a week here and there, when they felt like it. He had to keep showing new guys how to do the same job. I believed Pete wasted precious time giving the same instructions to a new face every week. He would spend a lot of his own welding time keeping an eye on their progress and answering questions.

I avoided bringing up the time management issue because Pete tended to get defensive if he perceived a threat to his ego. Well, I thought, the chickens had now come home to roost. I wondered how Pete would handle IGT on this matter. I decided I would have no comment if they asked me about it.

The meeting began on time. Bob Rosenberg and Dean Deitrich from IGT ushered us into a conference room. Two representatives from Northern Illinois Gas Company were already seated at the table with paper cups of coffee in front of them and tight smiles on their faces.

Bob tolerated the usual greetings before he got down to business. To my surprise there was no discussion of the lack of progress or ballooning budget. No one identified problems with the project or speculated about possible ways to speed things up. We didn't negotiate. We didn't look at options. Bob simply stated that IGT was appointing Dean Deitrich as the new project director. He was slated to take charge on January 1, 1970.

"Do you agree with this arrangement?" Bob asked us.

"Yes," Dick and Pete answered immediately and in unison.

Everyone looked at me.

I was stunned. What happened? It felt like I was the class idiot and had just been sucker punched. How did I end up in this position?

CHAPTER 5

HIGH SCHOOL DAYS AND ARMY RESERVES

1956

It was easy to get away with it.

"Knuck. Knuck. Knuck," John Marek chanted quietly.

Marek's signal was almost lost in the relentless rumbling and screeching of the Illinois Central Commuter Train as we jostled and tumbled toward downtown Chicago on this frigid December morning. The windows were streaked with splattered slush kicked up by the wheels on our morning journey to various Catholic high schools in the city. The IC was crammed with commuters and students, as usual, so I was sure that Marek and his football buddy would succeed in throwing Knuck (short for Knucklehead) off of the train at the next stop.

"Riverdale station!" the conductor barked as he pushed his way through the clog of high school boys standing in the small area between the cars. His eyes were dark and scornful underneath his black-billed hat. I never knew his name, but he was the type of conductor that earned himself the wrath and pranks of the teenage passengers. The girls would wait until he went to the next car and zigzag a rope across the doorway between the train cars so he could not get back in. They also wrote not so complimentary messages in chalk on his back.

We stood between the cars to have easy access to the station platforms and look cool and cavalier to the high school girls who sat in their seats watching us as they traded homework. Maybe we were hoping they would flirt with us and maybe we saw what they wrote on the conductor's back and needed to keep our brown and white Mt. Carmel letter jackets out of their reach.

The boys went to Mt. Carmel or Mendel. The girls went to St. Louis Academy, Mercy High or Aquinas. We met each day in the train cars and occasionally at Diocese-sponsored dances and social mixers at our respective schools. Each Catholic school had a sister or brother high school that provided attendees of the opposite sex so that the Catholic teenagers could mingle with the appropriate crowd and not be corrupted by Protestant social norms.

My best friend, Tom Sannito, elbowed me hard in the ribs and nodded toward the conductor's receding dark blue uniform. Knuck was a nice guy, but namby-pamby enough to be an easy target.

The train doors swooshed open and Marek edged closer to Knuck. Another football player, Dave Beran, sidled up to Knuck, whistling a few bars of "Don't Be Cruel." Just before the doors shut Marek and Baron each grabbed an elbow and cried, "Knuck!" They shoved the weaker boy off of the train. The culprits quickly backed up to blend in with the rest of the boys standing in the small vestibule.

"Off you go, Jagoff!" Baron turned and smiled at the first row of giggling girls in the car behind him. Knuck's face was visible through the doors as he frantically tried to claw his way back in. The train picked up speed and Knuck was left on the Riverdale platform to wait twenty minutes for the next train to swing by and take him to school.

"He'll end up in the Jug," Tom announced, "Luke will give him time for being late!"

The Jug was Mt. Carmel's version of detention. A classroom was selected at random to hold miscreants who violated any number of rules during the day. Being late for school could get you time in the Jug if the teacher was in a bad mood. Knuck had Trigonometry with Father Luke first thing in the morning. "Luke" as we called him, was notoriously hungover and cranky until mid-afternoon. After that he was just plain vindictive in the name of the Catholic Missions.

Luke would pass around a tin can for Missions donations each day. Any student that didn't drop in a few coins would live to regret it. The most common thing was that they would be given a math problem to work out while standing at the blackboard in front of the whole class. The problem assigned was normally one that hadn't been covered yet, so unless you had worked ahead, you were a dead duck and Luke made you look foolish in front of everybody. It was funny if it was someone else up there, but not if it were you.

"Aw, Luke won't even see him come in. He's drunk by the time he gets to school and if Knuck gives him a quarter for the Missions, Luke will let him in," Marek laughed and made a motion like he was throwing back a bottle of liquor. All of the students joked that Luke spent the Mission money on booze. We thought we could smell it from our desks as it oozed out of his evil pores.

■ ■ ■

Mt. Carmel High School is an all boys Catholic high school on Chicago's south side. Today the students have to wear uniforms, but when I attended Mt. Carmel we wore any clean shirt and pants that we had. Since we did not have to have gym shoes for physical education class, we wore street shoes to school. We just removed our shoes for phy ed and worked out in our socks.

Every boy wore a scapular. A scapular has two cloth rectangles about one inch wide and two inches tall. The cloth rectangles are decorated with religious insignias and attached to a string, so it can be worn over the shoulders. It is supposed to symbolize a priest's robe, sort of a miniature version. One cloth rectangle hangs forward over the chest and the other hangs over the back. The scapular I wore was a Carmelite Scapular, which is made of brown cloth because when the Virgin Mary appeared to the Carmelite monks she was wearing brown robes. We rolled up the cloth part of the scapular so that it would not get in the way when worn under the shirt next to the skin. The scapular did take on a strong body odor after years of use.

The reason for wearing the thing was that the Virgin Mary promised that anyone who died while wearing the scapular would be given the chance to confess his mortal sins before dying. This of course would save you from going to hell. This was a big plus to those of us who were committing many mortal sins every week as a result of going through puberty. The scapular took away the threat of hell, but not the threat of going blind, which was instilled in us by the Catholic Nuns in Ascension grade school in Harvey, Illinois. Those were days of living on the edge for us young guys of the '50s.

Carmel usually had good football teams. In fact there are a few famous alumni that went on to play in the NFL such as Donovan McNabb, Simeon Rice and Chris Calloway. Carmel played all away games since we had no football field of our own. Girls from some of the city's all-female high schools attended the games, and this provided enough motivation for me to make the trip, especially when Carmel had the chance to borrow the turf at the Chicago Bears' Soldier Field.

I was a swimmer. Swimmers were nobodies in sports. No one ever came to see us, not even the priests. The only school official in attendance was the swimming coach. Swimmers were not popular. The only way anyone would know if you were a swimmer was if you wore your school sweater with your swimming letter on it. You were on the swimming team for the love of the sport and the satisfaction of knowing that you were a good swimmer. It appears that swimmers are still on the lower end of the sports totem pole at Mt. Carmel because the online photos for the current swim team show the same small pool I used in the '50s!

Track was another interest for me, but I wasn't allowed to run because swimming and track were during the same season. Swimmers need long loose muscles and runners need tight muscles, so swimmers get leg cramps in the pool if they try to do both. Mr. Jacoby, my social studies teacher, was the coach and I really liked him because he made the effort to connect with his students and I thought he was an interesting teacher. He mentioned that I would be a good candidate for the track team so I decided to try it. The only event I entered was pole vaulting because it wouldn't require me to run for a significant distance and no one else wanted to do it. The spot was open.

I was the lone pole vaulter for Mt. Carmel. Our team only owned one pole, so I had to make sure I didn't leave it at a rival school after a meet. No one gave me any instructions about how to pole vault. I ended up competitive, but not exactly a champion. My training was, "Grab the pole, run down there and get yourself up and over the crossbar." I decided to figure out how to do it on my own and I developed my own style which proved to be unique and quite entertaining at track meets. I was only about 145 pounds, but I had great arm and shoulder strength from so many hours doing the butterfly stroke in the pool.

In order to get over the bar I didn't have to race down the track. I sort of jogged down the track, hooked the pole in the pole vault slot and pulled myself over the bar with my upper body strength. Everyone used to stand and watch because they had never seen anyone do that before. I would observe the athletes from other teams at our track meets to try to get pointers. I noticed that the other guys ran as fast as they could to use the momentum to get themselves high enough in the air and over the bar. Over the years I improved my performance and my best vault was just over ten feet, which in the days before flexible poles was pretty good. I was able to win the event at one track meet and most times was able to place second or third.

Our teachers were either Reverends or Misters. The Reverends were Carmelite priests and the Misters were lay teachers. On the morning Knuck had the misfortune of being tossed from the train, my buddy Tom Sannito and I headed into Mr. O'Connor's physics class to find him running late. Our laughter at Knuck's inevitable tardiness preoccupied our thoughts.

I found a seat in the front row and decided to plop down immediately so I wouldn't appear unprepared when Mr. O'Connor eventually walked in. Today was lab day. Tom was lingering at Mr. O'Connor's desk, trying to stretch his neck around the corner to see if Mr. O'Connor was approaching the door. A quick grin snaked across his face and he reached under the desk and flipped the loaded switch.

"Aaaaaaah! Jesus!"

A few rows behind me Gary Pawlish yelped in pain and bolted out of his desk. Mr. O'Connor had an electric generator hooked up to his desk and told all the students from the time they were Bennys (freshmen) that he would use it to shock any student who was daydreaming or otherwise not paying attention during his physics lab. There was a switch system which enabled Mr. O'Connor (or a daring student such as Tom if the teacher was running late) to shock any desk at any moment. Mr. O'Connor, according to the 1957 Mt. Carmel Oriflamme yearbook, had instructed Carmel men in the science of physics "since Mt. Carmel's early days." He had developed quite an effective classroom management style over his long career.

"Mr. Pawlish."

Mr. O'Connor stood in the doorway. Gary Pawlish shook his right hand violently to get rid of the aftershock and grimaced in an effort to look obedient and attentive. He was unsuccessful because his face was screwed up like he was chewing on tinfoil.

"Yes, Mr. O'Connor. Sir, I realized I left my lunch on the train," he stumbled over his excuse. Telling on Tom Sannito would ensure weeks of harassment.

"Yes. That is certainly distressing. Take your seat," Mr. O'Connor replied with a level gaze.

Gary glanced down at his chair as if vipers were slithering back and forth across the seat.

"Yes, sir."

"Very well."

I never got shocked by Mr. O'Connor because I liked science and I generally paid attention because of my interest. He didn't appear to shock people randomly or for the fun of it. He did it if it needed to be done. I figured if I did what I was supposed to do I wouldn't get shocked, and that's how it worked out.

After physics lab Tom and I parted ways for the remainder of our morning classes and decided to find each other during lunch to talk about the upcoming "Winter Whirl" dance because we would probably ride together. I reluctantly headed toward Luke's room for my daily dose of mathematical torture and frustration.

Luke was a major academic roadblock for me. He taught very important math classes I needed to get anywhere in college. His ridiculous and punitive teaching style not only made me bitter, it made me shut down and resent even stepping foot in his classroom. Needless to say my grades were not great and I rarely understood the homework. My father, an electrical engineer, helped me with my homework, but even his help couldn't support me through the long classroom hours with Father Luke and his arrogance.

I did not ask Dad to confront Luke for me, but one time he did. He went at the request of Mother. I don't think I remember what he said except that he basically told him he was a crappy teacher and asked to have me transferred to another math class with another teacher. It didn't work and I was forced to remain in Luke's class. I wonder how many other boys Luke affected in such a disastrous way. I also wonder how things would have turned out differently had I had an effective caring math teacher at Mt. Carmel. But it was not meant to be. I have since learned that I am a very visual-spatial learner and that the traditional sequential style of math teachers can be like hearing a foreign language and without translation the subject matter can be indecipherable.

Visual-spatial learners learn in systems and patterns, not step by step directions. I have always had trouble "showing my work" in math because the answer just comes to me all at once and it is difficult to trace the answer back to certain 1-2-3 steps. In the 1950s this difficulty was unknown and kids like me had two choices: struggle or give up.

At lunch I made my way outside to eat in the cold. Before the school cafeteria was built all of the students had to eat outside no matter what the weather had in mind for the day. I always took my lunch in a brown bag. Usually the same brown bag. I brought the bag home with me every day, until it became worn out. Bags of the proper size were harder to come by in those days. None of the guys carried a lunch box. This would have been a source of ridicule for sure.

"What the hell? Tell me which assholes threw me off the train," Knuck dropped his stack of books beside me and started to unroll his brown bag before his backside hit the curb.

"Knuck, you know the gang. Probably the football players. I was watching the girls from Aquinas because they were whispering and getting ready to do who knows what," I replied, because staying out of it with a vague lie seemed like the better choice here. Good thing I was wearing my scapular.

"Bunch of assholes," Knuck grumbled as he jammed his hand into his brown bag and pulled out some carrot sticks wrapped in wax paper.

"Hello, ladies!" Tom Sannito punched my right shoulder and sat down on my other side. "Guard your skirts and sandwiches."

The worst part about eating outside was the biting Chicago wind and whipping snow. The second worst thing was dealing with the bums that wanted part of our lunch. Bums and hobos would wait around for leftovers or handouts during the Mt. Carmel lunch hour because teenagers threw away a lot of food and generally had a hard time saying no.

Knuck, Tom and I ate our lunch quickly and talked about who we would like to invite to the Winter Whirl in our soon to be completed student center. The new student center was highly anticipated because when not being used for dances and other events it would double as a cafeteria and our curbside lunches would be history.

At the moment I didn't have any ideas about who to ask to the dance, so I mostly concentrated on my lunch. I usually had a cheese or meat sandwich, and a banana and a homemade peanut butter cookie. That day was no different. After just a few minutes all three of us jumped to our feet, stuffed our brown bags back into our pockets and headed inside to the warmth of the hallways, and with any luck, the gymnasium.

Rockets were not on my radar during high school. I guess my mind was too occupied with sports and girls. During this time I started to help my dad with his arrowhead collection so my hobby turned to archaeology. My dad had been given the collection by his father. It was amassed by Dad's Uncle Orb while living on my great grandfather Henry's farm north of Milford, Indiana. When Grandpa Bert died Dad got the collection and gave it to me since I had an interest in Indians and Indian lore for a long time. I always played the role of the Indian in Kankakee when we played Cowboys and Indians. I think I was an Indian in a previous life.

Dad and I would scour the farmers' fields of Indiana and Illinois after the plows went through and cherry pick the artifacts that were churned to the surface. Many times I would go out alone if Dad was at work and I had some spare time. I continued this tradition when I had children. I took my kids on frigid windy walks each spring to search the ruts and valleys of Wisconsin fields near our home.

■ ■ ■

"You should join the Reserves, Ray," Mother paused to gauge my reaction as she sipped her coffee and wiped the table in front of me. She hovered momentarily while I considered her idea.

"What?" I was confused at this turn of events and not sure how to respond. Stalling seemed to be the best choice here. It was eight months before I would graduate from Mt. Carmel and I figured that I would enroll in college for next fall.

"Six months. That's all, Ray. You'll get to travel for free and avoid the draft."

These tidbits sounded compelling. Knowing Mother, however, there could be drawbacks and fine print to be excavated.

"The Army?" I asked, trying to picture myself gunning down an escaped Nazi war criminal or Communist sympathizer. Could I spend my time eating food from a tin can, crawling around in muddy foxholes or marching in formation for hours at a time?

"Of course the Army."

■ ■ ■

From Fort Leonard Wood, Missouri Company C

Saturday, July 20, 1957

Dear Mom and Dad,

Well, today ends the first week of basic training. Time is starting to move faster now than it did at first. So far we have done things like dismounted drill M-1 rifle instructions, marching, first aid, safety, and most of all clean the barracks. Almost every day we G. I. the barracks on our hands and knees with scrub brushes. Last night we worked from 8:00-12:00 A. M. The night before that I got about 3 hrs. sleep because I had K. P. that day. If you draw K. P. you get up in the morning at 3:30 and work till 8:00 P. M. I sure warshed a lot of dishes that day. We have a lot of classes every day on different things such as first aid, etc. Oh by the way, in the last first aid class we had to give each other shots of sugar water. I also had 2 shots yesterday for tetanus and typhoid, these were booster shots. I had a small reaction to the vaccination I received a couple of days ago. That tetanus shot sure gives you a sore arm.

We had an inspection this morning and our platoon got 2ⁿᵈ place. We had the rest of the day off and it is about 6:30 P. M. now. The food is good and you get all you can eat. I think I am gaining weight. The days are still very hot and humid, but I am getting used to it now. All our classes are held in an air conditioned theater.

I just came back from the show. I went with Roy and Bill, a couple of guys in my platoon. Bill graduated from Purdue. He majored in horticulture. Bob Crowhurst who lives in Joliet is my best buddy. We plan to fly to Chicago together when basic is over. All the guys I have met so far are very nice and everyone helps everyone else, I guess it's because we are all in the same boat. I know my other letters were short, but it is because I had no time to put into them. Oh! I bought a swimsuit today and Bob and I are going swimming together tomorrow. I went to mass Sunday at 11:00 A. M. and boy it must have been 110 degrees in the shade. I sent my laundry to the Laundromat today and will be able to get them tomorrow.

If you come to see me I am in the 1ˢᵗ platoon and the number of my barrack is 1077. Bring a watch and a camera. I have about $4.00 left but I think it will be enough. I still have 2 weeks to go before I get paid. On second thought maybe you should send me some.

The training is really pretty easy so far, but the heat is what makes it hard to take. We were issued two more uniforms besides our regular khakis. They are the new green winter uniforms and the khaki Bermuda shorts and short sleeved shirts. I have on my Bermudas now.

I am running out of things to say and I should clean my rifle now so I will sign off. Be sure to write again.

Your son,
Ray

■ ■ ■

From Fort Huachuca, Arizona

September 10, 1957

Dear Mom and Dad,

I just came back from the show a little while ago, and am now in my bunk writing this letter. We arrived in Arizona about 8:00 A. M. Monday morning. It took us about 36 hours to make the entire trip. We traveled Pullman all the way and we had private rooms from El Paso to Herford, Arizona which was our last stop. We went through Oklahoma, Texas, New Mexico, and Arizona. I saw a lot of these states from the train. I was impressed with the size and the flatness of Texas. Here in Arizona we are surrounded by low mountain ranges. The highest I think is about 9,000 feet. The Fort is situated about one mile high and you can sure tell the difference in the air. It is much thinner. It is sure beautiful scenery though. I wish I had a movie camera.

At Leonard Wood there were 3,300 men, here there are about 6,000. As a result it is a much nicer place. Everything is clean and neat. I am assigned to the 93 Battalion Signal Corps. In our whole company there are only about 100 men. All the men are in for two years except us and are mostly PFCs or specialists.

The duty is much easier than before. So far all we have done is draw details. That's all anybody does. In the morning formation all the men are assigned to a detail, and that's all they do for the rest of the day. One of these days they are supposed to start training us. Instead of radio repair they put us in an operating section. We learn to operate radios instead of repair them. Because we are six months I don't suppose we will get much of it though.

Today I signed up for a 12 week correspondence course in the fundamentals of radio. If I don't get it here I'll go to school for it. The course only costs $2.00. This course should help me later on.

The weather is really great. Sunshine all the time and it is a dry climate, nothing like Illinois, you can sure tell the difference. Down here we wear sun helmets, the ones the African hunters use on safari. Our duty hours are from 5:30 a. m. to 4:30 p.m. The rest of the time is ours. We can wear civilian clothes after duty hours. I already have some. Please don't bother to send me any. We can get a pass any time we want it, and we can also go to Mexico, which is only 30 miles away. As soon as I can I will send you some pictures of the camp.

We have it much better here and now maybe I can relax and take life easy.

Love,
Ray

■ ■ ■

Dear Mom and Dad,

Well we just finished another day and boy am I tired. Today Harold Harrison and I went mountain climbing. We had the aid of what were supposed to be mountain horses. The horse I had must have been a mule, because I spent most of my time and energy pushing or pulling the darn thing up and down the mountainside. Its name was Sugar, and I see why they call him that, you probably have to offer him sugar whenever you want him to move. Oh well! We had fun anyway. The highest we went was about 8,000 ft. I took some color pictures with my camera. I don't know how they will turn out. I'll send them home when I get them developed. I'm sitting here recuperating now. I just took a shower and shave and I feel pretty good. I can't find your letter so I won't be able to answer your questions. I think you asked about us being mistreated because we were 6 mo. men. Nothing could be further from the truth. All the guys here are all real nice to us and now we have a lot of friends here.

Do they have the flu going around there? It has spread all over the post here and they call it an epidemic. I think about 1,000 men are in the hospital now. I went once myself, but they said I didn't have it. Out of the eight that came down here with me three are in the hospital. By next week it should be about licked.

This is like a four month vacation being here at Huachuca. We have it made. The only thing that we have to do is look sharp for the Saturday inspection. During the day they give you some light detail. Just something to keep you busy. Since there is no war or anything like that now there is not much to do on any Army post now.

Last week we had a full week of radio procedure class. We learned how to converse on the air and how to use radio language such as Roger, out, and things like that. We operated a radio net using four different radios the ANGRC/6, (handy talkie) ANGRC/10 (walkie talkie) ANGRC/9 a larger set and the largest on the ANGRC/3/8 series. It was a real interesting class. I got a 91 on the final test.

I haven't received any correspondence course work yet, but I should get it any day now. I am sort of anxious to get it so I can get started.

I am getting the newspaper now and I get the news about a week late, but I don't mind. I hope everyone is feeling fine at home.

Well I have to sign off now.

Love to all,
Ray

■   ■   ■

Dear Mom and Dad,

I've got a little time now so I will write. It was sure nice to hear from you again. All those letters help a lot. My watch arrived in good condition and keeps good time. Now I can be sure just what time it is when I awake in the morning. I received a letter and stamps from Nola and got all the news from Chicago. She sure is a great sister. The stamps will enable me to send this letter. I will enclose some Chinquapin Oak leaves for Dad.

I am learning a lot about electrical engineering and both calculus and analytic geometry from my E. E. friend. His name is Harvey Friedland and he is a graduate of the New York City College and knows his subject inside and out. I haven't received my second assignment from correspondence course yet but it should be along any time now.

I hope that reserve money comes because I can sure use it. If I had some money I could get a very good camera very cheap. I don't know the exact date of my discharge yet but is probably around Dec. 15.

Tomorrow I am going mountain climbing with some buddies in Garden Canyon. By the time I get out of here I plan to climb most of the mountains on Fort Huachuca's 77 sq. miles of area (1,000,000) acres. For the last week I have been going to driver's school. Now I can drive any jeep or truck that is made. This evening Harold Harrison and I are going to get a deer license. The season opens the 15th and we want to be the first ones out. We will draw a carbine out of supply and set out. The mountains around here are full of deer and wild pigs. I suppose we can get one.

I enclosed some pictures I took in basic and some taken here in the mountains. The colored pictures are the first ones I took with my camera so the next ones will be better.

Well I have to go now.

Love,
Ray

■ ■ ■

Dear Mom and Dad,

Well it's Sunday evening and I have time on my hands so I can write. I hope everyone is well and feeling fine, I am. I sent Harold a newspaper from Tombstone, Ariz. I suppose he has it by now. I will send some pictures later. I am going to the show soon. I was in the mountains again today. It is about the only thing I can do without spending money. I have about $30.00 left now and I expect to have about $120.00 at payday. If you want a camera or something I will be able to get it then. I can pick up a 30 cal. Rifle that has only fired 11 shots for $45. I can't decide whether to do it or not. Ask Dad about it. I put my name in for deer hunting again because they lowered the price of a license to six dollars.

I have a chance to see California, Las Vegas and other places, but I won't be able to be home for Christmas if I do. I have only been thinking about it though. What do you think? I met a guy from Winamac, Ind. and made plans to go relic hunting on his farm soon as I go to the lake.

I can't wait to get some home cooked meals and sleep in a real bed again. These 54 days left will go very slow. I have taken up cigar smoking now. Tell Harold I have a stone I took off of Bat Masterson's grave I will bring home with me. I can probably sell it for $50.00. I have not received any mail from the relatives yet and *have not written any. You just don't care about anything anymore after you have been in this army very long. The only reason I read books and study is to keep my mind from decaying. You lose all your incentive to do things after 6 months of being told what to do.*

Say hello to everyone for me. By the way, when are your birthdays, I still do not know. Please write.

With love,
Ray
P. S. Keep this money for me.

■ ■ ■

Dear Mom and Dad,

I just finished lunch, if that's what you could call it. I am now sitting on my foot locker writing this letter. Before I say anything else I will ask you to send me my $20 back. I need some money to put down on my plane reservation. I have $10 now and if I use it for that I won't have any left. I got air-coach now instead of first class so I will save $10. I will tell you more about when I will arrive when I get everything set. I will do this Saturday.

I spent last weekend in Los Angeles with Harvey Friedland. I got a ride with some guys who lived there. We had a good time visiting all the different places. We drove all around Los Angeles and Long Beach. We went to Disneyland Saturday night. Sunday we went deep sea fishing at Long Beach. I caught 1 barracuda! Harvey didn't fish. There were 183 barracuda caught in all.

I am going to mail my clothes home instead of parcel post. A package will follow this letter with souvenirs.

As for Christmas presents I always need clothes.

I will write again to tell you what I forgot to say this time.

Love,
Ray

■ ■ ■

Mother was right. I didn't get any useful training, but the train ride didn't cost me a thing. My interest in rockets was rekindled during this time for a couple of reasons. Fort Huachuca was the Army's missile testing ground. They did a lot of things out there like shooting anti-aircraft guns and occasionally, very occasionally, you'd hear a roar and a whish and somewhere way off in the desert you'd see a streak of smoke going up in the air. They were launching small rockets of various types, mostly ground to air missiles of some type or other.

Just prior to my conclusion of duty at Fort Huachuca in late December 1957, the Russian Sputnik Satellite was sent into orbit around the earth and the event was publicized on the radio and TV. I remember listening to the beeping sound of the Sputnik on the radio. You were supposed to be able to see the Sputnik as it passed over at night at the published times. I did try on several occasions to view the moving light in the sky, but I never saw it.

I returned to Chicago to start the next chapter in my life. I was now a well-traveled man with radio repair and jeep driving skills. I was ready to face my future.

CHAPTER 6

First Date and Soul Mate

1958

"Ray. Rita's friend wants to meet you," Tom Sannito assured me during a phone conversation a few months after I returned from my stint in the Army. His girlfriend, Rita, sometimes asked Tom to match his friends with her friends.

"How does she even know about me?" I asked, not convinced of Tom's latest scheme.

"Well, she doesn't, but once she does she'll be glad she met you! Let's double on Saturday at Willowbrook," said Tom. Willowbrook was a popular dance hall in the south suburbs of Chicago.

"Who is she?" I asked.

"Her name is Phyllis Gerdes and she's Rita's best friend. What do ya say?"

"I don't know, Tom. What's she like?" I asked.

"Tell you what. I gotta go over to her house and return a book for Rita. Come with me and see for yourself. I suppose she could use a preview of you, too!"

So that's what we did. I wanted to look presentable, so I changed into a fresh pair of khaki pants and a green and black argyle sweater. It was early springtime in Illinois, so I grabbed my brown leather jacket and shrugged it on as I walked out the door. I drove over to Tom's house and picked him up. We showed up at the Gerdes house in Riverdale and I stood on the front stoop, smiling, next to Tom. He was dressed in jeans, black t-shirt and a black leather jacket. Neither of us were wearing gloves, so we stuffed our hands in our pockets to keep them warm.

"Here goes nothing," said Tom.

He rang the doorbell and we waited. I rocked back and forth on my feet, trying to look casual. We heard footsteps approaching almost immediately. Phyllis opened the door, and we both got our free look at each other to help us decide if we'd like to double with Tom and Rita.

Phyllis was a beautiful girl. Stunning, really. She had shoulder-length light brown, wavy hair and green eyes that twinkled when she smiled. Phyllis was wearing a blue and white print top and navy blue skinny pants. Her eyebrows arched playfully as she looked back and forth between Tom and me.

I fell for her right off the bat.

"There you go, Phyll. Rita told me to say it's a great book and thanks a lot for lending it to her," said Tom. He held the book in his outstretched hand. She took it.

"Thank you, boys. I'm happy Rita liked it. Will you ask her to call me, Tom?" said Phyllis.

"I sure will. This is my friend, Ray. He just got back from the Army and agreed to give me a ride over here."

"Nice to meet you, Ray," said Phyllis.

"Thank you. It's nice to meet you, too." I couldn't come up with anything more creative than that because her smile had really gotten to me and I was having trouble forming words.

"So, Phyll, I think Rita wanted to talk to you, too, about your plans for this weekend. She really wants to go dancing at Willowbrook."

Phyllis grinned. She glanced at me and said, "I'd like that."

My face felt hot and my heart pounded because I knew this was my chance. We all knew why we were here.

"Well, Phyllis, I'd really like to help round out the couples, so would you be willing to be my dance partner?" I asked. I looked into her green eyes and tried to give her a charming smile. I'm afraid it looked more like a wince because I was so nervous. Not my smoothest move.

Phyllis didn't say anything at first. I thought I had blown it. She looked down at her blue and white pointy shoes and leaned against the door jam. I looked at her shoes, too, wishing I had waited for Rita and Tom to set up the date over the phone. Now I had forced an answer and I was afraid Phyllis wouldn't like being asked out by a boy that only knew her for less than a minute.

She finally looked up at me with an answer.

"I would. That would be nice, Ray," said Phyllis.

"Okay! Saturday it is," I said. "Tom, I can pick you and Rita up and then we can come by and get Phyllis. Just tell me what time."

"Sure, sure. Why don't we let the girls decide the time and when Rita tells me I'll call you," said Tom.

"Okay," I said. "Phyllis, I will see you Saturday. Nice to meet you!"

I turned around and headed towards my car parked in the driveway. Tom wasn't far behind. He slapped me on the back of my head.

"Way to go, Ray. Thought you were going to ask her to marry you the second you met her. Good thing she's Rita's best friend or she might have slammed the door on us!" said Tom.

My grin stretched from ear to ear and I shoved him away from me. We got in my car and went home.

Our first date was indeed that double with Tom and Rita at the Willowbrook Ballroom. Phyllis greeted me with a warm friendly smile when we picked her up and my attraction to her was strong from the start. I didn't give anyone else a second thought after that. We danced and laughed like we had known each other more than just a few hours. In fact we entered a dance off that first night for couples and on our entry card wrote that we had been together for 25 years. We thought it was hilarious to hear a voice booming, "Congratulations to Ray and Phyllis, together for 25 years!" No one seemed to question how that was possible as we danced on by, obviously still teenagers with wicked grins and conspiratorial giggles.

The music swirled around us.

Blue Moon, now I'm no longer alone
Without a dream in my heart
Without a love of my own

Phyllis and I started dating after that first night of dancing. There was an A & W Root Beer stand halfway between my house and Phyllis's house in Riverdale. We would meet there and talk in the car as we ate our hot dogs and sipped cold root beer. Over the next several months we went to movies, drive-ins and spent time in her parents' basement watching TV and talking. My mother liked Phyllis a lot and of course that didn't hurt.

I didn't go out with anyone else. It was either Phyllis or no one. But Phyllis would go out with others and I would get jealous and worried she liked someone better than me. She did that deliberately numerous times to get me worked up. She liked to get me going.

CHAPTER 7

BEACH BOMBING AND COLLEGE CALCULUS

1959

College Days. I am in the middle. My old friend Tom Sannito is on the right and my friend Melvin Pommerance is on the left. Melvin attended the Purdue Extension with me. We had just launched one of my homemade rockets. It just came back down and the rear end of the rocket is sticking out of the ground just in front of me. You can see the tail fins.

"We might as well go ahead and launch it," I told Dale as the warm East Chicago wind whipped across my face, causing me to squint at him in the darkness.

"Yeah. We drove all the way out here."

We had a very good plan…

After my discharge from the Army Reserve I enrolled at the Purdue University Calumet Center in Hammond, Indiana. My major was going to be electrical engineering. I met fellow freshman Dale Carpenter in my first chemistry class and before too long found out that he shared my interest in rockets and explosives. Dale and I got together outside of class to talk about rockets and how we could build and launch them.

One day he came up with a book on rockets and missiles called *Rocket Propulsion Elements* that was written in 1949 by George P. Sutton. It was sort of a handbook on rockets and contained detailed information on how to build rocket engines. It is in its seventh edition today. There were chapters entitled *Flight Performance, Liquid Propellant Rocket Engine Systems, Components of Solid Rockets* and *Rocket Testing*. There were a number of charts and graphs that enabled the reader to calculate maximum altitude and such things as thermodynamic relations or thrust coefficient. The text was very technical and involved a collection of variables and abbreviations I had never seen before. Fortunately, in the back of the book there were a number of example calculations that explained how to design rockets and calculate thrust.

When Dale and I weren't studying we used to look through Sutton's book and debate what kind of rockets we could build. We weren't interested in seriously studying rockets or switching our majors. Dale and I just wanted to build some small rockets and launch them ourselves.

We found out that one of the best and easiest propellants for rockets was a combination of two things: zinc dust and sulfur powder. Dale and I experimented and we found if you mixed those two things in the right proportions and lit it with a match it would burn very rapidly. This particular reaction would liberate a lot of heat and smoke. So we experimented with things like how much of this and how much of that works the best. After we decided on the best design, we packed the stuff in some aluminum tubing and secured a nose cone to it with some pins. We would mount it on a steel rod and point it up in the air. Then we would stick a fuse in it and light it off. Dale and I made sure to get out of the way quickly so we could stand back and see if it would do anything.

For a while nothing really happened other than the zinc and sulfur dust would burn. It wouldn't burn fast enough to lift the rocket off the ground, so all we were doing was making a lot of smoke, although it was an impressive quantity of smoke. So then we came upon a new idea. In order to get the dust to burn all at once we would make little paper bags of rocket fuel. We took some brown paper bags and cut them up into pieces and made little paper tubes. We'd pour dust into the paper tube until it was filled halfway. We left the other half of the tube empty. Dale or I would twist off both ends of the little tube. We made a bunch of these little packets of fuel. In between each packet we had a fuse and then we'd put each of the packets inside the rocket one by one. The fuse went right up the middle of all the packets so that when the fuse lit the bottom packet it would burn and then ignite the next one and so on in a rapid reaction sequence. That new approach worked very well. From then on we were launching rockets.

ZINC & SULFUR
ROCKET

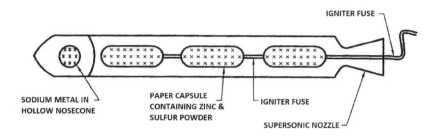

IGNITER FUSE

SODIUM METAL IN
HOLLOW NOSECONE

PAPER CAPSULE
CONTAINING ZINC &
SULFUR POWDER

IGNITER FUSE

SUPERSONIC NOZZLE

SOLID PROPELLANT
STATIC TEST ROCKET

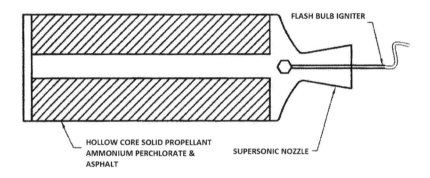

FLASH BULB IGNITER

HOLLOW CORE SOLID PROPELLANT
AMMONIUM PERCHLORATE &
ASPHALT

SUPERSONIC NOZZLE

*Zinc and sulfur rocket design I used with my friend Dale Carpenter
in my college days*

They started out small. Dale and I kept making the rocket components bigger and bigger and they kept going higher and higher. But they were just tubes, there was no rocket nozzle or anything like that. It was more like a mortar shell type of propulsion rather than rocket propulsion, but we were satisfied---for a while.

The biggest and most interesting launch was on this windy summer night on the sand dunes of East Chicago on the shore of Lake Michigan. Our homemade hollow rocket nose cone contained about two pounds of sodium metal, and this, our most impressive rocket to date, was housed in a two-inch diameter tube about eight feet long. It even had guidance fins. Earlier in the week Dale and I had decided to bring our new rocket to East Chicago, Indiana because it had a nice swimming beach with large sand dunes. We figured that if we launched it at night and used a long fuse we would not be observed.

"Dale, give me a hand, will ya?" I was a little annoyed that he was just staring toward the picnic area, rocking back and forth on his heels while I tried to unload our equipment. Dale was a few inches taller than my 5 foot 10 inch frame and had blond hair combed back from his pale face. He had a quick laugh and darting blue eyes. Right then they were scanning the beach.

Danny and the Junior's faint lyrics were drifting across the sand layered with sharp bursts of teenage laughter and the savory smoke smell of campfires and barbecue.

You can rock it you can roll it
*Do the **bop** and even stroll it*
At the hop
When the record starts spinnin'
You calypso and you chicken at the hop
Do the dance sensation that is sweepin' the nation
at the hop

"Yeah. How many people do you think are over there? What if someone sees us?" Dale asked, eyes narrow in the wind.

"Ah. No one will see us! It's dark. I can barely hear anything with this wind." I tried to assure Dale because I didn't feel like packing up and returning home without even trying our luck with our new rocket design.

"That's just it. The wind must be twenty, thirty miles an hour. How do we know how that will affect this situation? Maybe we should just come back tomorrow," said Dale. He tossed his blond hair off of his skeptical forehead.

"We don't know what will happen. But there's only one way to find out." I wrapped the fuse into a coil and gathered as much of our rocket gear as I could from the trunk of Dale's bright blue and turquoise 1956 Ford Parklane Station Wagon. I am pretty sure it was his mother's car. It wasn't what you'd call "cool," but it certainly had enough space to stash all of our homemade rocket parts. That's all that mattered to us.

The purpose of our launch was to find out how high our new rocket would go. We could calculate the rocket's trajectory in the dark because the sodium metal in the nose cone would burn when it came into contact with water. We would see flashes of light when the sodium metal exploded in the lake. The plan was to record the elapsed time between launch and lake explosion to figure out how high the rocket went. It was a very good plan.

We had an eight foot long steel rod that we pushed into the sand at a 45 degree angle pointing towards the water. We slid the rocket onto the rod. The rocket tube had sturdy screw eyes bolted to it at three points: one near the top, one in the middle and one near the bottom of the rocket tube. This was our standard launcher system for all of our rockets. The 45 degree angle was important in our distance calculations.

"Okay. Get back. No, no, no! Dale. Get back!" I shouted above the wind.

"We have to know when it launches!" he screamed.

"We'll hear it!"

I was wrong. We didn't hear anything as we approached the safety of the big blue Parklane. I stood next to the car looking out at Lake Michigan, waiting for this big flash of light somewhere way out there. Nothing happened.

"Maybe the fuse went out," Dale offered, "I'll bet it never went up. Let's go get it."

Another popular hit was playing on the beach as we trudged across the sand to recover our dud rocket.

I chew my nails and I twiddle my thumbs I'm real nervous, but it sure is fun C'mon baby, you're driving me crazy Goodness, gracious, great balls of fire!!

The beach party picnic area lit up like daylight with two or three sudden explosions about thirty or forty feet offshore. Bright white, blue and green flashes erupted as chunks of sodium metal exploded in the water, dropping on the parking area behind the picnic area with increasing speed.

The rocket had launched, but almost immediately after the launch the nose cone must have come off, spraying the area with sodium metal. One piece would explode and shatter into a number of smaller pieces and those pieces would go up and come down, hit the water and explode. For several seconds there were explosions all along the shoreline, much to the consternation of the teenagers on the beach.

"Oh my God!"
"Debby! No. Wait for me!"
"Holy shit! What the hell?"

The beach erupted as teenagers grabbed their blankets and coolers of beer and ran towards their cars.

We watched in horror, fascination and pride mixed together in a cocky cocktail of, "Let's do this again!"

Well I saw the thing comin' out of the sky
It had the one long horn, one big eye
I commenced to shakin' and I said "ooh-eee"
It looks like a purple people eater to me.

■ ■ ■

Dale and I got tired of the zinc and sulfur powder rockets, so we decided to get more serious and try to introduce a solid propellant to our rocket design along with a rocket nozzle.

In order to build an actual rocket we had to use solid propellants. The rockets we were interested in used burnable powders with rocket nozzles that were built to produce a certain amount of thrust. I needed to calculate and design the dimensions of the rocket nozzle to produce the correct amount of thrust or our rocket wouldn't amount to anything.

"I'll go through the book and see if I can build something for solids," I told Dale as we walked through the math building after class one Friday afternoon.

"Yeah, Ray, see what kind of fuel core you can cook up. When you have it ready we can take it over to my buddy Rick's and fire it off in his backyard." Dale grinned and gave me a half wave as he ducked out the side door to the parking lot.

We decided to use a combination of asphalt and a white powder called ammonium perchlorate. The asphalt would be the fuel and the perchlorate would serve as an oxidizing agent. Ammonium perchlorate was used in explosives such as military weapons, so I knew that we had to be careful here because mixing a strong oxidizing agent into hot, flammable asphalt could be dangerous. I didn't want to be disowned for setting fire to my dad's workbench.

Dale and I picked up some asphalt from a local constructions site and bought the perchlorate from a chemical supply company in Hammond, the source of all our chemical needs in the past. For several nights in a row I went down into our basement and fiddled around with little portions of this asphalt and perchlorate. I'd make a batch and light it on fire with a match to see how rapidly it burned. When I found the right proportions I decided I had to make a larger quantity for the rocket.

I needed about a cup of this concoction to fill the rocket chamber. My parents had a little gas-fired burner down in the basement that my mother used for boiling water for some reason. I decided I was going to use this to melt the asphalt until it was soupy and then mix in this other material, mix it up good and then pour it into the rocket chamber while it was still hot. When it cooled down it would be a solid block of rocket propellant. Then I would screw my rocket nozzle to one end and the other end was sealed shut. My idea was to run a fuse through the rocket nozzle to ignite the bottom part of this rod of rocket propellant and let it burn from one end to the other.

I got a metal pan from the kitchen and put a chunk of solid asphalt into it with a clunk. I started heating it up. After it got soft enough, I added the rest of my supply of smaller chunks of thick, gummy asphalt. I kept stirring the pot of molten material. About that time my mother happened to come down to the basement. I think she smelled the odor of a burning car down there and wanted to know what the heck I was doing.

She said, "Well, you know, if the asphalt gets too hot it might catch on fire all by itself. Instead of putting the pan directly over the flame, why don't you put a pan of water on the burner, boil the water, and then put the pan containing the asphalt in the boiling water and let the boiling water heat the asphalt. That way it will only get up to 200 degrees and that would be as high as it would go."

I knew that would be hot enough to melt the asphalt, and this would eliminate any contact of my pan with the asphalt with an actual flame.

I smiled and said, "That's a good idea."

Mom said, "That's what they call a double boiler. You can use mine, just make sure you put it back in the cupboard."

When I got the asphalt sufficiently hot I started mixing in the powdered ammonium perchlorate. I stirred it up for a while and then I took it out of the double boiler and poured it into my rocket chamber, screwed on my nozzle, and let it sit there and cool down. I was ready to go.

By this time one of Phyllis's friends from Thorton College had introduced me to Bill Jouris. Bill was interested in rockets, too, and he worked at the Armour Research Foundation in Chicago. He was a technician in the physics department in the nuclear reactor facility there. When Bill got wind that Dale and I were involved in launching rockets he got interested. Previous to my mixing this fuel he had told me, "Well, when you're ready, we can take it over to my friend's house and fire it off in his back-yard. He lives over in Crete."

The day after I got the rocket all cooled down Dale, Bill and I made plans to go out to the country where Bill's friend lived. We got some cement blocks and built a crude circular test bunker without a cover. If something blew up, it would explode straight in the air, but no frag-ments would come shooting out at us. We mounted the rocket on a long wooden stick.

"Who wants to light the fuse?" I asked, matches in hand and grin on my face.

"I'll do it!" Dale offered quickly.

Dale lit the fuse and all three of us ran away and hid behind the house. All of a sudden there was this tremendous explosion. We stepped out from behind the house and the whole thing was completely gone. There was no rocket to be seen. It must have shattered into a million pieces.

"Dale! It's gone! It's gone! Do you see any of it around here?" I shouted as we looked into the blackened bunker.

"No! Holy shit! You made a Ray-grenade," Dale joked.

That was the first catastrophic failure of our rocket engine. Either the rocket nozzle was designed poorly, or the rocket fuel had burned too fast. If the rocket fuel had burned too fast, it would have released too much gas faster than the rocket nozzle could let it out. So the thing blew up. Actually, I had made a bomb.

It was back to the drawing board.

Dale and I had hired a machinist in Hammond to make our rocket nozzle in his machine shop. His name was Helmut Mueller and he said he had made rocket parts during World War II for the German Army.

I decided to try it one more time, this time using a different approach. This time Dad got involved.

"Mother told me you're planning another launch," he said. I hadn't even heard him come down the stairs and there he was peering over my shoulder as we stood at his basement workbench.

"Last time we had massive rocket failure, so I need to make some adjustments. I think I've got a better design now," I answered.

"I can take you down to the big lot behind the Public Service Building and we can build a bunker there. We just use it to store all the telephone poles, transformers and things like that for the line gangs."

"That would be great, Dad. Thanks," I said, surprised at the offer. "We should be ready by this weekend."

I was grateful because there would be more than enough room and we wouldn't have to drive all the way to Bill's friend's house again. We'd have to walk all of three blocks from my house to our new test launch site.

By this time it was winter. Dale and my father stood around in the snow while I mounted our rocket on a table we had dragged inside the bunker. This time I had it configured so the exhaust gas would go straight up and the rocket would push straight down on the table. In case it did want to fly it wouldn't go anywhere. The idea here was just to see if the rocket would generate any thrust or explode again.

I had varied the fuel combination a little bit and I had changed the shape of the solid rocket fuel. I think there were numerous cracks in the solid cartridge of rocket fuel we had used in our first attempt. When the flames shot through all these cracks the whole fuel charge burned at once. In this second attempt I had made sure there were no cracks and I had allowed for a hole down the center of the fuel cartridge. I figured this would allow the fuel to burn down the center of the charge instead of just on one end.

It didn't explode. It didn't really generate much thrust, either. We could tell because we set the rocket on a bathroom scale on top of the table. The scale retained the maximum scale reading when we stepped off of it. It was sort of a flop, but at least we didn't have a complete catastrophic failure.

Things were looking up.

Dale Carpenter is on the left and I am on the right

■　■　■

My studies at Purdue, however, were sinking fast. Electrical engineers had to take several math courses, and I struggled to keep my grades up. I asked for extra help from my instructors, but still my grades didn't reflect my hard work. Purdue gave me a few chances to get acceptable grades in my math courses, but I couldn't do it. First Purdue warned me that my grade point average was dangerously low and gave me half a term to correct the situation. At the end of the semester my grades were not better. I was dropped.

For years, I tried to come to an understanding about why I did so poorly. People always asked me, "Why?"

For at least five years all I could say is, "I am not sure".

I now know why.

I was not properly prepared to do college math. I could do algebra and trigonometry, but not calculus. Calculus was essential to solving electrical circuit problems. Electrical circuits were the heart of electrical engineering. I just did not get calculus.

Today, students have calculators. We did not have them. End of story. I just did not fit into the mentality of memorizing facts and spitting them back out on a test. I am best at learning by doing. I checked the Purdue Calumet Center website today to see if there are still engineering programs available. The majors are now called Engineering Technology where there is an emphasis on incorporating hands-on experience with engineering concepts. I would be more successful in the present day Purdue program instead of the 1950s version because I did well in lab work where you learn by doing experiments. I always struggled with memorizing facts which was how things were taught in 1958. The harder I studied the worse I did until I just gave up. I thought I should take a break from school and get a job.

I intended to go back some day and finish my degree.

CHAPTER 8

RESEARCH LAB AND WEDDING BELLS

1961

I got a job as a research technician at Armour Research Foundation in the chemistry department. After about two years the Foundation was sold off to Illinois Institute of Technology. It was renamed Illinois Institute of Technology Research Institute. IIT was the school and IITRI was a separate research institute. Bill Jouris had heard there were some openings in the Chemistry Building so I filled out an application. My salary was $350 per month. Chicago teachers were getting about $500 per month. For the first year or so I lived with my parents in Harvey and commuted into the city every day by car.

IITRI is located at 3100 South Michigan Avenue in the near south side Chicago Loop. Traffic was bad. The Dan Ryan Expressway was being built, so there wasn't a quick an easy route into the city until it was finished. I took State Street most of the way from Harvey. It took 30-45 minutes. The train would have taken longer.

My duties included research on high temperature molten salt electrical power sources. It was a project for the US Navy. They were paying to have someone find out whether or not it was possible to build a device to generate electricity from the waste energy from the engine in a jet fighter plane. Could the jet engine generate electricity to use in an emergency situation? The jet exhaust pipe is about 1500 degrees Fahrenheit, so this device had to operate in an extremely hot atmosphere without being damaged. We built very small prototypes to show the feasibility of such a device, but the project didn't get past that stage.

I also learned about several other interesting projects. I could visit the other labs and observe research on how to disperse chemical agents into the atmosphere like nerve agents. There was also a program to see if medical checkups could be performed by sniffing the body odors of people confined inside a large glass bottle. A patient would remove his or her clothes and go into the bottle, which contained chemical sensors to collect and store the human odors emitted from the patient. Healthy and sick people would be tested and odors analyzed for type and chemical composition. The goal was to identify "healthy odors" and "sick odors."

Researchers were investigating the idea that each malady might have a signature odor or chemical compound. They were trying to determine if medical professionals could sniff somebody and form a diagnosis. I don't think that project went too far. This was only a sample of the type of work the federal government was paying to have done during this period.

I learned some things about rocket propellants there, and I gained experience handling exotic chemicals. My job taught me how to get results in a scientific way rather than creating a haphazard design and hoping for the best.

I worked with a lot of very intelligent scientists. I realized that I learned the most when I surrounded myself with people who were more knowledgeable and talented than I was. Since then I've operated under this guiding principle: If you're the smartest one in your group, you're not really learning anything, so it's a good idea to be with people who are essentially more talented than you are.

I worked part of the time for Ted Erickson, a chemist who was attempting to develop a new liquid propellant for rockets. Ted Erickson is better-known for his marathon swimming exploits. He held the world record for double crossing the English Channel for ten years. Erickson also swam across Lake Michigan, Lake Ontario and San Francisco Bay.

My job at IITRI taught me that I could still work with science and intelligent people without a college degree. When I was dropped from Purdue I was afraid I wouldn't be able to find a job that was interesting and challenging. I was glad to be proved wrong.

Phyllis and I had been dating for three years. She was the one and I knew it. My sister Nola helped me find a good jeweler so I could pick out a nice ring. I popped the question one night while we sat in my car in front of her parents' house.

We got married in June, 1962. We drove to Quebec City for our short but memorable honeymoon. We splurged on a romantic stay at Le Château Frontenac overlooking the St. Lawrence River. After a few days we returned to our new apartment in Chicago and settled in to our newlywed routine of work and starting a family.

Our wedding day, June 9, 1962

CHAPTER 9

DRAG STRIP AND BRIGHT IDEA

1963

"Did you say drag race?" I asked, looking at Dick Keller. He was approaching me in the hallway of the Chemistry Research Building at the IITRI where we be both worked.

"Sure I did. So have you ever been to a drag race?" Dick smiled, eyebrows raised.

"No, I'm not interested in racing," I answered.

"Well, I'm going up to Great Lakes Dragaway in Union Grove next weekend. It's up near Milwaukee. Do you want to go with me? I mean, what else do you have going on?" Dick said.

"Nothing, I guess." Phyllis and I spent most weekends at our apartment or socializing with Dick and his wife Nancy on the IITRI campus since they lived right down the hall. Nancy babysat for our daughter Cheryl while Phyllis worked as a teacher, and our wives spent many hours together over coffee and toddlers in tow. Occasionally our small family ventured up Chicago's Lake Shore Drive to the Art Institute and a lazy walk along the blustery lakefront grasping the edges of our coats together against the Windy City's namesake gale.

Phyllis and I spent many summer weekends at my parent's lake home in Rochester, Indiana, surfboarding and lolling about in the lake. In the evenings we usually visited The Flagpole ice cream stand for paper cups cold with orange slush, gooey banana splits in ample dishes or hand-dipped chocolate ice cream cones. It was also a chance to visit with my aunts, uncles and cousins and reconnect with my family.

I didn't know it then, but this conversation with Dick was the beginning of the story of the Blue Flame journey.

"I don't even know what a drag strip is!" I admitted as we rode the elevator down to the cafeteria.

I knew that guys with hot souped-up cars often got together at night on some deserted road and had side-by-side races to see who had the fastest car. I also knew that occasionally these encounters proved deadly to the drivers or their passengers who were almost always the girls they were trying to impress.

"Now it's a sport. I guess there are still unsanctioned drag races, but that's for stupid teenagers. I'm talking about the real racing machines," Dick grinned.

He informed me that there were privately-owned drag strips like Great Lakes Dragaway where guys could pay an entrance fee and compete with others on a quarter-mile asphalt strip with timing devices to accurately measure their elapsed time and speed. There were official national records kept for various automobile types.

"That's a good idea to get that kind of activity off the public streets," I answered, wondering what I was getting myself into.

"There are also cash prizes and trophies given out for the quickest cars at some of the major events every year. In fact, some guys are drag racing full time."

"You mean that's their job?" I asked.

"Oh, yeah. They appear at tracks in almost every state. The very best get sponsors and everything," Dick said as the elevator doors pinged open. We headed toward the cafeteria. I didn't know what to say or how to get out of this.

"Well, then do you want to ride up with me on Saturday? They'll have the exhibition cars and all the engine roar you can take in one day."

I really had no interest in going, so I had to justify going for some other reason. In my mind, I figured that since Nancy was our babysitter during the day when Phyllis was teaching school, I should be nice to Dick and try to be a good neighbor.

"Okay, I'll ride up there with you just to see it," I shrugged, "but I really have no interest in cars or auto racing."

"Me, too, I'm just a spectator. My sport is team bicycle racing," said Dick.

While we waited in line to buy coffee, Dick told me that he belonged to a team that raced at a bicycle track in Northbrook, Illinois. He went on to regale me with his exploits in the sport. He was not considered a professional racer and only competed in the amateur ranks. He loved to do it for the feeling of speed and danger and it kept him in great physical condition. I guess I was surprised to learn that there was so much danger riding a bike. He corrected me, saying that it was common for serious injuries to result from falls during a race. Guys could get run over, suffering concussions and broken bones.

"So, is Nancy going? Should I ask Phyllis to get a babysitter?" I asked.

"Nah. It would be just us. If we leave right after dinner we can catch the evening races. You'll like it." Dick assured me.

Since we got stuck in drive-time traffic, we didn't arrive at the drag strip until the first events got under way at seven that evening. During the drive up it became apparent that maybe the only reason I was asked on this trip was that Dick wanted to show off his new Pontiac GTO. He obviously had more interest in fast cars than he let on during our initial conversation about this trip, since we made the trip mostly in excess of the posted speed limits.

Dick purchased a pit pass in addition to the normal spectator admittance ticket.

"We need to get into the pits so we can see the action and talk to the drivers," he said.

The first thing I noticed about drag racing was the sound. Everything was loud. Noise assaulted me from every direction: engines revving, crew members shouting, fans squealing, music blaring and the excited chatter of the announcer as each car was prepped for the starting line. As we walked through the pits looking at the cars and the pit crews, engines were being "tweaked" for optimum performance.

"All the drivers tweak their cars even if they don't need it. It's part of the fun," Dick said.

Crews would always arrive at the strip well ahead of race time to play with the cars and their engines. "Rails," a type of Top Fuel car, burned a special type of fuel called nitromethane. "Nitro" was an expensive chemical, which was also used as a rocket propellant. In a properly altered Chrysler "Hemi-head" V-8 engine, this fuel could increase the engine horsepower.

"Do the nitro engines explode a lot? Seems kind of dangerous." I was wondering just how safe the pit area was.

"Sure they do. Sometimes."

I nodded and quickened my step as we continued our tour of the pits. The thunder of the engines as they were revved up was deafening. The ground actually shook. I wished I had brought along a pair of the ear protectors we used at the lab when working in the machine shop. During tweaking, huge blue flames shot out of the exhaust manifold on each of the eight cylinders of the engine. Dick explained that all Top Fuel owners used Chrysler engines exclusively, since they had the largest cylinders. Each of the stock engine cylinders were then bored-out to create even more room for burning the nitro, thus producing even more horsepower.

Another aspect of drag racing that caught my attention was that each crew seemed to have a "Honey," sometimes more than one. A Honey was a wife or girlfriend who seemed to be dressed in a manner to attract maximum attention from bystanders or members of the racing fraternity. These women were usually dressed in short-shorts and tight-fitting t-shirts with the racing team logo on the front and back as well as some phrase with sexual connotations in appropriate locations. In short, their job was to keep everyone happy that they had attended, even if the job of tweaking had become boring. Honeys were always very friendly and in many cases knew as much about drag racing as their "associates" (boyfriends). In some cases the women were the car owners and drivers. In those cases they had male Honeys.

It crossed my mind that this might be my last tour of the pits. It seemed like a place I only needed to see once.

We took our seats in the grandstands to watch the racing. As I watched the brightly painted cars hurtling down the quarter-mile strip trailing a white plume of smoke from burning rubber tires, I thought of my home-made rockets streaking into the blue sky with a thrilling roar and trail of white smoke. In both events large quantities of power were being released followed by a vehicle streaking away into the distance.

I was surprised to see so many people at the races. There must have been close to a thousand at this event. Most were young, but about a quarter were middle-aged. About half were female. Most race crews seemed to have a following in the ranks of the spectators. After races involving the more famous drivers, the winner would return to the pit area via a side road parallel to the strip. The winner would sit on top of the car waving to the cheering crowd while being towed back in front of the grandstands, by the pit crew. The loser usually didn't get much attention when he passed by.

I liked what I saw. I was most impressed with the cars that made the most noise and smoke. But as we sat there, I asked myself if I would make the effort to come again on my own.

"Let's get going!" Dick shouted before the last race started.

"What?" I couldn't hear him over the roar of the engines blasting their power into the stratosphere.

"It gets pretty hairy if we wait to leave with everyone else," Dick told me.

After watching hours of racing, most spectators left the track pretending that they were drag racing heroes driving Top Fuel rails and shooting down the strip in their family cars. Driving out of the drag strip could be hazardous to your health, especially since most of the spectators had been drinking for several hours.

On our way back to Chicago, Dick looked at me and asked, "So did you like it?"

"Sure, sure. I probably won't go back, but I appreciate your invitation and it was entertaining!" I assured him. I was impressed by the sound of the top-fuel engines as they revved up for a run. I thought of the steam engines in the rail yards in Harvey as they released the steam in their boilers.

I also thought about the similarities between rockets and drag racers. Both had the possibility to produce raw power, shock and awe. Was it possible to create a hybrid of the two?

Just after we crossed the state line into Illinois, I told Dick, "If I were to build a drag car, it would be rocket-powered."

He didn't say anything right away, but then asked, "Why rocket-powered?"

"Rockets have the highest power to weight ratio of any moving vehicle. We spent all night watching guys trying to pack as much power as possible into their drag cars to achieve as much acceleration as possible down the strip. Seems to me that most of the power was used in burning up their tires from the friction of the rubber on the asphalt road."

"How is that different with a rocket?" he asked.

"A rocket would not use wheels to push the car forward. All the rocket power could be used to drive the car down the strip."

We sat in silence for a while and I mulled it over some more.

"Another advantage of the rocket," I said, "would be to eliminate the problem of keeping the car going straight when one of the two driving wheels is driving harder than the other one. Several drivers had lost control of their cars during the race and had run off the strip tonight. Luck played a part in their not killing themselves or someone in the grandstands."

"There is a class of drag cars called jet cars," Dick said, "they use surplus military jet engines as their power plant."

"How come we didn't see any of those?" I asked. "A jet couldn't beat a rocket, but that would be interesting to see."

"There's not many running, since the weight of the engines turns the car into a very heavy dragster," said Dick. "Most drag strips are too short to allow for the car's parachutes, so the car can easily run off the end of the drag strip and crash. Some of those guys aren't around anymore. They ended up either dead or seriously crippled."

"A rocket engine would be less massive than any of the car engines we saw running tonight and would have more power." I said. "It would also not need to be tweaked. Plus a rocket is a lot less expensive and has zero maintenance compared to the continual adjustments required to maintain an automotive engine. You wouldn't have expensive parts to replace after every run—no exploding engines at $4,000 a crack!"

Dick shrugged and kept driving, not too impressed. Maybe the absence of tweaking would be a negative to most gearheads, but not to me, since I had no interest in pistons, valves and superchargers…or acquiring another Honey.

We did not say much for the remainder of the ride back home to Carman Hall, our apartment building on the IITRI campus. I spent the rest of the trip thinking about the advantages of a rocket car vs. a jet-powered car for the ultimate drag racing machine. The rocket would produce twice the power-to-weight ratio than a jet-powered car. The rocket motor would have less maintenance. The rocket-powered dragster would have no tire wear due to tire slippage.

The hydrogen peroxide rocket dragster would also be safer to operate and less dangerous to the spectators than the automotive engines, which frequently explode when the crews used nitromethane fuel. Overall, I decided the rocket-powered dragster would be safer, less expensive and produce more power than either the automotive engine or jet engine. Finally, the rocket machine would be a novelty and draw more interest than the jet-powered cars which were already well known to drag racing fans.

It was close to midnight when I walked in the door of our apartment. Phyllis was sleeping. As I crawled into bed she asked how it went.

"It was ok," I told her.

I thought that was the end of it.

CHAPTER 10

Baptism by Rocket Fuel

1963

The next week, Dick came in the lab at IITRI and he said he had thought about my comments about the rocket-powered dragster. "What do you know about rockets, and if someone did want to build a rocket-powered dragster what kind of rocket do you suggest they use?"

"Well you'd have to use something that was controllable." I said. "You don't want to just bolt on some solid-propellant rockets that are basically like sky rockets, where you ignited a fuse and the vehicle went out of control until the rocket engines burned out. You need something where you could control the thrust of the engine."

"Is that even possible?"

"You could design it where either you turn it on or shut it off when you wanted to. You know, modify the thrust during the run. That way you'd have the same amount of control over the power that the people with auto engines do."

"What kind of fuel would make that happen?" Dick asked.

I thought for a second. "It would require a liquid-propellant rocket."

"Well what would be our options if we wanted to do that?"

"The only one I know of that I would consider safe enough to use at a public place like a drag race would be hydrogen peroxide. You would have hundreds or thousands of people lining the raceway. You wouldn't want your car to explode and shower them with red-hot high velocity shrapnel or gas them with toxic exhaust!"

Dick nodded and said, "True. That would be bad…"

I chuckled. "You need a very safe liquid propellant. Hydrogen peroxide is the way to go."

Dick was intrigued by our conversation and didn't say much more about it until sometime later that week. Again he brought the subject up and said, "I would be interested in possibly building a drag race car using a hydrogen peroxide rocket. Would you consider sketching up a design of a rocket engine that I could look at?"

"Well, I don't know. I'll try."

So at some point I went back to my George P. Sutton book, which I had used to design my earlier rockets with Dale Carpenter. I used Sutton's equations to design a small 25 pound thrust rocket engine which would of course be way too small for a race car. But since I had never built one of these before the thing to do would be to build a very small scale engine and test it to see whether we could get it to work. If it did work, we could scale it up to a much bigger size and use it for our drag racing engine.

Fortunately I had been working at IITRI for a while and part of my duties were to go to the chemistry building's machine shop from time to time and fabricate various types of metal parts. The parts were for electrodes used in high temperature molten-carbonate fuel cells to be used in U.S. Navy fighter planes. Sometimes our experiments required us to make prototype experimental models so I had some experience in using a metal turning lathe, band saws and various grinding tools. I was well equipped to make this engine. It was just a matter of finding the material and going into the machine shop after hours to make it.

All the materials I needed were in the shop. Across the hall from the Chemistry building machine shop there was a room with a scrap bin where scientists tossed their leftover stainless steel rods and remnants from lab trials. I pulled out a few stainless steel rods and got to work.

"If I'm successful in making this miniature engine," I said to myself, "then maybe we could see about trying to find some 90% hydrogen peroxide to use for fuel. We'd also have to find some type of silver mesh to use as a catalyst and to decompose the hydrogen peroxide into steam and oxygen."

It took me several days to finish my rocket engine, and in the meantime Dick had been searching the chemical supply houses to see who sold 90% hydrogen peroxide in small quantities. He had come up with a source called FMC Corporation in Buffalo where we could buy one pint bottles of 90% hydrogen peroxide at an affordable price.

We bought one pint. We found a company that sold pure silver wire cloth, so we decided to buy a little bit of that for our experiment.

Before long I had assembled the rocket engine. We had the fuel. Now the question was how did we test it?

I talked to Phyllis about the rocket project one night after work. Cheryl was sleeping on a blanket on the living room floor while Phyllis and I sat down to a dinner of chicken and dumplings. I poured myself a glass of milk and a glass of beer for Phyllis. She scooped steaming dumplings, dripping with gravy, onto my plate. She fished around in the pot for a few large chunks of white meat for me and plopped them down as well. She served herself, looked up and smiled.

"So what *are* those drawings you left on the coffee table? Are you working some overtime hours this week?" she asked.

"Actually they are just something I'm working on with Dick." I said. "We might build a rocket-powered dragster. I don't know. Dick is pretty interested in racing and he asked me to build a prototype to see if it would fire."

Phyllis took a sip of beer and shrugged. "What do you mean a rocket-powered dragster? What's that all about?"

"Well, when we went up to Union Grove we saw all these dragsters and I mentioned to Dick that a rocket-powered car could outrun them all!"

"Oh. Huh. I didn't get the impression you were all that impressed with the races. Do you plan on racing it around here?" Phyllis glanced at Cheryl, who had started to roll towards the living room couch. She was chewing on the edges of her pink and white blanket. It looked like she might roll herself up like a little pink and white burrito.

"I'm not sure where this is going." I said. "Dick and I are just going to see if I can make a miniature rocket in the shop and if it fires without blowing up maybe we will keep going and build a bigger rocket for a car."

"I remember you liked rockets. Didn't you and Dale almost blow up the south side of Chicago one night fooling around with rockets?" Phyllis laughed and scooped another bite of chicken and gravy into her mouth. I could see she was just giving me a hard time.

"Well, this time I will find a better testing spot with no witnesses." I said.

■ ■ ■

Dick and I still hadn't agreed on building a rocket-powered dragster. I think maybe Dick had decided in his own mind, but to me it was just an experiment. We were going to build a rocket engine and test it. The possibility of actually building a car using this as a power plant was sort of remote to me because I wasn't that interested in racing and Dick, at this point, was approaching this very casually. He didn't really press that issue with me.

We decided we had to find a place to test this rocket engine. "I know some drag racers that live out in Blue Island." said Dick. "They said we can use the vacant lot across the alley from their garage. The neighbors shouldn't complain too much about the noise because they're used to loud engines and people working on cars. No one will call the police or anything—they're so used to the drag cars they will think we're another set of dragsters."

It turned out the vacant lot in the Chicago suburb was in a residential / commercial area, so it didn't appear as though the neighbor problem was going to be too big. It was nice because the actual lot itself was recessed maybe six or seven feet right along the alley, sort of like an embankment. So we thought we could put our rocket engine in the vacant lot on the embankment area and be out of the line of fire, so to speak, if the engine were to blow up or something.

We set about trying to design some kind of a test device. We had to get the engine to fire, and at the same time measure the thrust to see if my calculations were correct on the nozzle design, which would create 25 pounds of thrust. In addition we needed to find out if we used enough silver catalyst or if we needed to enhance the silver mesh to improve reactivity.

Our first engine was very small -- about 1 ½" in diameter and about three inches long. I think we put in enough silver mesh to have a catalyst pack that was maybe an inch in diameter and ½" in depth. I had no way of knowing if that was enough or not. For all I knew you might need a catalyst pack that was an inch in diameter and 12 inches long or 24 inches long. I had no idea, but since silver was very expensive I decided we'd start out with the assumption that it didn't take very much.

The engine, high pressure fuel tank, fuel lines and valves were all made of stainless steel. The hydrogen peroxide needed to be contained in stainless steel or pure aluminum otherwise it would start to decompose all by itself in the container. We added a bottle of compressed nitrogen to attach to the fuel tank to force the hydrogen peroxide out of the tank and into the rocket engine. Dick and I had to save money, so we borrowed a high pressure tank of air, a small stainless steel container to put the hydrogen peroxide in and a valve from our labs to add to the rocket motor and complete our design.

The trick was going to be figuring out how much hydrogen peroxide to run into the engine in order to get the proper 25 pounds of thrust. In other words, we had to put in so many gallons per minute. We couldn't just push in an unlimited amount. In order to get the right amount of thrust not only did I have to design the nozzle just right, I had to have the flow of the fuel through the catalyst pack at a uniform and proper rate in gallons per minute. I calculated the chamber pressure of the rocket needed to be 300 pounds per square inch.

I decided we would use a needle valve to control the flow of the hydrogen peroxide into the engine. To prepare for our experiment we did some preliminary work in the lab at IITRI. We pre-calibrated our rocket using water at 300 psi tank pressure in the system because we couldn't afford to run hydrogen peroxide through every time.

When I decided we had all these things figured out and we had designed a thrust stand that would measure the thrust at the same time, we were ready to test the engine. It was a warm summer morning in 1964 when Dick and I packed up our equipment and drove out to the vacant lot in Blue Island, Illinois.

We decided to mount the rocket engine pointing downwards. What is normally the bottom or back of the rocket engine would point upwards. This would cause the engine thrust to push the tiny engine downwards on the top of a bathroom scale. The amount of force would be displayed on the scale as pounds of thrust generated. We could eyeball how much push the engine had during its operation by looking at the scale.

Dick was in charge of reading the scale during the rocket test, so he stood along the embankment above the alley about 30 feet away from our test stand. He gripped his binoculars tightly and watched me assemble the test stand. Dick had also mounted an 8mm movie camera near the test stand so we would have secondary data in case he couldn't actually see the reading through the binoculars. If the engine did blow up then at least it would just hurt the camera, but maybe not do damage to Dick.

I double checked the equipment and made sure the angle was good for the rocket to thrust directly against the scale. I ran the fuel line up the embankment and to the bottle of compressed air in the alley. I stood on the embankment, out of harm's way. The rocket engine and test stand were mounted almost directly below me with the nozzle pointing up. I was just about to give the signal to Dick that we were ready to fire.

At that moment Dick got up.

"I'm going to go down in the lot. I can't see the scale from here," he said. So he went down to the vacant lot and got close enough to the rocket engine so he could see it through his binoculars.

Now we were all set to go. I opened the needle valve to the proper point. The hydrogen peroxide rushed out of the storage tank, down the fuel line into the engine. It proceeded right through the engine and shot up into the air in a nice stream.

So as soon as I saw what going on, which only took a fraction of a second, I immediately shut the valve to stop the flow of hydrogen peroxide that had just shot right through the catalyst back without decomposing and out the rocket nozzle and into the air.

Much to my surprise I felt this liquid splashing down on my head. I was in exactly the right spot for this stream of peroxide to come back down and land right on me. I sort of panicked at this point because I knew that hydrogen peroxide was such a strong oxidizing agent that it could very easily start my hair on fire.

"No! Damn it!" I shouted and quickly turned around to look for help.

Luckily, there was a garden hose across the alley in the backyard of the nearest house. I ran over to the hose, turned it on and doused my head, trying to dilute the hydrogen peroxide.

Dick came running up. He was peering through the binoculars at the scale and by the time he figured out something had gone wrong I was spraying water all over myself.

"Ray! Ray! What the hell are you doing?" he screamed at me.

"Did you see the spray? Did you? The hydrogen peroxide came gushing out and sprayed all over me! I had to spray it down or else start on fire!" I answered. I squeezed my eyes shut tight and kept waving the hose.

"No! No, I didn't see it. Holy cow, Ray. That is crazy. Is it over? Are you going to start on fire?" asked Dick, stunned.

"Okay, okay. No. I'm fine." I said. "Maybe the ratio of hair to hydrogen peroxide wasn't enough to ignite."

I stood there, relieved and soaking wet from head to foot.

Giving up was not an option because we had done so much planning and experimenting with the rocket system in the lab. We decided that the problem was due to the catalyst. There just wasn't enough catalyst in there to do the job. There was still some peroxide left, so we decided to try again.

"Let's not put the full amount of HP in all at once this time," I suggested. "Maybe we should just sort of dribble it in, you know, open the valve just a little bit on a second try. I'm thinking maybe the decomposition will happen if it were allowed to percolate for a few seconds before we shoot the full amount in."

"You mean preheat the catalyst and get some steam first?" said Dick.

"Yeah, then we can open the valve all the way and fire it once it gets hot enough." I said.

This whole thing was not all that well conceived, but we were more interested in getting the experiment done than in safety. Sometimes you just have to take a chance and see where it leads.

Dick grabbed his binoculars and assumed his position. "Go ahead." He nodded.

This time I just cracked open the valve a tiny bit and waited. There was sort of a gurgling sound and all of a sudden a big cloud of steam started pouring out of the rocket nozzle. It wasn't jetting out, it was just billowing out of the nozzle. I thought it must be pretty hot by now, so I opened the fuel valve to the proper position and Bingo! Instead of a jet of hydrogen peroxide we heard a loud exhaust sound from a high velocity jet of steam and oxygen shooting out the nozzle. It lasted for a good ten seconds. Then the rocket shut off automatically, the fuel spent.

"Yes! Yes! That's it! It worked!" Dick ran up the embankment and slapped me on the back.

"It worked! The noise is the key. The scream of the rocket means it worked!" I was thrilled.

We were out of hydrogen peroxide and the question remained: did the engine generate any thrust, and if so how much? Dick had gotten so excited from the noise of the rocket he missed getting a visual reading. Maybe he had been a little frightened at the noise and lost his focus. Fortunately the camera was running. The only way we were going to know for sure if we had hit the 25 pound mark was to get the film developed.

Testing our 25 lb thrust rocket engine in the Blue Island alley

We picked up our stuff, packed the car and headed back to Chicago. After a minute or two we looked at each other and started to laugh out loud.

"You and the hose, Ray. You and that hose. Classic. Ha! Good thing you have quick reflexes!"

I chuckled. It was pretty humorous in retrospect. But at the time it happened I was sure I was going to lose my hair.

We took the film in to be developed and picked it up a few days later. Sure enough, the camera did pick up the dial on the bathroom scale. The dial shot immediately to 25 lbs. As soon as the fuel was exhausted the scale dropped back to zero again.

The test was a success.

Dick and I had a pretty good feeling that we knew enough about rocket engine design to go ahead and scale the engine up to a bigger size -- if we wanted to -- for powering a drag racing car.

CHAPTER 11

PARTNERSHIP AND PROTOTYPE SKETCHES

1964

"Get busy and draw up a drag racing rocket, Ray!" Dick said as he took a drink of his beer. We were sitting at a picnic table on the edge of the local park near IIT. Phyllis and Nancy were sitting near the table on a blanket, playing with Cheryl and Ricky Keller, both still infants. It was nice that Dick and Nancy had a child about Cheryl's age. Both families' responsibilities and social lives now involved small children, so we saw a lot of each other.

Did he have this in mind all along? I hadn't been sure if we were really going to go further than our test engine. I have a feeling that Dick had the idea of a land speed record car in the back of his mind the whole time.

"So we need a couple thousand horsepower for that," I answered, not committing just yet.

In my spare time I started thinking about it and went through the calculations. For a 2500 pound thrust engine I could use a factor of 100 greater than the 25 pound thrust engine I had just built. I spent time looking through my George P. Sutton rocket manual and talking to some of the people at the Research Institute. I found out how many pounds of thrust would equal a horsepower for an automotive engine traveling at about 200 mph, and that's where I came up with the 2500 lb of thrust to get 2000 horsepower. I started sketching up the dimensions and drawing a picture of that engine over a number of weeks.

■ ■ ■

"Ray, can you get that?" Phyllis asked. I hadn't even heard the knock at the door. I'd been poring over pages in the Sutton rocket manual to make sure my equations were accurate.

I got up and answered the door. The curry smell that perpetually lingered in Carman Hall's corridors greeted me as well as Dick's grin and enthusiastic, "Got a minute?"

"Sure, come on in. I was just double checking some calculations," I answered.

"Would you like something to drink?" asked Phyllis, bouncing Cheryl on her hip and walking over to our small kitchen. "We've got some lemonade or beer."

"Nah, thanks, Phyllis. Nancy is expecting me. I just stopped down at the lab for a few hours so I have to get back pretty soon."

"Okay, tell Nancy that I will meet her downstairs in the morning, probably by nine," she answered. Phyllis and Nancy often took the kids outside and talked while the kids giggled and pointed at each other while propped up in their play seats. There was a place to sit in the shade beneath the Mies van der Rohe first floor design, which had the concrete building hovering over a covered area just outside the lobby with the elevators and mailboxes on the ground floor.

"I found a guy to build the frame, Ray. His name is Pete Farnsworth. He's got a lot of experience and drag racers respect his skills," said Dick.

"Is he a driver?" I asked.

"No, no, well…he does drive his friend's car once in a while, but nothing full time. He's well known for building drag racing cars with automotive engines. Pete has excellent welding skills and can build just about anything," said Dick.

I hesitated, knowing that if we contacted Pete then we were committing to this project and I would be setting aside a lot of my free time. Phyllis knew I was interested in rockets and she wasn't fazed by this turn of events. She was always very amenable to what I felt I needed to do and since we had been married a short time we didn't have a rigid routine that I was interrupting if I signed on to this endeavor. I glanced over at her just to check her reaction and she just raised her eyebrows.

"Dick, you sure know a lot of people!" Phyllis said with a laugh and signature twinkle in her eye, "I'm sure you know an astronaut who can drive the car, too!"

Dick joined in her laughter. "I'm working on it! I'm working on it! Hey, Ray, what do you say we call Pete and see if he is interested?"

I thought for a few moments and realized that since Dick and I lacked the welding and fabrication skills to produce a car we would need someone else to team up with if we were going through with this rocket car idea.

"We might as well, because there's no way you or I could be in charge of that end of the project," I said.

"Oh, I know a thing or two about welding, Ray. I just think we should have a full time guy that has built cars before," said Dick.

"Of course, Dick. Of course. Give him a call," I agreed.

Dick contacted Pete. They had met twice before. Once at an auto repair shop and once at Oswego Raceway in Illinois. The first conversations were tentative negotiations. Pete wanted to buy a rocket engine from us for a dragster he and his wife Leah were building in their garage. They had already been looking around to buy a rocket engine, so he thought he could hire us to build one for him. Dick tried to convince Pete to build a whole new car for us and we would supply the engine. Dick explained that we couldn't pay him, but he assured Pete that we would all split the money when the rocket dragster started to rake in the winnings at the track.

The talks were going nowhere, so Dick made an appointment with Pete for the three of us to get together and work this out. One Saturday Dick and I made the two hour drive to Milwaukee. At that time Pete and Leah lived on the north side near 35th Street and Center Street, a blue collar area.

We knocked on Pete's door and we sat down and talked about it. Pete was a stocky, muscular guy with a sardonic smile, thick eyebrows and blond hair that he wore neatly combed back. He was an intelligent man. My first impression was that he had no problem speaking his mind. The three of us sat down in the den while Leah and their three young children were in the kitchen baking a cake.

"I've heard about using a rocket engine, so I sent away for this information. The concept is pretty intriguing. It's hooked to the rear axle and contains a small jet turbine. I didn't buy the thing, just had them send me their brochure," said Pete. He passed a glossy pamphlet to me that explained some sort of turbine engine configuration. I smiled and passed it over to Dick.

"What does it burn for fuel?" I asked.

"Gasoline…no, maybe alcohol," said Pete. "Like I said I didn't buy it or anything."

"Ah, so it's not a rocket engine, but it definitely works differently than your typical dragster," Dick added.

"Yeah. I've been thinking about this for a while. It's a big coincidence you called me, Dick, because this idea has been running around in my head for more than a year."

"That's good news, then. We all have interest in moving forward with this project. With everyone's input and skills I think we can do it." One of Dick's greatest strengths was to organize people towards the same goal. His encouraging style could border on "schmoozing," but to his credit Dick was very effective at persuading others to join forces and mobilize toward a common interest---even if some of the people didn't know they were interested in the first place!

"You're right, Dick. I need a rocket that I can use in front of a crowd. I can do everything else on the car, but I don't have the equipment to fabricate a rocket."

Dick and I spent most of the morning at Pete and Leah's. We shared ideas and debated if collaborating on a rocket car was feasible. The three of us went back and forth explaining our experience and what we felt we could bring to the table. I liked Pete's deliberate style and open-minded attitude. Before we left Dick pressed Pete for an answer.

"So, what do you say, Pete?" said Dick. "Ray and I are game if you are."

I felt the need to speak for myself.

"Pete, between the three of us we've got all the skills covered," I said. "I think we can work out a way to split up the job so we all have input and a fair workload."

"But let me think about it a while," said Pete. "My part will be building the car. You two would have to come up and help on weekends since I'll be doing this in my spare time off of work, you know."

"Sure, Pete. We will help you, and while we're in Chicago we'll build the rocket engine, test it and see about fuel," I said.

"Yep, Pete, we'll help in any way we can," said Dick.

"Leah and I will have to decide," said Pete. "I'm sure you understand. Your wives have had a chance to talk this over with you already. Just give me a few days and Leah and I will give you a call."

Dick and I exchanged a glance at the mention of our wives. Phyllis and Nancy were somewhat aware of the project, but it would be a stretch to say that either couple had talked it over thoroughly.

At the sound of her name Leah breezed in from the kitchen, smiling wide. She turned briskly to Pete. Her eyes were sparkling and her wide grin lit up the room. Leah was a friendly woman, and she was very affectionate and attentive with Pete.

Pete and Leah were best friends throughout high school and had many pals in common in their local hot rod club. On many weekends

Pete and Leah would go to the stock car races at Soldier Field in Chicago. After graduation he attended University of Illinois at Urbana Champaign for engineering for two years before leaving school to enter the tool and die industry.

Pete knew Leah was the woman he wanted to spend his life with when she offered to help him bleed the brakes on his 1934 Ford roadster. She was used to helping her dad take parts from one of his 1936 Buicks to fix the other two that took turns breaking down, during World War II, when new cars were not being built. Leah was a good match for Pete in intelligence, wit and work ethic.

The Farnsworths started their married life in Evanston with Pete working as a tool and die apprentice. A recession led to his company eliminating the apprentice positions, so Pete and Leah moved north to Milwaukee so Pete could start his new job as a truck mechanic at C & J Transport's repair facility. The couple continued their passion for cars and racing by building dragsters together in their spare time. Leah had a love of the sport and a deep understanding of mechanics and racing technology.

Contrary to Dick's initial information, Pete was a driver. In fact, he became a local superstar at the drag strip. Pete was such a good driver that he could make more money racing on the weekend than working 50 hours per week at C & J Transport. Pete was used to building cars and breaking track records. I hoped he would agree to join forces with us. He knew everything about racing that Dick and I didn't.

"Oh Pete, now what are you boys planning? I heard my name. You didn't tell these boys I would drive their crazy rocket car, did you?" Leah asked.

Pete laughed and grabbed her around the waist and pulled her toward him. "No, dear. Ray and Dick want me to give them an answer today, but I told them I wanted to talk to you first."

Leah put her hand on Pete's shoulder and said, "Well, we have talked about it and we already know how we feel about it."

She went back into the kitchen and the three of us stood silently.

"Well," said Pete.

"Do you need a few days?" I asked.

Pete looked down. He looked up at the ceiling and cleared his throat. Dick and I waited for his answer. It took just a moment more. He lowered his gaze to meet my eye and then to glance over at Dick. Pete pondered a bit before he answered.

"Let's do it."

■　■　■

Another of Dick's talents was in drafting. He had taken a number of drafting courses and was pretty good at making engineering drawings. He volunteered to take my rough sketches and turn them into something we could take to a metal fabrication shop to get an estimate of how much it would cost to build and fabricate the rocket engine. Meanwhile, I set about finding out where we could acquire 90% hydrogen peroxide in large containers. We weren't going to be able to get by with the little pint bottles.

I started searching for sources of commercial high concentration hydrogen peroxide. The question of the silver catalyst pack also came up. We would need a lot more than we used for the 25 pound thrust motor. I was able to find a wire cloth manufacturer that sold copper, aluminum, silver, brass, nickel, and silver wire cloth. I got busy and priced out what a catalyst pack of a similar thickness for the big engine would cost. I had to figure out how many square feet of silver wire cloth we would need for how much money.

My source for the hydrogen peroxide was at the FMC Corp. in Tonawanda, New York, near Buffalo. FMC had developed a process for making the 90% HP for NASA. At that time they had been selling it to NASA for a number of years for reaction control units in small peroxide rockets on the satellites and space capsules, and the stabilization rockets for launch vehicles. So FMC had a ready source of 90% hydrogen peroxide in 30 gallon aluminum drums.

I could order however many drums of this material I wanted and it would be delivered to my door by a truck for $300 per drum. FMC had designed a special pure aluminum drum with all the accoutrements required to safely store concentrated hydrogen peroxide, so when I bought the HP I had to also put down a $100 deposit on the drum. At this time neither of us had much money. I was making $300-350 per month, fairly decent pay for a lab technician, since professionals were making $10,000 a year instead of the $70,000 or $80,000 they make today. Because Dick and I didn't have a lot of money, we'd have to fund this project out of our grocery money somehow.

By the end of October 1964, Dick had finished converting my sketches to engineering drawings. We took them to a few different fabrication shops in the Chicago area to get quotes. The combustion chamber and most of the rocket engine wouldn't cost too much to make, but the rocket nozzle was a fancy piece of machinery. The run-of-the-mill fab shop didn't have the experience or machinery, so we had to go with a specialty shop for the nozzle. Two shops, two prices, but we were satisfied that our grocery money was being spent efficiently.

The stainless steel tank to store our HP turned out to be our easiest purchase. Every local war surplus store had piles of stainless steel tanks and we bought one that was exactly the right size for $50. During WWII, the tanks were used to supply oxygen masks worn by the bomber crews as they flew at ultrahigh altitudes to evade the German air attacks.

In the meantime Pete and Dick had several phone conversations to start planning our next steps. We needed to decide what type of business arrangement we would have. There was a financial investment involved, so we decided not to leave it as three buddies working on a car together. Of course Dick said he knew an attorney who worked in the Chicago Loop. He promised to call and find out what would be required for the three of us to form a legal partnership.

In January of 1965 the three of us went downtown and talked to an attorney named Clarkson Loucks. He was a very distinguished looking gentleman, although by the appearance of his office I got the impression that he wasn't doing all that well. The early 20th Century furniture and wallpaper didn't match. The carpeting had a well-worn traffic pattern from the door to his desk. The walls were bare except for a few diplomas in thin wooden frames mounted behind his cluttered desk. Attorney Loucks didn't have a secretary or fancy knickknacks, but at least he was interesting to talk to.

After some debate on the name we decided to form DFK Enterprises—Dausman, Farnsworth, and Keller. I'm not sure Pete was too happy about the order of the letters, but in the end we decided in all fairness the letters should be in alphabetical order. A month or so later we got our paperwork back and we were officially in business as DFK Enterprises with the prime purpose of building a rocket-powered dragster. Our land speed quest had begun.

CHAPTER 12

X-1 Testing and Accidental Igniting

1965

In April of 1965 Dick and I visited Jim McCormick at FMC Corporation near Buffalo. Jim was a rocket scientist of considerable experience. He had a generous nature. He was in charge of not only making the hydrogen peroxide reaction jets for FMC but also of helping to design equipment for manufacturing the hydrogen peroxide. Jim was an expert in hydrogen peroxide decomposition and had worked on many projects for the government involving the use of HP in guidance rockets for NASA. He was very helpful because we were trying to figure out how to design the catalyst pack for the X-1 engine. It was a challenge to scale it up properly from the 25 pound thrust prototype engine.

On the way to Buffalo we stopped at Niagara Falls. This was my first time seeing such a spectacle. The force of the water and the loud crashing of the falls reverberated in my mind and renewed my hope about life's possibilities. It reminded me that amazing things happen in nature and that our project of designing an innovative rocket car was our way of doing the incredible. The energy of Niagara Falls impressed upon me that strength and power could accomplish amazing feats.

We interviewed Jim McCormick at his home in Buffalo and laid out our plans for the X-1 rocket car. He gave us good information on how thick he thought the catalyst pack should be and how it should be composed. This was the first time I found out we didn't need all silver mesh.

"This rocket just needs partially silver mesh and partially nickel metal mesh as long as the mesh was coated with a high temperature samarium oxide to give it strength."

"We don't have to go pure silver?" I asked with relief. Pure silver was expensive and I always had our budget in mind.

"The samarium oxide will enhance the reactibility of your mesh with the HP to prevent a wet start," Jim assured us.

A wet start is what I had when we tested the prototype engine in the vacant lot and I certainly wanted to avoid that! During our discussion Jim agreed to help us with the catalyst pack for our X-1 motor. Later, he sent us some sketches of how he thought the catalyst pack should be designed and how to apply the high temperature samarium oxide coating using samarium nitrate. We were able to apply the samarium oxide in one of the high temperature furnaces in the chemistry building at IIT. We were lucky to have access to all the equipment we needed to build this catalyst pack correctly. Of course we would have to wait until after hours to work on it, but Dick and I were willing to put in the time.

During our collaboration on the X-1 rocket, Jim gave us a lot of background on hydrogen peroxide rocket engines and shared the rocket designs he did for NASA. Jim informed us that there were actually two types of processes to make 90% hydrogen peroxide and he advised us that we should use the electrolytic method of 90% hydrogen peroxide production since the other method tended to contaminate the wire mesh after some usage and led to a very short lifetime for the catalyst pack.

■ ■ ■

On May 12, 1965 Pete, Dick and I formed Reaction Dynamics Corporation. We felt a corporation would provide more financial account- ability and protection than a simple partnership such as DFK Enterprises. Another advantage to a corporation was limited personal liability. It was important to us that we protect our families.

During the development of our X-1 rocket car Dick and I spent a lot of our spare time working on the car. We drove to Pete's house in Milwaukee just about every weekend and spent most of a Saturday in his garage helping him build the car. I spent countless hours sitting around making little metal parts for Pete or holding the metal parts for Pete while he welded or clamped them to the chassis.

I am sitting in the incomplete X-1 chassis in the Farnsworth's garage
(Photo courtesy of the Ray Dausman collection)

We would run out for hamburgers at George Webb's. One of the pluses of visiting Milwaukee was constant access to Webb's. I thought the burgers at Webb's were excellent -- way better than McDonald's. Webb's was open 24 hours a day and served everything from omelets and hashbrowns to cheeseburgers and fries to soups and club sandwiches. There were a lot of George Webb restaurants around, so we didn't have to go very far to find good food at a reasonable price. Sometimes we worked well into the evening before we jumped in the car, stopped at Webb's for take-out burgers and drove back to Chicago.

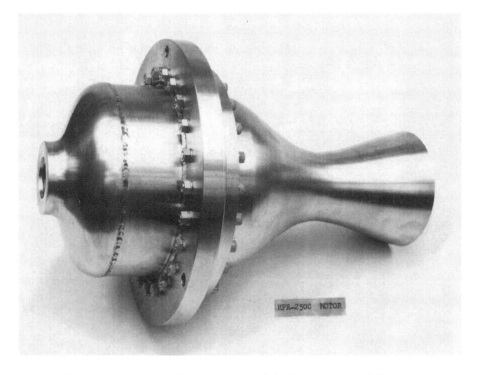

The X-1 rocket engine (Photo courtesy of the Ray Dausman Collection)

It was July 1966 when Dick drove the X-1 at Union Grove in unfinished condition for its first run. This was the first time we fired the engine mounted in the car. In fact we hadn't fired it when it *wasn't* mounted in the car. This was also the first full drum of HP we used, which cost about

$480. We borrowed the money from Dave Anthes, a long-time friend of ours at IITRI. The owners of Great Lakes Dragaway had given us permission to use their track while it was closed. One weekday afternoon we loaded the X-1 onto our new company truck and headed to the track.

We pulled into the deserted drag strip in our modified Chevy flatbed truck with the X-1 strapped in the back. It was a very basic truck; it was just a cab and wheels. Pete Farnsworth built a truck bed on the chassis and we decided to paint it black so it would look like steel, which seemed like a good idea at the time. Pete made some aluminum rails so we could push the car up a pair of inclined planes from the ground to the truck bed. The X-1 was attached to the truck bed with some chains and hooks.

This was our first experience filling the X-1 with fuel, so we knew we had to proceed with caution. The hydrogen peroxide was highly reactive with combustible materials such as cloth, hair, paper and wood. I had done some research to find out the safest way to fill the X-1 from our 30 gallon aluminum drum would be to transfer the hydrogen peroxide into a polyethylene bottle that was large enough to at least hold the amount of fuel we needed to fill the HP tank in the car. I procured some siphoning hoses and the polyethylene bottle and brought them all to the track with our other supplies. I put marks on the outside of the bottle to indicate the level of one gallon, two gallons, all the way up to the ten gallons we would need to fill the car.

There was some danger of spilling some hydrogen peroxide somewhere along the line, so we also had a WWII fire extinguisher with a five gallon tank and hand pump on the top attached with a hose. If we spilled anything, we would have to dilute it down to at least 50% hydrogen peroxide with the water.

Dick and Pete rolled the car down the inclined planes so it was safely on the ground. We kept the hydrogen peroxide tank on the truck. Our plan was to siphon the hydrogen peroxide into a polyethylene bottle (also on the truck) and measure off our ten gallons. Then we were going to roll the car alongside the truck and siphon the hydrogen peroxide into the top of the fuel tank where we had stainless steel fixtures that we could seal it off with a large nut on top of the tank.

At first I noticed a little bit of liquid on the truck bed, but I thought it was water. I was focusing on the siphoning job. No one noticed that a little bit of hydrogen peroxide dribbled off the end of the siphoning hose at the 30 gallon aluminum drum.

"Jesus! Ray! Jesus! Look out, gimme that hose!" Pete was frantic, grasping wildly for our handy WWII fire extinguisher. I turned around and saw that our truck bed was on fire!

Pandemonium reigned for a few seconds. A blaze was burning where the HP came into contact with the wooden truck bed and it was growing rapidly. Pete waved the fire extinguisher over the widening hole in the plywood and I struggled to push the polyethylene bottle filled with ten gallons of hydrogen peroxide – and weighing 90 pounds – off of the truck bed. I had to move fast but made sure not to spill anything on myself.

If Pete couldn't put out that fire we had a whole drum of hydrogen peroxide sitting on this truck bed that would overheat and explode. It was not a good situation.

Dick stood there and watched then tried to roll the car out of the way so nothing would get on the car. Pete finally doused the fire and I managed to get the bottle off the truck and onto the ground. But in the process I spilled hydrogen peroxide all over my hands.

"Ray! Look at your hands! They're all white!" Dick exclaimed.

I glanced down at my hands. They were covered with hydrogen peroxide.

"Pete! Spray my hands before they blister! Spray me! Spray my hands!" Pete swung the hose in my direction and drenched my hands immediately.

This was another potential problem we hadn't run into before. When you get a high concentration of hydrogen peroxide on your skin it soaks in and decomposes and forms billions of tiny bubbles of oxygen, which get lodged in the pores of your skin and makes your skin appear to turn pure white. Fortunately none got on my clothes, but my hands were white for about three or four hours until all the oxygen dissipated out of the pores.

At the time, I didn't know exactly what had caused the whiteness. I thought maybe I had burned my skin. My hands began to tingle and itch. But they didn't catch on fire or anything so I thought I would worry about it later.

Once we finished siphoning the fuel we thoroughly hosed down what was left of the truck bed and all of the hoses, tanks, bottles and rails. The damage wasn't too bad; there was a hole in the bed about a foot in diameter. We decided it would be prudent to fill the X-1 with just three or four gallons of fuel instead of the entire ten. We also had to set up a bottle of high-pressure nitrogen gas we brought along to provide pressure to drive the HP out of the fuel tank in the car and into the rocket engine. Thankfully, this process went smoothly with no hitches.

After about an hour of courting disaster (and in the process learning a lot about how to handle hydrogen peroxide), we were ready to try running the car. Our next task was to decide who would drive.

"Whoever drives it should make sure it's not at full throttle in case something happens you won't be going too fast," I said. "We just need to see if the engine works right and if it's mounted right on the chassis. If it's unstable you don't want to be going at full throttle."

"Yeah, if it veers you're in trouble," said Pete, looking at Dick.

"What do you mean me?" asked Dick.

"I need to watch it run down the track to watch how it moves and if it needs adjustments to the chassis," said Pete.

"Ray?" asked Dick.

"I'm not driving it," I said.

So Dick got the job by default. I didn't want to drive it because I was very concerned for my safety at this point. The engine was fairly large and I knew enough about rocket engines that I didn't think it was wise to just stand close to one under any circumstances. We rolled the car up to the starting line on the drag strip. I was glad there was no one at the drag strip except us to witness our earlier ordeal with the car. If the owners had seen our truck start on fire we certainly would never have been able to run that car at their drag strip!

Dick got in the X-1, put on his helmet and gloves, and pressurized the fuel tank with the nitrogen. I took my position some distance back, hiding behind a telephone pole so that if the engine did blow up, hopefully the shrapnel from it wouldn't hit me.

I tried to warn Pete about the possibility that something like this might happen, but he didn't seem to be concerned. He stood right next to the car as it was poised on the starting line like it was any other dragster. I think the reason he wasn't worried was that he had seen many jet-powered dragsters in the past and of course none of them had blown up. He was thinking of jet engines and the relative safety of their operation. So, I didn't press the issue. I just stood behind the telephone pole and waited to see what would happen.

Everything was ready to go. Dick was in position to see how the car was going to run and ride down the strip. When Pete waved his hand Dick opened up the throttle slightly to let just a little bit of hydrogen peroxide into the engine and then closed it up. He did this as a form of preheating the catalyst pack so we wouldn't have a wet start. We didn't know for sure whether this catalyst pack was going to work right. It was the first one we had ever put together correctly. So he shot a little hydrogen peroxide into the engine, closed the valve and waited.

All of a sudden a big puff of white steam came shooting out the back and then stopped. It didn't come out very fast, it sort of billowed out the back of the rocket nozzle. Dick waited a few more seconds for the heat from the decomposition to permeate the catalyst pack and then he opened the throttle again part of the way. The engine started almost instantly and a loud bang and a little wisp of white steam shot out then it disappeared. At this point the car jolted ahead, down the track.

We didn't record the speed. But it didn't go real fast because Dick only ran the motor for about three or four seconds. Even so it caused the car to accelerate rapidly as it shot 200 feet down the strip. Dick closed the valve and the engine shut off and he just coasted for a ways until he hit the brakes.

The rocket engine didn't blow up, and the car didn't run off the drag strip. Everything seemed to be just fine. Dick jumped out and we ran to check everything over.

"Yes, she did it! It works - we're going to do it!" shouted Dick.

"Woooohooo! Baby!" Pete yelled.

"What was it like?" I asked.

"Like a dream. It's amazing. Loud! Amazing---I can't imagine the power if it's all out! I only had it out a quarter of the way. Not even halfway. It wasn't even at half power. A quarter of the way!" Dick beamed at us with his winning smile.

We didn't use all the fuel, so we decided to remove what was left and let it go at that, not wanting to push our luck by trying to run the car faster. We wasted so much time setting up and putting out the fire and it was late in the day, so we loaded the car back onto the truck, secured everything in place, and drove back to Pete's house, smiling all the way.

All three of us were encouraged by what had happened. Even though it didn't go smoothly, the car and the motor together performed very well. We knew we were on the right track. And there wouldn't have to be any major changes in either the car or the rocket engine in order to follow through with our project.

*Pete and I and our Reaction Dynamics truck. We are transferring HP to the X-1.
This shot is taken on a day after we set the truck on fire. We decided it was safer
to transfer the fuel on the ground instead of on the wooden truck bed!
(Photo courtesy of the Ray Dausman Collection)*

CHAPTER 13

PROFESSIONAL DRIVER AND FIRST WORLD RECORD

1966

"I'm your driver," a voice said from behind me. I swiveled around and took a look at the well-dressed, clean cut young man with a confident smirk-smile and dark crew cut regarding me from the shop doorway. It was a sunny Saturday afternoon in September, 1966, and I was measuring some parts for Pete while he ran into his house to make a phone call.

"Hello," I said carefully. Was this guy in the right shop?

"Chuck. Chuck Suba." He said, walking toward me. "Pete and Dick told me to come by and take a look at the car this weekend."

"Oh, right, right," I had never heard of him. I wasn't too surprised, though, because I knew that Dick and Pete were trying to round up a local drag racer who already had experience driving his own jet-powered car. This must be him. Dick had decided he wasn't going to drive the X-1 anymore so we were in search of a professional.

"Is Pete around? I can come back later if you're busy," said Chuck.

"No, he's here. I'll get him. The car is right over there," I said, pointing to the X-1 chassis. It still didn't have the exterior body attached so it looked somewhat skeletal.

Just then Pete came in the door and saw Chuck. He smiled and said, "Chuck! So glad you could make it. Any trouble getting here from Calumet?"

"Nah, piece of cake. Nice operation you've got here," said Chuck, looking around at Pete's garage jammed with tools, machines and one underdone rocket car.

"Just wait until we've got the body on her, Chuck. You will love her. The body will be streamlined, so the car will be out of sight! I guess you met our rocket guy, Ray, huh? Dick was going to be here, but he cancelled, so it's just me and Ray this weekend."

"And last weekend," I said to myself, under my breath.

Pete showed Chuck the car and afterwards the three of us sat down at Pete's kitchen table to negotiate a business arrangement over a bag of George Webb takeout burgers and Mountain Dew. Chuck was a well respected driver in the local drag racing community. He was a quiet bachelor in his late twenties who was well versed in the science of drag racing and spent a lot of time staying current on the trends and innovations. Turns out that he knew Pete and Leah for years. All three graduated from Evanston Township High School, Class of 1955, in Evanston, Illinois.

Chuck lived in Calumet City, Illinois, which is just a few miles east of Harvey, my last hometown. He lived in a commercial building that he rented from a guy he called his "Godfather." It turns out that this man he rented from used to be active on the Calumet City strip back in the '40s and early '50s. Calumet City was sort of a red light district near the south side of Chicago where people went to gamble, drink and visit houses of prostitution.

That whole operation was run by the crime syndicate. And evidently this "Godfather," who was a good friend of Chuck's, took him under his wing and gave him a place to live. The building was big enough that Chuck could also use it as his shop and work on his dragster. Chuck lived in his machine shop in a little room off to the side where he had a make-shift bed, a sink and a little gas hot plate. Chuck evidently had nothing on his mind except drag racing. He slept all day and worked all night on his drag car, keeping it up to speed and just puttering around all night long.

Chuck took these things he called "Bennies." I never did ask him what the Bennies consisted of, but my first guess was they might have had something to do with Benadryl. I later found out the "Bennies" were slang for amphetamine pills. That was his only vice as far as I could tell. He didn't seem to hang around with women and he didn't seem to be involved in anything illegal. He was just a nice, clean-living guy with no other interests besides drag racing.

Our kitchen table negotiations resulted in Chuck agreeing to drive the X-1 for $500 per event. He would run it as many times as possible to gather attention and set speed records. We agreed that Chuck would also be our driver for Reaction Dynamics's future land speed record car when we got to that point.

Reaction Dynamics quickly hired a booking agent named Ira Litchey. He was a small booking agent but had a good reputation in the local drag racing circuit. Ira would book the X-1 and charge us a 15% booking fee that we could pay him after we had been paid from the drag strip.

Later that month, Chuck drove the X-1 for the first time and clocked a quarter-mile time of 203.39 mph at the U. S. 30 Drag Strip in our first exhibition run at full power. The elapsed time for the run was announced at 5.41 seconds. We set the world record in the quarter mile our first time out!

The car's exterior was still unfinished; it didn't have the aerodynamic envelope over the chassis. It was also the first and only time Phyllis saw the car run. It was an exciting time because Reaction Dynamics was moving forward towards our land speed record goal - just over the horizon.

I left my job at IITRI almost immediately.

CHAPTER 14

Fresh Start and AGA Sponsorship

1966 - 1968

"What do you think about moving to Milwaukee?" I casually asked Phyllis.

We were watching The Ed Sullivan Show in our hot and sticky apartment while Cheryl slept and we sipped lemonade in ice-filled glasses in an effort to keep cool. The heat was nearly unbearable, even after dark, but especially so for Phyllis, who was almost seven months pregnant.

She didn't say anything at all. Jimmy Durante's growl came over the airwaves, "Corn that really packs a punch! All American! All American! Kellogg's! ...Corn Flakes!"

I wondered if she hadn't heard me.

"I don't know," was all she said. "I don't know."

The Beatles were about to perform, so I guess I didn't have great timing. I waited until they finished "Ticket to Ride" to bring it up again.

"IITRI isn't going anywhere and I think I can do better. The cost of living is lower in Milwaukee and we could find a bigger place in a safe area. You could teach again next year when the baby is born," I said.

Phyllis liked teaching, but would often come home in tears because the situation in the Chicago schools was 60% behavior control and 30% paperwork and 10% actual teaching. Maybe the Milwaukee schools would be more pleasant.

"Who would look after the kids when I'm working?" she asked.

"I don't know," it was my turn to say this. "I don't know."

"Right. We don't know anybody," she said.

"We know Pete and Leah," I reminded her, "and maybe Dick and Nancy would like it there too."

"Now that would be something if we all moved up there," said Phyllis, finishing her lemonade. She pushed herself up from the couch, walked over to the kitchen and placed her glass in the sink.

"So I could start looking around and see what kind of lab job I can find up there and tell Nancy to start packing," I chuckled.

"Fine. Fine," she answered, "go ahead and see. Go ahead and see." When Phyllis is anxious she tends to repeat her short-lipped answers as she walks away. But I knew if she truly disagreed with this idea she wouldn't hesitate to say so.

In 1966 I left IITRI to work at Ampenol Connector Corp in Cicero while I looked to relocate to Wisconsin. The job at Ampenol paid better than IITRI, but I did not enjoy the task they gave me, which was to test electrical connectors all day. The commute from IITRI across town to Cicero on the "El" train was long and difficult. I quit after six weeks because I had a firm offer from Allis Chalmers in Milwaukee to be a lab technician in their fuel cell department. The plant was located in a close western suburb called West Allis.

Our new apartment was located near 36th Street and Lisbon Avenue on the northwest side of Milwaukee. It was a very quiet neighborhood; a lot nicer than where we lived in Chicago. We lived in the upper flat and Mr. Hoehne lived in the lower flat.

Mr. Hoehne was about 90 years old and lived by himself. He owned the house and charged $80 per month, which was fine with us because we had paid $200 per month for our van der Rohe hotbox. In fact we never had high energy bills because Mr. Hoehne kept his lower flat so hot that all of his heat seeped through the floorboards to heat our home.

The best part about that place was that half a block away was Kehr's Candy. It was just a little storefront, and in the back the owner had a shack where he made his candy. Mr. Kehr was very nice but very overweight. People came from all over Milwaukee for his candy. Any time I wanted something sweet all I had to do was walk across the street and down the road a little bit to buy ice cream cones, chocolates, jelly beans and hard candy. The store wasn't any bigger than our living room in our upper flat. Kehr's Candy still has their "factory store" on Lisbon as well as a few other locations around the Milwaukee area.

We adjusted to life in Milwaukee as I started my new job and Phyllis gave birth to our daughter, Cathy, in December 1966. Luckily, Leah Farnsworth offered to take Cheryl in while we went to the hospital the night Cathy was born. Phyllis and I were grateful for her friendship since we didn't have any family in town to help.

Our family fell into a routine of work, children and occasional visits to Chicago or The Lake in Indiana to see relatives. My job was interesting and involved in-house research and projects for the government. I worked on six or seven fuel cell projects during the two years at Allis Chalmers. I tested and built high-temperature molten salt fuel cells. For another project I tested fuel cells for changing methane gas into electricity for use in machinery such as industrial lift trucks. These fuel cells were intended to replace the batteries to generate electricity for the lift trucks. I was involved in trying to develop a type of fuel cell that could be used to power a passenger car rather than using a conventional automotive engine.

Phyllis was a substitute teacher in the Milwaukee Public Schools. She reported that, yes, the Milwaukee schools were more pleasant than their Chicago counterparts, and we had a nice new life in Wisconsin.

■　■　■

The X-1 rocket car (Photo courtesy of the Ray Dausman Collection)

Pete finished the bodywork for the X-1 in April of 1967. The completed car was a beautiful machine. It was classified as a single-seater, enclosed cockpit, open wheeled "unlimited dragster." Its aerodynamic body is similar to a Formula One car—low and sleek. It had a Plexiglas windshield and a chassis made from welded steel tubing and aluminum plates housing our Reaction Dynamics HPR-2500 liquid monopropellant rocket. The thrust was controlled by the driver with a 0-2500 pound thrust range. It sported Goodyear tires on Halibrand magnesium casting wheels with four wheel disc brakes on dual master cylinders. Two eight foot emergency parachutes with a single 16 foot diameter chute were packed in the back for protection.

Chuck Suba fulfilled his end of the bargain by making exhibition runs all over the drag racing circuit to garner attention and awe for our land-speed record prototype. He drove the car at about a dozen different locations and impressed audiences from Union Grove, Wisconsin to Los Angeles, California with our rocket car. I would try to attend if Chuck and the X-1 were appearing in Wisconsin or northern Illinois.

Leah and Pete Farnsworth and me at Oswego Raceway with the X-1
(Photo courtesy of the Ray Dausman Collection)

There were a few drag strip personalities that made strong impressions on me. I was fascinated by this passionate and boisterous population. The pits were so new to me that sometimes I felt like I was trying to make my way around a foreign country. I think I must have stuck out like a sore thumb, my eyes wide with people watching and my mouth clamped shut so I didn't embarrass myself with poor attempts at the unfamiliar language of racing.

One of the more amusing fixtures of the Union Grove drag strip was a character named "Black Bart." Shortly after the drag races started for the evening, Black Bart would make a spectacular entrance in his long, black Cadillac limousine. His car would come screaming into the drag strip, horn honking, and speed along the spectator section so all of the race fans could welcome Black Bart.

Black Bart was a cross between Zorro and Black Beard the Pirate, with long black hair and a bushy black beard. He was always dressed in black from head to toe. He wore black cowboy boots, cowboy hat, pants, shirt and topped it all off with a black bandana tied around his neck. In his hand was a long, wooden handle with straw at the business end, his trademark broom.

Black Bart would rush out to the starting line waving his broom wildly in the air. It was his job to make sure the two competing dragsters were in the proper position at the start of the race and to clean up after the cars were headed down the track. The cars would leave the starting line with huge clouds of smoke, and Bart would furiously sweep away any oil or debris that might have been left on the starting line. He always made a big deal doing this after every race.

We showed up one Saturday night with the X-1 rocket car to do an exhibition run. Our driver, Chuck Suba, forgot to preheat the rocket engine so we had a wet start. When Chuck opened the throttle to start the race about a gallon of hydrogen peroxide passed through the rocket engine before it got hot enough to generate thrust. The HP landed on Black Bart's clean swept pavement. As the X-1 rocket car tore down the drag strip, Black Bart and his broom promptly attacked the clear puddle of liquid, which he mistook for water or other harmless discharge.

The hydrogen peroxide was bubbling away and Black Bart tried valiantly to sweep it onto the grass alongside the drag strip. But within a matter of a few seconds the straw part of his broom burst into flames. Bart just stared at his broom, unsure what to do.

As his prized broom turned into a torch, Black Bart stood in a puddle of hydrogen peroxide. Suddenly the bottom of his shiny black cowboy boots burst into flames, shooting sparks in every direction. Bart was dumbfounded. "This can't be happening!" he seemed to say, throwing down his broom and running to the side of the track where he tried to get his boots off before he burned the bottom of his feet. But he must have stepped in the hydrogen peroxide with his cotton socks, because they caught on fire too! This was more than Black Bart could take. He ran back to his car with his socks on fire and left his broom and boots burning away at the starting line, gunning his black Cadillac as he raced out of the drag strip. No one ever saw him at the strip again. He never came back.

From that day on we made sure the X-1 engine was preheated before we got to the starting line so no one else would find himself in that position, although I have to admit it was the most hilarious thing I ever saw.

Doug Rose was another memorable character we would run into while exhibiting the X-1. Doug had wooden legs because part of each of his legs had been amputated. Evidently Doug lost his legs in a crash while driving Art Arfons's jet-dragster "The Green Monster." The parachute system failed, so the car didn't slow down when it came to the end of the drag strip. It kept right on going into a telephone pole or a tree and crushed his legs so badly they had to be amputated. He learned to improvise and it wasn't too long after he got his wooden legs that he was able to start drag racing again.

Doug was a clean-cut, good looking guy and very well-spoken. His wife Stephanie was also very good looking. He had a day job, but he did a lot of exhibitions around the country, much like Chuck Suba did. After his legs were amputated Doug built his own jet-powered car called "The Green Mamba."

All the women hung around Doug because they thought he was handsome; a real sexy guy. He had this habit of standing next to a car talking to some people and all of a sudden he'd bend over and take his wooden leg off and put it up on top of the car. Of course the kids would come running over and want to know how he could take his leg off. I could see how this would appeal to the ladies.

Years later, in 2006, the Green Mamba was stolen from Doug Rose's residence, chopped up and later found in pieces at a recently deserted

Florida body shop. The jet engine was found in a scrap yard in Tampa. Incredibly, Doug was able to reassemble the Green Mamba and return it to the drag strip for a welcome back performance in 2007.

Near the end of the X-1 exhibition, we got involved with a couple of Cubans. Russell Mendez was a fairly tall guy and his Mutt and Jeff type partner, Ramon Alvarez, was very short. Both men could speak English pretty well, but with heavy Cuban accents.

I was told was that this Cuban Mutt and Jeff raised money for racing their cars by selling marijuana at drag strips. Ramon would go around the pits with his briefcase of marijuana and stop at the various cars and make his sales. His size may have made Ramon insecure because he went to great lengths to protect himself. In addition to packing a pistol under his shirt, he also had this huge Great Dane on a chain that he sort of dragged along behind him to intimidate people, I guess. It was a huge dog. It stood taller at the shoulders than this guy was tall. It looked like he was leading a horse around the pits.

Mendez bought a rocket engine from me, a few years later. After The Blue Flame project I worked on a few rocket-powered vehicles with a dragster designer named Arvil Porter. In fact, Mendez was our first customer. Arvil, Mendez, and Alvarez, who carried the briefcase, and I would meet at the Holiday Inn in Racine, Wisconsin to discuss plans for Mendez's rocket car. I designed the rocket and Arvil built the rocket for him while Mendez built the car himself and named it "Free Spirit." I had heard Mendez had plenty of money because he and Alvarez were bringing tons of marijuana across the border stuffed in semi trailer frames. Supposedly they had a trailer specially made so they could pack the pot into the metal framing of the truck. They allegedly got so wealthy they purchased a big farm near Atlanta, which they called their "ranch."

I lost track of them for a while and then one day Arvil called and said the car had crashed at a Florida drag strip and Mendez had been killed. A rumor circulated that it looked like the car had been tampered with. Some people felt his little partner might have been responsible in order to take over the drug thing full time, alone.

Mendez's fatal crash was on March 16, 1975 at the Gator Nationals in Gainesville, Florida. He ran the only exhibition car that day, which means he wasn't racing against another car. Mendez was just going to show off or "exhibit" his car for the crowd. The spectators were excited to see his car, Free Spirit, run at predicted speeds of 325 mph. The run started out without any problem and Free Spirit shot down the track in front of the cheering crowd. Tragedy struck when the car veered sharply to the right almost at the same time as the chutes deployed and hit a guardrail. Mendez was ejected from the car.

I don't know what happened to the short guy. He's probably in jail or dead by now. I wonder if he still has a Great Dane on a chain following behind him wherever he goes.

■　■　■

On one occasion Art Arfons refused to race his Green Monster against Suba in the X-1 unless he received a time handicap. Suba allowed a half second handicap to the Green Monster and still roared past Arfons to beat him in the quarter-mile in an elapsed time of 6.32 seconds.

In June 1968 Rislone, a maker of oil additives, became a sponsor for the X-1 which was then nicknamed "The Rislone Rocket." It was unclear why they would be willing to be our sponsor because our car didn't use oil. Dick had convinced Rislone representatives that the X-1 was for the future and so was Rislone. From there it was a small leap to sponsorship and, while they didn't give us any money for the right to apply their logo to our slick red and white dragster, Rislone did give Reaction Dynamics a large supply of Rislone products.

Dick was still living in Chicago and responsible for making connections and obtaining sponsors for our land speed record attempt. He had the best negotiation and networking skills of the three Reaction Dynamics founders and was effective in securing the interest and later the sponsorship from the American Gas Association. Dick worked for the Institute of Gas Technology and convinced his employers that including their natural gas as fuel in a land speed record car could greatly promote the natural gas industry and bring its options to the forefront of American society. The natural gas industry wanted to move beyond the household heating fuel market and start focusing on sales of liquid natural gas. They were in the process of developing ways to ship liquefied natural gas overseas to customers in Europe and Asia. Liquid natural gas is cryogenic, so in order to ship it they needed to build special insulated tanks to ensure that their gas would stay in liquid form enroute. Once the liquefied natural gas reached its destination (a city in Europe or Asia) it had to be stored in special underground tanks that would freeze the ground outside the tank for insulation. The frozen layer around the tank made sure the gas wouldn't evaporate.

The second project the natural gas industry was looking into was persuading the airline industry to convert their aircraft fuel systems to liquefied natural gas instead of jet fuel, while the third goal was to convince automobile companies to redesign automobile engines so they could use liquefied natural gas instead of gasoline. When Dick approached the AGA and let them know that liquefied natural gas could be used in the Blue Flame, officials realized that our rocket car could be the vehicle, literally and figuratively, to help bring their goals to fruition.

The AGA sponsorship, in essence, was one huge promotional stunt to gain the world's attention and persuade the public that liquefied natural gas could be used as an alternate high-tech energy source in various international markets and products.

In September, 1968 Chuck Suba approached the starting line at the Oklahoma City drag strip, ready to rock and roll toward another track record. In the stands were natural gas industry officials who were looking to learn about the power of the X-1 rocket and streamlined design. The chassis had been altered slightly to allow for the car to be lighter and a larger fuel tank took up residence on the tube and panel chassis.

The Green Monster declined the challenge to race head to head with Suba, so the X-1 simply raced against the clock. The car screamed down the track and scorched its own best performance with a speed of 265 mph and an elapsed time of 5.9 seconds.

Natural gas officials gave the green light to The Blue Flame. The Bonneville Salt Flats appeared on the horizon - the place where world records were set.

Unfortunately, Chuck Suba would not be our driver. A few weeks later one of his friends had asked him to check out a handling problem he was having on a car and to suggest what changes needed to be made to correct the problem. Chuck took the car to the Rockford Dragway and did this favor for his friend. The car went out of control, ran off the edge of the drag strip and hit a 55 gallon drum which was marking the finish line. The drum bounced into the air and landed on Chuck's head, killing him instantly.

In an interview Chuck's dad (Chuck Sr.) told reporter Robert Markus, "There was a drum on the track that shouldn't have been there. It was windy and Chuck's car was sliding sideways and it hit the drum; it went out of control and then there was a car parked where it shouldn't have been. He hit that. I'm sure he saw it all happening, but there is only a fraction of a second to try to make things better so that these things don't happen."

No one seemed to know what to do, so I took it upon myself to write a letter on behalf of Reaction Dynamics to his parents to extend our condolences. I'm sure Pete and Leah were in contact with Chuck's family too, but we were all too stunned to talk much about it.

Chuck's parents went out to the salt flats to watch The Blue Flame's record attempt in 1970 because they knew how important it had been to Chuck. Gary Gabelich, The Blue Flame's driver, carried a picture of Chuck Suba in the cockpit when he broke the record. I wonder if Chuck's parents gave the photo to Gary so their son could ride the rocket after all.

*"Team X-1" (from left to right) Me, Chuck Suba, Pete Farnsworth and Dick Keller
(Photo courtesy of the Ray Dausman Collection)*

CHAPTER 15

GARLITS AND THE SPITFIRE

1968

"Garlits. It's gotta be Garlits," Pete said.

The three of us were in the Reaction Dynamics shop, wondering what to do with the setback of not having a driver. AGA had given sponsorship to Reaction Dynamics based on the performance of the X-1 in Oklahoma City, which included the skill of our driver, Chuck Suba. The AGA was expecting a world land speed record with Suba in the driver's seat.

"Yeah. He's the best. Dick agreed. "Garlits is the perfect choice. He's the most famous driver out there."

I didn't say anything. Of the three, I had the least experience or know how when it came to actual drag racing. If Pete and Dick thought Garlits was the best choice, who was I to put in my two cents when I didn't even have that much?

"Big Daddy" Garlits was considered the father of drag racing. He was from Florida so he was also nicknamed, "Swamp Rat." In fact Garlits named his cars after his nickname in a series of Swamp Rat vehicles. The most famous of which, Swamp Rat XXX, is on permanent display at the Smithsonian Institute. Dick and Pete considered Garlits a hero and were sure he was our best option.

"So, Dick, are you going to contact him?" I asked, just assuming that our best motivator and promotion guy would be the one to do it.

"I can do that," he said. "I'll talk to AGA and let them know and see if their contract conditions will be the same and so forth."

I was happy that he would take care of finding a driver because I didn't have the first clue where to look. Turns out, perhaps our best option called our office herself a few days later and I managed to overlook an amazing opportunity for us all.

Part of my office duties included the clerical work involved in running a business. One Friday afternoon in the Spring of 1969 I was in the office paying bills and the phone rang. A woman's voice greeted me with a chipper hello and I missed it when she announced her name.

"I've heard about The Blue Flame and want to know if you have a driver yet," she asked with a crisp, cheerful voice.

"We don't know yet, we're looking for a driver," I answered.

"I'd like to pay a visit and see your car. We can talk about the possibility of me being your driver!" she said.

"Well, that would be great," I said, proceeding to give her our address and directions to the shop. She told me she and her husband were living in Michigan and she would see me early the next week.

I guess I figured she wouldn't show up.

I was wrong.

The following week there was a knock on my office door and there she stood.

She was a trim and slender woman in her late forties or early fifties with blonde, slightly graying hair. Her eyes were sharp and her smile was quick. I had no idea who she was.

Unbeknownst to me, I was looking at one of the most famous pilots in the world. Here we were trying to set a world land speed record and who shows up ready to drive? Betty Skelton aka "The First Lady of Firsts." What a perfect match it would have been. I did not know anything about stunt aviation. In hindsight I wish I had. An experienced record-breaker with nerves of steel (just what we needed) was standing in my office doorway and I was completely unprepared. I stumbled my way through the visit. I dropped the ball on signing the perfect driver for The Blue Flame.

We didn't have the car built yet, so I showed Betty what we had so far. I spread out a few documents on my desk for her to review. I had several drafting sketches of the rocket engine and an artist's rendering of the future Blue Flame. She placed her index finger on her chin as she bent over to scrutinize our conceptual models and drawings. Betty asked a lot of questions about the design of the rocket as well as the body of the car and the timetable for the record attempt. I told her as much as I knew at the time and informed her that we weren't ready to make a decision about the driver yet, but we would definitely keep her in mind.

"Well, then, I do need to get back to the airport. Could you arrange a cab for me, Ray?" Betty asked.

"I can take you back, no problem. I'm not doing too much today. I really appreciate you coming all the way here from Michigan." I hadn't realized she had taken a taxi to the shop since I didn't see her drive in.

When we arrived at Timmerman Field, Betty waved to a spot over to our left.

"I'm parked over there," she said.

I was a little confused, not realizing she had flown herself here. There wasn't anything in the spot she had indicated except this tiny stunt plane. It was a little biplane called a Pitts Special with double wings that was adept at aerial acrobatics.

"I'm surprised you're flying a plane like that." I told her.

"Oh, yeah, that's my plane. Do you want to take a look inside?" she offered. She was perfectly casual about piloting such a powerful piece of machinery. The engine was enormous. In fact, it seemed like the plane was just a huge engine and a couple of wings. I just looked at it in amazement.

"Are you sure?" I asked.

"Yes, go ahead and climb up on the wing," said Betty.

I did just that and peered into the cockpit. I couldn't even imagine this plane flying, much less having a woman pilot. I guess I was guilty of not being able to picture a woman flying such a machine, for which I regret. My first thought was there's no way *anyone* could control this thing in the air. It had short stubby wings and a little tail and one seat mounted on top of the gigantic 2000 horse power engine! The cockpit was just big enough for one person. There were no dials or instruments of any kind.

"How do you fly this thing? There aren't any instruments." I said.

She chuckled. "Ha! There's no room for instruments, so we fly by the seat of our pants."

I was stunned at this whole situation and only managed to say, "Well, okay…it was nice of you to come…"

Betty gave me a smile and a wave and she climbed onto the wing. I turned around and started walking back to my car, shaking my head. Wait until I tell Phyllis about this, I mused.

Suddenly there was this tremendous roar as Betty started up her engine. I turned to watch her. Betty taxied a short distance to one of the runways and just roared away. She didn't go much more than a hundred feet and her plane took off. It went *straight up*, absolutely *straight up in the air* and disappeared in a matter of moments, headed back across Lake Michigan. I stood there, completely shocked at the whole experience. As I watched the spot in the sky where her plane used to be, I asked myself why I didn't ask her more about her flying background.

I later found out Betty Skelton was already legendary by the time she visited me at the Reaction Dynamics shop. She set 17 aviation and automobile records, and she has been inducted into ten halls of fame, including the National Aviation Hall of Fame, International Motorsports

Hall of Fame, Women in Aviation, Pioneer Hall of Fame and the latest Motorsports Hall of Fame of America.

The airplane she flew to Wisconsin that day in 1968 was a Pitts Special stunt plane Betty called 'Lil Stinker. It is on permanent display at the Smithsonian National Air and Space Museum.

When I was rifling through my records and recollections for this book I decided to contact Betty and let her know she had made a huge impression on me. I also wanted her to know that I did truly think she would have been an excellent choice to drive The Blue Flame.

From Betty's Response:

"*Dear Ray: NOW you tell me. I would have given my life for that ride! … I will say just hearing from you and your saying I might have had a chance to drive that marvelous vehicle has given me goose bumps all over again…*"

~Betty Skelton

CHAPTER 16

Doctors Torda and Uzgiris

1968

Reaction Dynamics negotiated a deal with the American Gas Association (AGA) where the three of us partners – Pete, Dick and myself would be paid a monthly salary for the period of time it would take to build the car, which we figured would take one to two years. I doubled my salary by quitting Allis Chalmers and going to work on The Blue Flame project full time.

One of the advantages to my career move was that my wife and I could buy a home. We bought a house in Germantown, Wisconsin, at the end of 1968 with my increased salary of $10,000. Germantown is a suburb about thirty minutes northwest of Milwaukee with good schools, wide lawns and fresh air. Our house was a green and brown three-bedroom ranch with a two-car garage attached to the house with a breezeway. Our large corner lot had room for a vegetable garden and our kids had ample space to jump and play.

Reaction Dynamics found a shop to rent on 124th Street in Butler, Wisconsin and moved our headquarters from Pete's garage to our new location. The building was about 50 yards long and separated into six or eight shop spaces that were narrow but deep. We had the second slot from the north end and were very close to an auto parts business. Our total shop space was approximately 20 feet wide and maybe 60 or 70 feet long. The front was comprised of the entrance and small office and bathroom facility. The rest of it was the shop area. On the rear of the shop area there were some overhead doors you could raise to get large objects in and out. The rent was about $100 per month.

Pete, Dick and I had agreed to divide the project into two general areas of responsibility. I was to concentrate on designing, building and testing the rocket engine. I also was assigned the role of office manager and would have to be the one to pay the bills and handle our correspondence. Pete and Dick were responsible for hiring people to help with the building of the car, locating outside contractors to fabricate parts and materials that had to be built outside of our shop, and to generally get the car built. Pete Farnsworth was certainly an expert car builder and we had confidence that he would be able to create a spectacular body for our LSR vehicle. But who would design it? Reaction Dynamics needed to find mechanical and aerospace engineers to design not only the aerodynamics of our car to make sure it didn't roll over on the salt flats or take off into the air when the 360 degree shock wave enveloped the car during the dangerous transonic stage of our land speed quest, but also build it strong enough to withstand the many forces that would be exerted upon its chassis (frame).

Any vehicle that is intended to travel at a supersonic speed must deal with the perils of the transonic zone. The transonic zone is an unstable transition period because some parts of the car will be traveling faster than the speed of sound, but not all parts of the vehicle are traveling at the speed of sound just yet. The transonic zone is between 650-750 mph. Shockwaves and vehicle instability are guaranteed in the transonic zone. The vehicle could roll over, start to pitch upwards or downwards, buffet, or there could be a combination of all three. It was crucial that the vehicle was designed to withstand the transonic zone without rolling, flipping or taking off. Our Blue Flame's rocket engine could easily tilt upwards and provide lift off and therefore propel the driver towards space with no hope of a safe landing if the car's dimensions were not perfectly calculated to prevent it.

In 1968 Reaction Dynamics hired Dr. Paul Torda, a professor in the IIT Department of Mechanical and Aerospace Engineering, to act as a consultant on The Blue Flame project. The next month another expert, assistant professor Dr. Carl Uzgiris, was asked to join forces with the WLSR project. Dick was instrumental in finding the engineering experts because he had many contacts at IIT through his job at IGT.

According to the professors, the question of aerodynamics on The Blue Flame was perfect to pose to their graduate students, who were all in search of thesis topics. Hundreds of pages of graduate work and Master's Thesis documentation was produced at IIT to solve the problems of pitch, yaw, lifting moment, body design, covered wheels vs. simple struts and the like. Each detail on the aerodynamic envelope of the car had to address the issue of making the car safe from lift off and crashing.

For instance, the front end of The Blue Flame was pointed towards the ground by one degree to keep the force from the rocket pushing the car towards the ground instead of encouraging the car to lift off and take flight. The graduate students suggested installing canard wings on the front end of the car to increase the stability of the vehicle as it streaked across the salt. This idea was later dropped due to wind tunnel testing results.

Other considerations were given to the metal panels on the car. The designers decided to use aluminum since it was very light. Direct attention was given to the size and shape of the panels to discourage buckling. The land speed record The Blue Flame had to beat was 600.601 mph, set by veteran Craig Breedlove and his jet-powered car, Sonic I in 1965 at the Bonneville Salt Flats.

Jet powered vehicles landed on the scene in the 1960s. Art Arfons and his Green Monster battled it out on the Bonneville Salt Flats with Craig Breedlove and his car Spirit of America. These dueling jet dragsters traded the record back and forth several times. There was evidence that the metal panels of the Sonic I buckled from the instability of approaching the transonic stage. This was important to us because we expected The Blue Flame to travel through the transonic stage and reach speeds of 900 mph or faster. The Blue Flame would definitely be at risk.

The transonic stage held the danger.

Torda and Uzgiris assigned their students to solve the questions about The Blue Flame and involved more than 70 undergraduates from IIT. The professors welcomed the chance to give their students real world problems to solve in their studies of engineering. Eight graduate students were involved in the project. Tom Morel, a grad student from Czechoslovakia, completed his entire Master's Thesis on the aerodynamic design of a land speed record car.

The IIT students were mostly young Indian men lacking in basic mechanical knowledge. They frankly didn't know which end of the screwdriver was used to do the work. But they did know their theoretical mechanical engineering. It took them a while to really comprehend what we were building, but about halfway through they finally were able to picture the vehicle.

As I recall one of the Indian guys was designing the wheels for the rocket car. Another was meant to design the suspension system. One was given the job, I believe, of designing the braking system. Everyone had their assigned project. So early on in the program these guys were all put to work trying to come up with the engineering drawings for the various systems in the car. Pete, Dick and I had regular meetings at IIT with Dr. Uzgiris and all of their students. They would ask questions, occasionally about the characteristics of the rocket system. How much thrust? How much would it weigh? Where would the component parts be placed in the vehicle? How much would the component parts weigh? It was very stimulating.

Design team from IIT's Mechanical and Aerospace Engineering Department working on the plans for The Blue Flame rocket car (from left to right) Harshad Parikh, Prahlad Thakur, Dr. Paul Torda, Manoj Adhikari, Tom Morel, Dr. Sarunas Uzgiris, and Krishna Pandey (Photo courtesy of the Ray Dausman Collection)

Occasionally the young students would come to Milwaukee to visit the shop to see what progress was being made. The visits gave them a hands on feel for what we were doing and what they were helping to create. They would typically stay all day and go back in the evening. So I was always faced with taking these guys out to dinner. Well, these Indians were vegetarians. It was always a challenge to take these guys to find a restaurant where they wouldn't violate their religious code as far as dietary restrictions. Generally I took them to someplace that served grilled cheese sandwiches. For some reason or other they were able to eat cheese, so they would eat grilled cheese and a salad or something. But there were always questions about the ingredients of the salad, and a lot of times they didn't eat it all.

During this time I built this very small rocket engine that I thought I might use as a demo after The Blue Flame project was over to attract new clients to Reaction Dynamics. I showed the IIT students this tiny rocket engine that only put out around five pounds of thrust. Some of the guys were curious and wondered if I could design and build something for their fluids lab at IIT.

"I guess you could just use the 25 pound thrust prototype that we built initially for the X-1." I told them. "I'd be willing to donate that to the cause."

So that's what happened to the prototype engine we tested in the Blue Island alley in 1964. I donated it to IIT Engineering Department and they set it up in their fluids lab and occasionally would fire it to demonstrate rocket propulsion to their students. And as far as I know it's probably still there today.

There were several reports written for IIT that provided the design for The Blue Flame aerodynamics and structure. Examples of Master's theses published in 1969 are *Structural Design of an L. S. R. Vehicle* by Shashikumar V. Kurani and *Aerodynamic Design of a High-Speed Rocket Car* by Thomas Morel. Professor Uzgiris and graduate student K. G. Pandey prepared a report called *Performance of The Blue Flame* in March 1970. *Design of the "Blue Flame" Vehicle - Structure* was written by graduate student M. C. Adhikari. Other graduate student reports include *Design of the "Blue Flame" Vehicle - Wheels* by H. Parikh and *Design of the "Blue Flame" Vehicle - Suspension* by P. T. Thakur.

Professors Torda and Uzgiris worked with graduate students Morel and Pandey to prepare a cumulative report called *Design and Performance of The Blue Flame*. This report was presented at the Second International Conference on Vehicle Mechanics in September, 1971 at Paris VI University. Torda and Uzgiris published their department's findings in several periodicals and journals including *Mechanical Engineering* in July 1970 and *The Indian and Eastern Engineer* in March 1971.

REACTION DYNAMICS, INC.
5254 NORTH 124TH STREET * MILWAUKEE, WISCONSIN 53225
* Phone (414) 462-6530
MEMORANDUM

11/5/68

TO: RICHARD KELLER AND ROBERT B. ROSENBERG
FROM: RAYMOND J. DAUSMAN
SUBJECT: REVISED ESTIMATE OF COSTS INVOLVED IN FABRICATING ROCKET SYSTEM

For the sake of future financial planning I want to make known to you the estimated cost of the rocket propulsion system for the LSR based on design work carried out to date. I want to emphasize that this is an estimate not a firm costing based on quotes from fabricators. The price breakdown is as follows:

Catalyst pack	$7,500.00
Combustion chamber	7,628.00
Heat exchanger	3,000.00
Fuel tank	2,000.00
Peroxide tank	750.00
Nitrogen tank	200.00
Valves and regulators	1,000.00
Lines and fittings	2,000.00
Controls	1,000.00
Testing	7,000.00
Total cost	32,078.00

In view of this cost I recommend that new and vigorous efforts be made to find a way to raise this amount by January 1, 1969 to prevent this phase of the project from falling behind schedule.

In the early days of The Blue Flame world land speed record (WLSR) project, I spent much of my time laying out the general parameters for the rocket engine in order to build it within the estimated cost I had reported in November, 1968.

Cost was always a problem, so I made every effort to find the best parts and materials at the lowest price. Our WLSR vehicle would need some fairly large, high pressure vessels for storing nitrogen gas in the car. These types of tanks were extremely expensive to fabricate, so I tried to solve this problem by seeking out parts that were already made. The notion came to me that I could find existing parts in the multitude of military surplus lots in California.

The West Coast surplus lots had treasures ranging from jet planes to rocket parts to military vehicles of all kinds. There were businesses out there selling military equipment and spare parts for a fraction of what it would cost Reaction Dynamics to have them made.

I went out to Los Angeles a couple of times and came back with some big spherical high pressure vessels, about 30 inches in diameter, which I had calculated would be about the right size for the requirements of The Blue Flame rocket engine. I believe I got two big titanium containers for the nitrogen gas and I bought one nitrogen vessel for storing high pressure helium for the liquefied natural gas fuel tank pressurization. I also found some gas pressure regulators that would have been exorbitantly expensive to buy elsewhere.

I found out early on in the game that Reaction Dynamics could get parts for free. The rocket engine needed several types of component parts such as pipe fittings, tubing fitting and hoses. These parts would surely add up and put some stress on our budget. I decided to try my hand at schmoozing. I would merely call up a company that made some of these parts and talk to someone in their sales department and tell them about the project for The Blue Flame.

The sales rep would be impressed in short order and wouldn't hesitate when I informed them we'd like to use some of their products in The Blue Flame. I would assure the person that in return for their donation of a sufficient supply of their widgets we would give them the right to use The Blue Flame in some of their advertising.

Much to my surprise I found out most everyone I called thought this was a great idea. So I was able to get thousands of dollars worth of parts for absolutely nothing. Jamesbury Corporation donated $1,928.60 of hardware, Marotta Valve Corporation donated $2,505.00 of parts, Norton Supply gave us $1,544.50 worth of valves and joints and Snap-Tite donated $452.80 worth of parts to our WLSR project.

The project was of sufficient interest that a lot of the sales engineers and public relations people from these companies actually made a trip out to our shop to observe what we were doing. They all thought they were going to see this big rocket-powered automobile, but really all they would end up seeing was our shop and the preliminary designs of the vehicle. I'd always give them some artist renderings of the proposed car and public relations items that we had gotten from the AGA, which were based on IIT designs.

If I wasn't working on the specific details of the rocket engine or working the phones to solicit free parts I could be found typing reports and organizing the accounts for Reaction Dynamics. I handled the routine bills and receipts for office supplies, phone calls to Riverdale, Chicago, Harvey, Calumet City and the like. I kept track of all of the money, even scribbling prices of train tickets and grilled cheese sandwiches on the backs of business cards to make sure our reimbursement records were accurate.

It was an easy decision to hire Jim McCormick as a consultant. His experience with hydrogen peroxide rocket hydraulics was top notch and I already knew he was reliable because I had collaborated with him before. During the X-1 days I came across his name in a bibliography for an article about using hydrogen peroxide in rocket engines. I found the number for his workplace, FMC Corporation, and asked him to do some work for our prototype engine. Jim was enthusiastic about our idea and designed the catalyst pack for the X-1. I enjoyed working with Jim because he was an extremely positive person who wasn't afraid to try something new. Jim thoroughly understood the science of engineering and was a very skilled designer. I think he had a great combination of a positive attitude and solid engineering skills to back up his "anything is possible" attitude.

"Hi, Jim. It's Ray Dausman. We've got a new idea down here in Milwaukee and I wonder if you would be interested in another rocket project."

"Of course, Ray. What's the plan?" asked Jim.

"This time we are going to break the world land speed record, Jim. The X-1 was just a drop in the bucket. I'm talking supersonic, here."

"Absolutely! Whatever you want, we'll find a way to do it!" said Jim, enthusiastic as usual. It was encouraging to work with someone who was so willing to put his energy and skills to the test in order to be the first to accomplish something.

"One thing, we need to use liquefied natural gas, Jim," I said. "Our sponsor is the AGA – American Gas Association. So we're talking much higher exhaust temps with the two fuels, and we need to make sure we don't melt the thing and start the crew on fire."

"Sure, sure. Two fuels are fine. I've done, let's see… kerosene and alcohol as secondary sources. LNG is just another fuel. We can make it happen."

Jim and I mostly talked over the phone to hammer out the details. He had his own consulting company, called Engineering Services. Reaction Dynamics hired him to be my consultant since I was in charge of designing the entire propulsion system. I explained to him what I needed him to do, and Jim would do some thinking about it. For example, we would have conversations about the appropriate chamber pressure for the rocket engine. Jim sent me a stack of papers shortly after our first conversation. The report explained his calculations on how to add LNG to our hydrogen peroxide rocket and make both fuels burn.

Jim's contribution to the rocket engine included designs for the combustion chamber, nozzle, catalyst pack and heat exchanger. The heat exchanger was crucial because it would take the cryogenic supercooled liquefied natural gas and heat it to an extremely hot gas that would ignite with the oxygen. Jim also designed the regenerative cooling of the rocket engine nozzle.

"Ray, we're going to spiral the tubes around the nozzle." Jim assured me over the phone. "The HP will absorb heat from the nozzle and go into the catalyst pack in a heated condition."

"Good, good. That way the nozzle won't melt during operation of the rocket," I said.

The exhaust temperatures were going to be much higher in our WLSR rocket because we were introducing two propellants. A hydrogen peroxide rocket (such as the X-1) has an exhaust temperature of about 1,300 degrees Fahrenheit. Jim and I expected exhaust temperatures to be approximately 5,200 degrees Fahrenheit with the WLSR rocket because we would be burning gas and the oxygen from the hydrogen peroxide decomposition.

Had we not been able to cool the stainless steel rocket nozzle of the Blue Flame engine, it would have melted almost immediately upon emission of the gases. We absolutely had to find a way to have a regeneratively cooled rocket nozzle.

"We need to go from minus 262 degrees to about plus 1,600 degrees Fahrenheit for the methane gas," Jim said.

"Agreed. Think about it and let me know when you want me to come up and see your drawings."

Jim was a very positive influence in my life. He was about 30 years older than me, and was always very encouraging. In early 1969 Phyllis and I went to Buffalo to visit Jim and pick up the drawings he had prepared over the past few months. We stayed with him at his summer cottage, which was on the shore of Lake Erie near Buffalo. He and his wife treated us to a barbecue.

In addition to collaborating with Jim on the rocket motor design I was in charge of the rest of the propulsion system. This included making decisions on the correct fuel tanks, pressurized vessels, hoses, connections, pressure regulators, valves and hydraulics. I was also responsible for the complete testing of the engine after everything was assembled.

I worked on these tasks in my office at Reaction Dynamics and starting scouting for a testing location. We certainly couldn't use an alley or local drag strip this time!

CHAPTER 17

The Gee Whiz and NASA Visit

1968

The China Lake Naval Weapons Center is located about 150 miles northeast of Los Angeles on the edge of the Mojave Desert. I stood next to a standard railway track that extended more than a mile towards the horizon. The track was laid on top of a heavy concrete bed to provide stability for the 1,500 pound sled that would zoom across the rails in an effort to study the effect of dramatic deceleration and g forces on the human body. This was the famous rocket sled track at China Lake. It was installed to test the V-1 rockets and repurposed once the military needed to research the effects of human deceleration in aviation situations.

The rocket sled was basically a rocket-powered seat mounted on rails. Scientists would strap a person into the seat and fire the rocket off and shoot the guy down the track out into the desert to see how much g force the rocket rider could stand before they blacked out. The test subject had sensors affixed to him at various points that would by telemetry send back data on heart rate, blood pressure and various other parameters they were interested in measuring.

Perhaps the most famous test subject was Colonel John Stapp. He took repeated rides on the rocket sled in the 1950s and proved that humans can survive extreme conditions when strapped to a rocket. He holds the record for the highest voluntary deceleration force of 45 g. He endured many injuries including broken bones, repeated broken blood vessels in his eyes and even a detached retina. Stapp helped advance the research about air travel, seat safety and pilot and passenger harnesses. As a matter of fact Colonel Stapp signed my Student Member "American Rocket Society Certificate of Membership" in December, 1959.

Stapp certainly wasn't afraid to put himself out there to try something new. At the time of our WLSR attempt he was actually the "fastest man on earth" since he achieved 632 mph on the rocket sled. He didn't qualify for the land speed record, however, since he wasn't in an automobile as defined by the Federation Internationale de L'Automobile (FIA), the world sanctioning authority for speed records. He supported technological advancement and knowledge by his willingness to take a calculated risk. He is known for Stapp's Law, which states: "The universal aptitude for ineptitude makes any human accomplishment an incredible miracle."

My first rocketry credential, signed by John L. Stapp

One day while I was eating lunch at my desk I came across a magazine article about the X-15 military rocket airplanes. I sipped my coffee and ate my ham sandwich while I read. The rockets used hydrogen peroxide, ammonia and liquid oxygen for propellants, so naturally I wanted to find out more. The X-15 rocket airplanes set altitude records and reached the edge of outer space, an altitude of 50 miles. Thirteen of the rocket propelled flights made it to outer space, therefore qualifying its pilots as astronauts. In fact, the altitude records were not broken until Space Ship One won the Ansari X-Prize in 2004.

Entire industries can be created by setting up a contest and promising a big prize. In 1927 Charles Lindbergh, in his plane Spirit of St. Louis, won the $25,000 Ortieg Prize for being the first pilot to fly non-stop between New York and Paris. Ray Ortieg, a New York hotel owner, sponsored the contest. Lindbergh proved it was possible and commercial flight became common throughout the world.

The Ansari X-Prize was modeled after the Ortieg Prize. The goal was to create a commercial space flight industry. The $10 million X-Prize was awarded to Burt Rutan's Space Ship One for being the first privately built and operated spacecraft to carry three people 100 kilometers above the earth twice in the span of two weeks.

Go right to the top. I needed to contact the X-15 rocket plane program at Edwards Air Force Base.

"My name is Ray Dausman from Reaction Dynamics in Milwaukee, Wisconsin. My company is working on a rocket-powered land speed record vehicle sponsored by the American Gas Association. I'd like to speak to someone about the liquid propellant rockets used in the X-15 program."

"One moment, sir." A brisk but friendly voice said.

There was a lengthy pause. I was routed to a few different people. Each time I repeated my interest in speaking with someone involved in the X-15 rocket engines. The personnel at Edwards either didn't know who could help me or they were avoiding my question.

"Brandt." A gruff voice said in my ear.

"Good afternoon, my name is Ray Dausman…" I repeated my spiel and was happily surprised when Mr. Brandt took the time to speak with me about his experience with hydrogen peroxide rocket engines.

"Containment of the HP is the key. Our team had a couple of transfer issues with getting the fuel into the plane. Make sure you have a strict plan for containing the fuel and then getting that HP into your vehicle. If it starts decomposing during transfer you've got an explosion on your hands. Literally."

Mr. Brandt was extremely helpful and he promised to send me information on the X-15 rocket planes.

"One more thing." I said. "Our previous rocket test sites will not be sufficient to test our Blue Flame rocket. In the past we've used a deserted drag strip. This time I will need sophisticated monitoring and safety measures. Do you have any ideas where I could test this rocket? We really need a site familiar with testing large rocket engines."

"I'd say you need to talk to Krzycki. He runs the rocket sled operation out at the Naval Weapons Center in China Lake, California. Krzycki can show you around so you can see if his facility is a good match for you."

In 1967 Leroy Krzycki wrote a book called "How to Design, Build and Test Small Liquid-Fueled Rocket Engines." Our rocket wasn't small, but Krzycki was helpful anyway. I talked to him a number of times on the phone about shock waves and how they might affect the Blue Flame operating so close to the ground. Krzycki had some data on shock waves as generated by this rocket sled installation. He said I could come out and talk to him sometime so I went out there and visited him for a few hours at the test station. He showed me some of their equipment including the famous rocket sled.

"This is what we call the 'Gee Whiz!'" said Leroy Krzycki, smiling ear to ear.

"Is that right?" I asked.

I didn't actually see anybody ride on the rocket sled, but Krzycki showed me a bunch of rockets and things they used for this purpose. He was interested in The Blue Flame project and gave me some technical papers about the effects of g-force on human beings. The papers also addressed what affect, if any, going supersonic close to the ground in some type of vehicle would have on the vehicle's stability.

It was an interesting trip, although it really didn't do me much good. After I studied over the material I found that most it wasn't going to help me any. But it was nice to meet him and see the installation. Leroy Krzycki was very gracious and went out of his way to help me, which I truly appreciated. My motto, go right to the top, helped me make an important contact to test our rocket engine.

Due to circumstances beyond my control we would never test the Blue Flame rocket at China Lake or anywhere else.

■   ■   ■

The American Gas Association (AGA) was striving to break into new markets. Liquefied natural gas (LNG) had been primarily used as a way to store natural gas in a safe and compacted form either in the summer months or for access in rural areas without their own pipeline. The gas companies could save money if they stored their natural gas underground in liquefied form during the summer since the households they serviced didn't need it until the weather turned cold. Natural gas could be transported to rural areas that didn't have pipelines and doled out as heating fuel after transferring it to gaseous form from the portable liquid tanks.

AGA was referring to LNG as the "cold fuel with a hot future" in their press releases during the Blue Flame project. The natural gas industry was hoping to incorporate their "safe to store and handle" fuel in both aviation and space race industries. According to AGA, one tidbit of exciting news was that "its feasibility as supersonic aircraft fuel has been confirmed by the Institute of Gas Technology." Another perk to LNG: "… its adaptability as passenger car fuel has been demonstrated by several companies, especially as a means of dramatically reducing pollutant exhaust emission."

Our country, of course, was in the midst of the Space Race. AGA decided that Reaction Dynamics should put their hat in the cosmic ring, so to speak. Industry officials at AGA informed an Illinois state senator that NASA needed to be alerted to our project. Contacts were made and a meeting arranged. One day while at the shop I was notified that I needed to accompany an AGA representative to Houston and pay NASA a visit. I thought it would be a huge waste of time, but AGA insisted that this might be a good idea for NASA to use a rocket similar to the Blue Flame engine in their lunar landing module. I agreed to go.

The senator set up a meeting with the Chief Propulsion and Power Division for the Manned Spacecraft Center, Joseph Thibodaux, Jr. He was in charge of the lunar landing module, which needed a throttleable rocket to land the astronauts on the moon.

We were shown into Thibodaux's office and found him sitting at a very large desk. He was a busy man with a serious expression, combed back hair and well groomed mustache. Mr. Thibodaux was a highly skilled chemical engineer who served as an Army officer in north and central Burma during World War II. He emanated the attitude that he wasn't interested in funny business. My AGA associate announced that we were here to show him the Reaction Dynamics liquid propellant rocket engine design that they may be interested in.

I unfurled a big drawing that showed the complete rocket engine.

"The Reaction Dynamics HP-LNG-22000-V is a 22,000 pound thrust rocket," I said. "This engine is completely throttleable and could conceivably be used on a NASA lunar landing vehicle."

I took a few minutes to explain to him how it worked, and he only asked me two questions.

"How long it would take to build this and how much would it cost?" he asked, with fingers tented in front of him on the massive wooden desktop. He leaned forward a bit to scrutinize my rocket diagram.

"Reaction Dynamics is now in the process of building the first engine. We expect the motor and propulsion system to be completed within six months and ready for testing."

"How much does this propulsion system cost?" he asked again.

"$35,000," I told him.

A strange look came over his face and Thibodaux leaned back in his chair. No one said anything. My AGA associate fiddled with his glasses and looked out the window.

"The engine is being built as we speak at Galaxy Manufacturing in Buffalo," I said. "It's a small fab shop run by a great family from the Ukraine, and I am confident that the project will be done on schedule and on budget." I glanced at my AGA friend for back up. He nodded.

Thibodaux looked at us. He looked at the drawing and then back at me. Awkward. For some reason I kept mentioning the Ukrainians, although in hindsight this probably wasn't the best plan.

"Our Galaxy fabricators are very adept at forming metal and have a fairly good machine shop," I added. "Oh, and they have sort of a sideline business steam cleaning the interiors of tanker trucks that run in and out of Buffalo."

Thibodaux stood up and walked over to my drawing, which was propped on an easel in front of his desk. He peered at them for a brief moment and immediately sat back down and folded his hands.

"Well, that was very interesting," he said. "But we wouldn't be able to use this engine because NASA plans call for using liquid oxygen and liquid hydrogen as fuels for the lander. We would need an engine that would use liquid hydrogen for fuel rather than LNG."

Essentially the meeting ended at that point.

"I recommend your firm consider working on a revised engine that would use liquid hydrogen instead of LNG. If you can come up with something I would be interested in seeing that," said Thibodaux.

I think what happened, though, was that Thibodaux heard the $35,000 figure and stopped taking us seriously. I had the impression that he believed it was obviously impossible to build a rocket engine of that sophistication for only $35,000. Thibodaux was probably thinking in terms of $35 million - not thousand! I think he got flustered and decided that this was not going to bear fruit.

In retrospect, I guess I shouldn't have provided so much information about our Ukrainian fabricators. I could have given the impression that a bunch of immigrant Ukrainian metal workers in a tiny machine shop in Buffalo would work on his sophisticated NASA engine between tanker truck steam cleaning gigs.

The whole concept must have been too mind boggling to Thibodaux to fit into his NASA mentality of spending the greatest amount of money possible for all NASA projects to secure reliability. NASA was obviously not in the practice of giving rocket contracts to the lowest bidder. I was about $30 million too low to figure in the picture.

The meeting was sort of a bizarre experience for us all. After we left Thibodaux was probably wondering, "Who in the hell arranged this deal?"

When the AGA guy got back to Chicago and reported on our meeting, I believe a few in the ranks in AGA were probably embarrassed for trying to involve NASA in this program.

The interesting thing is, after it all was said and done, NASA did not use a throttleable rocket that used liquid hydrogen and liquid oxygen as a fuel. Even NASA couldn't find anyone to develop or build such an exotic system as that, so they ended up using aerozine 50 as fuel and nitrogen tetroxide as the oxidizer. I'm glad I didn't spend a lot of time trying to redesign the engine to use liquid hydrogen.

In reality I think the Blue Flame engine would have worked just fine for NASA if they had decided to pursue it. It also would have worked out really well for the AGA's promotion of LNG.

■ ■ ■

I still needed to find a testing location for our rocket engine. At that time one of my idols was Wernher von Braun, the German rocket scientist that had helped develop the V-2 rocket for Germany during WWII. He was the premier rocket scientist of the twentieth century. Von Braun was working at the Marshall Space Flight Center in Huntsville, Alabama. He was in charge of our government's efforts to put a man into space.

I thought, well, why not go straight to the top and ask Wernher von Braun? I had known from reading about his early days in rocketry that he had done a lot of the same things I had been doing, such as building homemade rockets and testing them with friends. In addition we both flunked courses in mathematics as teens, so I felt we had a lot in common, Wernher and I!

I once saw a photograph of von Braun standing next to Fritz Von Opel's land speed record car in Germany. Opel's car, the RAK2, was an early rocket-powered car that set the land speed record of 238 k/h in 1928 behind 24 solid propellant rockets. Von Braun was very young as he stood next to the rocket car and I thought, well, maybe with that kind of a background he would take an interest in our project.

So I wrote a letter to von Braun at Huntsville explaining what we were doing and I sent along some artist concepts of what the car would look like and a brief description of the rocket engine. I indicated we needed a place to test the engine after we had built it and would he be able to help us out in this regard?

One day I received a letter, not from Wernher von Braun, but from one of his subordinates indicating they had received my letter and that they didn't feel the operation at Huntsville would be well suited for our needs. However, he did recommend the General Electric (GE) rocket test station out in Ballston Spa, New York. It was being used to test Navy rocket engines in the Space Race. The letter provided contact information for Dr. Al Grahm at the Malta Test Station.

I called Al Grahm and let him know my problem.

"Yes, I heard from Dr. von Braun and I was expecting you to contact me," said Al.

"We need a facility that can give us data on the Blue Flame rocket in order to assess how safe it will be to install in our vehicle." I told him "Maximum thrust is 22,000 pounds with both fuels."

"Come on out and take a look at our facility. I would say we have the equipment and the space your team will need," he said.

"Okay, that would really help the project move forward," I said.

I took a trip to upstate New York to tour the Malta Test Station. It was established in 1945 and used to test rockets, different types of fuels, explosives and atomic energy research.

Al was my tour guide around the test station and showed me the test stand and the launch pad. At that time the only rocket they had attempted to launch was called a Vanguard Rocket. It was a very nice looking rocket. The Vanguards were small three stage rockets just over 70 feet long. Unfortunately, every time they tried to launch it there was an explosion on the launch pad. So they were, at that time, in a holding pattern. They weren't actually trying to launch any more rockets because they had to figure out why their rocket design kept blowing up.

But I stayed overnight in New York and had a quite a long discussion with Al about what we were doing, and he seemed to think the concept was sound with the LNG peroxide engine.

"As soon as you're ready to test it, let me know," he told me. "We will get you a costing for the full testing and data analysis of the rocket."

I was confident that if we could get our engine built we could actually test it. The experts I had met with at China Lake and Malta confirmed for me that we could obtain good test data of the design and the safety of the engine for use in The Blue Flame. The rocket couldn't be used until we proved it was safe to install.

CHAPTER 18

GALAXY MANUFACTURING AND SUDDEN SAILING

1969

Jim McCormick had recommended we use Galaxy Manufacturing in Buffalo to fabricate the Blue Flame engine. This was a job for specialized fabricators with extensive equipment and expertise. The X-1 rocket was fabricated in the machine shop at IITRI, but this new and powerful engine was much more complex and expensive. The owner, Don Magro, had taken part of the down payment for the Blue Flame engine work and gone out and bought a sailboat.

I had been at Galaxy for several days when Don approached me and said, "Why don't you come sailing with me on Saturday? We can go out on Lake Ontario."

This was my hint that the fabricating work I was waiting for wasn't going to be finished before the weekend. I knew Don was a sailing enthusiast and had sailed several times with friends, but as far as I knew he had never captained a boat himself. I debated Don's invitation for just a moment before I called Phyllis and asked her to fly out for the weekend. She agreed and got busy finding a babysitter.

On Saturday morning Phyllis, Don, his wife Andrea and I got in the car and drove about forty miles north to a little marina in a quaint town called Niagara-on-the-Lake.

The four of us piled into Don's sailboat with supplies: beer, soda and cookies. Later I realized what we didn't bring: a map, first aid kit or flashlight.

"So, where are we going?" asked Phyllis, sunglasses perched firmly on her nose and blue and white scarf wound around her hairdo. She smiled pleasantly, awaiting our destination.

"Well, if we sail directly across the lake from here we will be in Toronto," said Don.

Since we had the whole weekend to mess around we decided well, yeah, we'll sail to Toronto today!

"We can stay overnight on the boat so we can spend some time in Toronto tonight," suggested Don's wife.

"Good thing we're leaving early," said Don. It was just past 8 a.m.

I popped the top on my first Mountain Dew of the day. The sun was shining and reflecting off of the water in a way that proved pleasant and promising.

"Sure, then we can sail back here on Sunday afternoon and make a weekend of it!" I said.

It occurred to us that we didn't really know where to point the boat in order to end up in Toronto. It was a big lake. I went down to the port headquarters and asked the guy what we should do to sail to Toronto. I asked him to help me with the compass setting from port here to the port in Toronto. He gave me the compass setting and we adjusted Don's compass on the sailboat. We decided we just had to maintain the proper compass setting and eventually we would sail into Toronto. It sure looked like a straight shot on a map.

"Let's head out!" announced Don, pumping his fist in the air.

We sailed and sailed and kept on sailing across that Great Lake, laughing and enjoying the wind in our hair and sunshine on our faces.

Our 4-person crew sailed into the Port of Toronto at 6 p.m. on Saturday evening. It seemed like no big deal. We just sailed across and there it was. So we sailed into the public docking area, got out and walked into downtown Toronto. It didn't take long before we discovered that nothing was open.

Everything was shut down. It was Labor Day weekend and for some reason Toronto had rolled up the sidewalk. We thought, my God we didn't have anything to eat. So where are we going to have dinner?

We finally found this little hole-in-the-wall restaurant. I think it was a Chinese place. We went in and had dinner. I think it was the only place in Toronto that was open. Fortunately it wasn't too far from the public dock.

After eating we walked around Toronto a little bit and then made our way back to the boat. We sat around talking and finishing our beer supply until dark and then slept on the boat. I didn't get much sleep because Don snored so loud. But other than that, it was fairly pleasant.

On Sunday morning we went back to the same Chinese place and got something to eat for breakfast before heading out again for New York state. We sailed and sailed and sailed and it got dark and we were still sailing. It never occurred to us that after dark you can't see too much. So all we could do was maintain the proper compass setting and hope that we ended up running into the shore – hopefully in the same place we started the day before.

It was dark and we also were trying to avoid getting run over by ships. Then, around midnight Sunday all of a sudden in front of the boat we saw a red light, way off in the distance.

"Maybe that's the port," I said, wishing it to be true.

"Let me steer a bit that way," said Don, making adjustments in the ropes and pulleys.

Sure enough, the red light was mounted on the post at the entrance of the Niagara on the Lake harbor. We breezed right into the harbor. Phyllis had been quiet for the last hour or so. She leaned against me and squeezed my knee.

"Good. We are back. Great job, sailors," she said. "Thank you for getting us back in one piece."

"Sure, Phyllis," said Don. "Thank you for joining us."

"It sure was an adventure." She turned to me. "Ray, let's pick up our trash. I think I see some pop cans behind your seat."

We tidied up the boat and got in the car and drove back to Buffalo. We were extremely lucky we didn't drown out there or get lost or never make it but somehow or other we just went over and came back and had a great time.

Monday, Phyllis flew back to Milwaukee and I went back to the shop and sat around for another couple of days before the work was finally done and I left for Milwaukee.

The sailing story is fascinating when I look back on it because I don't think any of us even asked how far it was to sail across the lake, I don't think we knew. It turns out that the distance from Niagara on the Lake to Toronto is about forty miles! None of us looked into that before we left. We just figured we'd probably be able to make it in the course of a day's sailing.

It would have been a lot wiser to ask ahead of time instead of just asking for directions. But that's how we lived in those days. If we felt like doing something we just went ahead and did it. I don't know, we were more risk-takers at that time. If you wanted to do something you went ahead and did it and hoped for the best. I've always liked to challenge myself to do new things. Our trip across Lake Ontario was a perfect example of deciding to do something new and just figuring it out along the way. A lot of times it can be done.

I'd never consider doing that now, at 74 years old. But it worked out and Phyllis and I laugh about it once in a while. We didn't even have a morsel of food. Had we gotten lost or disoriented out there we could have been in big trouble. There was no radio, or anything. We didn't even have any lights, just the boat's compass. We could have wandered around out there for weeks.

■ ■ ■

Jim McCormick had used the fabricators at Galaxy Manufacturing to work on projects for him at FMC such as nozzles and hydrogen peroxide thrusters. They were familiar with the parts of a rocket engine and had experience making them, although not on the scale of the Blue Flame rocket. Our rocket would be much bigger than they had helped to create in the past.

The Ukrainian immigrants I raved about to NASA had a shop adjacent to Galaxy. They were skilled welders and specialized in bending sheet metal and doing exotic welding and pressure testing.

Both companies gave me a very warm welcome, and treated me well. Many of the workers said they were excited about being involved with the rocket car project and hoped we set the land speed record. The Ukrainians were especially warm and the men presented me with beautifully decorated eggs that their wives had made especially for me.

According to Ukrainian custom, when a special person or somebody they held in high respect visited they would be presented with one of these hand decorated eggs. I was quite honored to get these eggs. You could tell by looking at them that it must have taken a long time to decorate them. I wondered whether they were hollow and they told me no, they still had the egg inside so I should be careful not to break them.

One of the big things with Galaxy was that they were also going to put together the catalyst pack for the Blue Flame engine, which was quite large, about 16 inches in diameter compared to the catalyst pack for the X-1, which was only 4-5 inches in diameter. So the amount of silver and metal cloth for the Blue Flame engine was very expensive. We needed $3,000 - $4,000 worth of silver alone just in the catalyst pack. The budget for building the entire propulsion system was over $32,000.

Part of AGA's plans for the Blue flame project was to produce a 30 minute documentary of the whole experience. One day when I was at Galaxy, the movie people showed up and wanted to take shots of the manufacturing process. The film and production crew spent one entire afternoon with their cameras and lights, having me pose with interesting parts of the engine. They showed me in various parts of the shop watching this or that being made and interviewed me about the progress of the rocket engine and how it worked.

The Ukrainians and the guys at Galaxy were quite excited to be involved in an actual movie project. As it turned out, in the final cut of the movie there was nothing whatsoever involving that day at Galaxy. In fact, I only showed up in about a second or two in the whole movie and it had nothing to do with the rocket engine. So at some point somebody decided to all but erase me from the movie. The only thing that made the cut was running The Blue Flame at the salt flats.

Many great minds and expert hands made that world land speed record possible. If I had editing rights to the AGA movie, I would have included more phases of the project so that the general public understood that it was a group effort that paid big dividends for AGA.

CHAPTER 19

DRIVER DILEMMA AND PRESS CONFERENCE

1969

A knock at my bungalow door interrupted "Mission Impossible." I had unpacked my suitcase and was waiting for Dick and Pete to let me know when they were ready to head to dinner.

We were staying at the famous Beverly Hills Hotel. Dick, Pete and I each had a lavish bungalow detached from the main hotel. The furniture, carpeting and bathroom fixtures were expensive, plush and more than a little excessive. Jim Chatfield from AGA's Public Relations Department had made all of our arrangements for our press conference the next day at the Los Angeles Convention Center. He told us to keep our eyes peeled for celebrities since there were several that lived at the posh landmark.

"Come in," I said as I walked over and snapped off my television set.

Dick and Pete came through the door, all smiles, ties and cologne.

"Ray, let's go! The Polo Lounge awaits!" said Dick.

"I'm ready." I grabbed my jacket that was draped over the bed. We were looking forward to a night on the town.

"Is Garlits here yet?" asked Pete. "Is he coming with us?"

I shrugged and Dick answered, "I don't know. Come on, Jim is waiting."

The three of us walked the short distance from my bungalow to the main building of the hotel. The grounds were lush and immaculately groomed, and I admired the sparkling water of the swimming pool, which was lined with green and white striped chaise lounges. The hotel itself was pink and had an adobe look to it. Windows with bright white trim lined the exterior and reflected the California sun, which was starting to set over the palm trees.

Jim had arranged this entire event as part of his public relations duties. He reserved a large room at the convention center to house our press conference and invited the media to send representatives to witness our good news. All of the television stations and several magazines were sending crews and correspondents. We were supposed to introduce the driver of The Blue Flame to the television audience, explain the land speed record project and answer questions from the media.

We entertained ourselves by trying to fake out the others with celebrity sightings. I swiveled my head around and whispered, "There's Elizabeth Taylor!"

"Where!?" Dick and Pete would hiss, searching the hallway.

"Oh! Right there, next to Robert Redford and Paul Newman!" joked Pete.

The three of us were practically doubled over with laughter as we spotted Jim waiting for us in the lobby.

He looked frantic. He was pacing the marble floor and rubbing his eyes and muttering to himself. He glanced up and saw me staring at him, then dropped his hands from his face and practically galloped over to me. I winced a little bit, taken aback.

"Ray! He's out! He's out! Ray! He's out!" Jim's shouts echoed off of the marble floor and domed ceiling with its enormous circular crystal light fixture looming over us.

"Jim…?" I started to say.

Pete and Dick stopped short when they saw the look on Jim's face.

"Garlits is out," Jim spat towards the gleaming marble floor.

"What happened to him? A crash?" I asked.

"No. I just got off of the phone with him. He's out. He changed his mind."

He looked nearly catatonic with fear, his eyes wide and staring at the wall behind me, his hair disheveled from the constant raking back and forth of his hands over his scalp. He was trying to find an alternative for this train wreck, but he seemed to be having trouble wrapping his mind around the possibility of cancelling the press conference.

We stood there for a minute, trying to process what we were facing. Elevators dinged, high heels clicked and clacked across the floor to the restaurant. The elegant doorman barked orders to valets and charming greetings to guests as they whisked through the glass doors into the lobby.

"You mean he can't make the press conference? Did something come up?" asked Dick.

"No. He won't do it." said Jim with clenched teeth and red face. "Garlits was supposed to be here today, but he just called and said he changed his mind." His eyelids started to twitch and he resumed his face rubbing.

We were in shock.

"What if we called him back and gave him time to think about it?" I asked.

"Do…you…know…anyone else?" asked Jim. He was having difficulty forming words and was nodding excessively to no one in particular.

"What's that guy's name, Ray. Do you know it? The guy who stopped by the shop?" Dick asked.

I visualized the spunky and skilled stunt pilot as she hopped into her Spitfire airplane at Timmerman Field and waved to me, standing there in disbelief. She lived too far away and certainly wasn't the "guy" Dick was referring to.

"Why did Garlits back out?" I asked.

"What? He said he changed his mind and won't do it!" Jim answered.

"But, why?" I persisted.

"Ray! He's out! He said he changed his mind. Who knows? Maybe his wife said it was too dangerous!" Jim was now starting to screech a little bit.

"Who can we get? What's that other guy's name? Remember the guy that wants to drive the car? Doesn't he live in LA?" asked Dick.

The only other person who had approached Reaction Dynamics with an interest in driving The Blue Flame was a man by the name of Gary Gabelich. Like stunt pilot Betty Skelton, Gary had also paid an unannounced visit to our Reaction Dynamics shop to express his interest in driving the Blue Flame. One day he just knocked on our door. I had no idea who he was. If he called ahead I don't remember that conversation.

He had brought along a large album with pictures and very detailed documentation of his experience in the racing world. He was a test astronaut at North American Aviation, an aerospace manufacturer. North American Aviation was a key player in several historic aircraft, including rocket-powered airplanes. There were photos of Gary being used as a human guinea pig to test how well the human body could withstand zero gravity and other extreme conditions such as being blasted into space. Several photos showed Gary driving high powered boats and cars; one or two even showed him out at the salt flats.

Gary had left a great impression on me. He was prepared and polished. I believed that he had taken the time to practice his presentation because he was deliberate and thorough when explaining his experience and describing his wish to drive The Blue Flame. He was well dressed, groomed and articulate, and he struck me as a very intelligent, sophisticated and determined man. It was clear he was not your ordinary drag racer. He had his sights on being much more than your typical high speed driver.

"Yes, he does. He does live around here," I answered slowly, glancing over at Jim. He eyes were locked on mine.

"Yeah, he's the guy who just showed up that day and you really liked him, Ray," added Pete.

"Gary. His name is Gary Gabelich and he's probably not too far away. I thought you guys weren't interested in him." I looked at Dick and Pete.

They didn't say anything. When Gary paid us a visit I informed Dick and Pete about it, and let them know I thought Gary was impressive. At the time Dick and Pete thought Garlits was a sure thing, so it was pretty much in one ear out the other. We had even met with Garlits at IIT during a meeting on the project. He had a contract to drive The Blue Flame.

"I'll give him a call," Jim said and dashed back to his bungalow to look up Gary's number.

Luckily Gary was home that day. It took no convincing at all to get him to show up for our press conference the next day. He lived a mere 30 miles away and would be happy to do it, he said.

Jim was able to breathe again, although a little nervously since he didn't know much about Gary Gabelich at all. I wasn't too concerned with who our driver was as long as no one suggested I drive it! We just had to make sure the driver had enough experience to work the controls and enough pure guts to get behind the wheel of an enormous rocket.

Gary Gabelich had guts. I knew he was our guy.

The four of us went to dinner in the Polo Lounge, and then Jim went back to his bungalow to rest. Maybe his panicked state did him in for the evening. Jim Deist, who was providing the parachutes for the Blue Flame, met us at the hotel and took us to a nightclub called The Pink Panther to experience an LA strip club as part of our whirlwind tour. It was the fashionable thing to do in those days, go to a strip club. It was actually just a place with loud, blaring music where people went to get drunk and watch women. I had a blinding headache and could barely see straight when we left, due to the pain, not the booze. We returned to our bungalows in the early hours of the next morning and caught a few hours of sleep before the press conference.

The next day Jim Chatfield introduced a beaming Gary Gabelich to KNXT, KABC, Design Engineering magazine and other journalists as we were all seated onstage facing the cameras and busy notepads. The introduction went off without a hitch and Jim didn't show any sign of concern or the panic that he was quaking with the day before.

I stood up and used a huge cutaway graphic of the Reaction Dynamics HP-LNG-22000-V rocket engine to explain how the rocket would produce enough thrust to beat Breedlove's record. I pointed to clearly labeled parts of the rocket and walked the audience through the process of firing and throttling it.

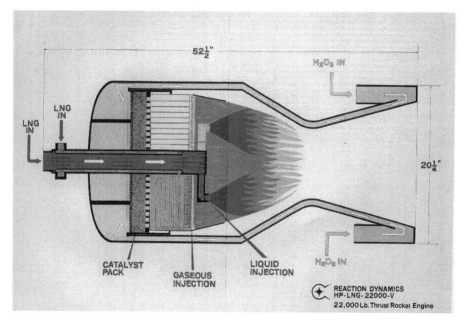

Promotional diagram for The Blue Flame rocket engine*
(Courtesy of the Ray Dausman Collection)

Pete and Dick used a conceptual model to show the crowd what the Blue Flame would eventually look like and they listed the specs of the car such as its weight, length and turning radius. Afterwards we answered questions about the project for the TV news crews and milled around with the reporters to be interviewed about the Flame's land speed quest.

The mission impossible was a success: the exchange was made. We all flew home with a collective sigh of relief.

The Blue Flame rocket motor being built at Galaxy Manufacturing.
This picture is the inner chamber of the rocket as it turns on a metal lathe.*

Pete (2nd from the left) during a meeting with the IIT engineering team (left to right) Dr. Uzgiris, Shashi Kurani and Monoj Adhikari.*

Gary Gabelich at the Reaction Dynamics shop during production of The Blue Flame*

Reaction Dynamics team working to build The Blue Flame (Front row left to right: Pete Farnsworth and Dick Keller; Back row left to right Gerard Brennan and Kenneth McCarthy). The Blue Flame's rocket engine is along the left side, waiting to be installed, and the X-1 is parked to the right.*

Promotional photo of part of The Blue Flame's propulsion system. Notice the perfect heat exchanger, which is the round section split into eight triangular segments.*

My father visited the Reaction Dynamics shop to see the rocket motor*

*Another promotional shot of me and the propulsion system for The Blue Flame**

My how far we've come! The small engine is the 25 lb thrust rocket that started it all and the large system belongs to The Blue Flame.*

*Me, with the unfinished Blue Flame in the Reaction Dynamics shop in Milwaukee, Wisconsin (*Photos courtesy of the Ray Dausman Collection)*

CHAPTER 20

CUSTOM WORK AND CHECKBOOK TROUBLES

1969

I remember one individual that was hired to come in and make just one single part for the car. We needed a sheet metal part that covered the driver when he was sitting in the driver's seat, and it required some fairly fancy work to form the aluminum sheet. It was basically the canopy and window that covered the driver.

Pete located a guy named Ray Besasie. He must have been in his sixties. Ray spent many years working on the fancy sporty car that was made in Milwaukee, called the Excalibur. It was an open cockpit car, a convertible with chrome exhaust pipes coming out both sides of the engine. It was an old time design with large circular headlamps, running boards and a spare tire mounted on the side. It was extremely expensive. Ray worked in a small shop in Milwaukee where the Excalibur Automobile Corporation handmade these cars.

We were going to pay Ray by the hour to make this piece of sheet metal for us. He was there for about a week or two, I would say, working on this a few hours here and a few hours there. He was one of these characters you never forget. He was a real colorful guy and all the while he was working he would be telling tales about his life and experiences he had, and it seemed like one story was more preposterous than the next. You knew he was telling a lot of lies but he always made the story so interesting everybody would sit around and listen to him.

He claimed he had a part in just about everything interesting that had ever happened in the history of Milwaukee. He was part of making the first airplane that flew into Milwaukee. He was involved in the first of this and the first of that. He also liked to regale us with tales of his sexual prowess in his younger days in the 1920s and 30s and how he became sort of an idol of all the women in town and how he would take them out in his car and do all kinds of things. Each story was more bizarre than the next. Everybody listening to Ray had to stand around and smile. He'd tell these stories as if they were perfectly true and he'd never crack a smile or anything, but you knew he was grossly exaggerating. Interesting, but way beyond the truth.

The problem developed when Ray was through with the project he made for us. He made the part and then said he would send us the bill for it. Since I was in charge of paying the bills, he walked in one day with his bill and presented it to me. The bill totaled around $2,000, and it was toward the end of the month so we had spent nearly all of the money. The sponsor allocated us around $10,000 a month for expenses. By the time Ray came in with his invoice, I didn't have enough money to pay him.

So I told him that. "Well, I just don't have any money to pay you, Ray. I'll have to wait until next month."

"Oh, no. You can't do that!"

He just wouldn't hear of that. He had to have his money and he had to have it now. He was going to have to call his attorney, he said.

"Well, we just don't have the money," I said. "I can't just write you a bogus check! I'll see what I can do."

He must have been there an hour arguing with us, telling me about all the things that might happen if he didn't get paid immediately and how he knew all these high-powered lawyers. He just was not used to not getting paid on demand, he said. This was a Friday, and I told him to come back Monday and hopefully I would have the money by then.

So I made a quick call to Chicago and explained the situation to IGT and they said okay, they would send us a check to cover his bill that same day and I should get it on Saturday. Ray came in first thing Monday morning and demanded his money. I was able to hand it over.

"Thank you, Ray. I'm sorry about the delay," I said.

"Next time, don't make me wait. You are the rocket man. Why are you not fast like your car?"

CHAPTER 21

ROCKETS STAGES AND GOODBYE WAVE

1969

I was no longer on the project. I wouldn't see The Blue Flame attempt to set a new world land speed record. My dream of owning my own business was over. We lost The Flame. What would I tell Phyllis? How was I going to make a living? Where do I go from here? Do I have to get back in the car with Pete and Dick? These thoughts and many more raced through my brain after the meeting at IGT where Reaction Dynamics lost ownership of The Blue Flame.

IGT named Dean Dietrich as the new project director for The Blue Flame. Pete and Dick agreed to the new arrangement, even though that meant their contribution to the land speed record attempt was marginalized to that of crew members. I felt that the sponsor was not justified in requiring Reaction Dynamics, Inc. to turn over ownership of The Blue Flame to them. IGT demanded ownership of the car for their continued commitment to properly fund the project as stated in their own contract with Reaction Dynamics.

I disagreed with IGT's new direction. The arrangement revoked Reaction Dynamics' oversight of the development of The Blue Flame. I also disagreed with IGT's position that the rocket motor didn't need proper testing. And I also could not overlook my fiduciary responsibility to Reaction Dynamics as Vice President and a member of the Board of Directors. I felt that losing Blue Flame ownership would doom the company to bankruptcy -- and that, unfortunately, is how it worked out in the end.

In fact, I told Pete and Dick exactly what I thought would happen. After the meeting at IGT where Dick and Pete agreed to sign over the car, I spoke with them briefly in the parking lot. The three of us stood next to Dick's car with hands in our pockets and chips on our shoulders. There had been no negotiations. I certainly would have tried to discuss a successful conclusion to the project with IGT. Negotiations occur all the time in the business world, and I believe it would have worked for us. I was not informed of the approaching doomsday until the matter had already been settled by others. I was shocked that I was not consulted until it was too late for any positive outcome to be achieved.

Since Dick had sold the project idea to the AGA, he was under pressure to agree to their demands. Pete had racing in his blood, so all he wanted was a shot at the world land speed record. My dreams of a business, properly testing my rocket and seeing it run, had just crashed in flames. Obviously racing was more important to Pete and Dick than our business future.

"We're in and you're out," Dick said. "The Flame is going to take the record, Ray, and you just decided to miss it."

But it was not how I saw things. "I think that even if you do get the car built and set a record -- without having the car belonging to you there's no way you're going to be able to keep the business going very long," I said. "Eventually you'll go bankrupt."

I couldn't believe that they didn't see this!

Pete spoke up. "That won't happen," he said. "We'll work it out so AGA lets us use the car again. We'll have the advantage of being famous for The Blue Flame."

"That's highly unlikely," I said to him, growing more and more frustrated. "Reaction Dynamics will go bankrupt, I guarantee. The only way around that is to keep ownership of the car."

■ ■ ■

As 1969 came to a close, I knew I needed to call Al Grahm from the Malta Test Station in New York to apprise him of the situation. Al was expecting to help us test The Blue Flame's engine so we could be sure the rocket was safe to fire. We had set a date of December 27th, 1969, to begin our tests. I dreaded making this call because I knew that Al would try to talk me out of leaving the project and remind me of the possible repercussions of sending such a powerful rocket to the salt flats without ensuring that it was stable.

"Hello, Al," I began. "This is Ray from Reaction Dynamics in Milwaukee. How are you?"

"Ray! Good to hear from you. We're all set for the 27th. When will you arrive? I can meet you at the airport." He sounded enthusiastic and I was anything but.

"The thing is, Al, I don't think it will work out," I told him.

"What do you mean?" he answered.

"IGT has taken over the project and I'm out of the picture as of January 1st," I said. "The guys that are taking over probably won't test it."

"So, are they going to wait until next year to test it? I can see what we have available after the first of the year. I've got a conference in the last part of January, but February is wide open. We could set something up." He was trying to be accommodating, but I couldn't offer him any words of encouragement. I was pretty sure the testing wasn't going to happen.

"Well, you see, I doubt they will follow up with any testing at all. They might just take the rocket to the salt flats as is," I told him. "They might not want to spare the time and money."

"I don't understand," he said. "The rocket…I've never heard of this. Don't they know it could be dangerous? I…are you sure?"

"No, I guess I'm not real sure about anything right now. I told IGT about the test date next week, but I didn't get the impression they thought it was all that important," I said. "Dean Dietrich is the new project manager, so I guess all decisions go through him now."

"Why aren't you finishing the project?" he asked.

"I'd like to, Al, but IGT took over the project and since I didn't agree to the new arrangement, I'm out," I said. "I'll leave the testing information with Pete and Dick. I wasn't sure if they were going to call you, so I thought I'd let you know what was going on."

As I talked to Al, I was seeing in my mind what I was going to miss because of the IGT intervention. I felt a huge surge of emotion and regret that it was never going to happen for me. I had invested so much of my passion and energy to build this rocket motor, the first of its kind. I would never see it in action.

"Ray, they can't take that rocket to the salt flats without testing it."

"Well, you're right. One of the reasons I'm getting out is that, without proper testing, someone might be killed by an engine problem, and I don't want to be a part of that tragedy. We need to know the car will be safe and produce the power we need before we put the engine in. I don't know what's going to happen. I can give you Dean's number at IGT if you want to get in touch with him."

Al had reason to be concerned. He had so much experience with the Vanguard rockets. This Vanguard rocket was the United States' second try to put a satellite into orbit. I had visited the Malta Test Station near Saratoga Springs, New York to set up a testing program for The Blue Flame rocket engine. During my visit Al showed me around the test facility, which consisted of several huge reinforced concrete bunkers with test equipment for measuring rocket thrust. The site was in a very remote location and took up a huge amount of acreage. There was a small room for the test crew adjacent to one of the bunkers. It was similar to a launch center at Cape Canaveral in Florida. This room was crammed with all types of recording equipment. There were several tanks for storing rocket propellants and high pressure gases. Heavy duty fire extinguishers and other related safety apparatus such as fire helmets and flame retardant clothing were stacked against the wall for easy access.

Al had showed me the shattered remains of many rocket engines that had exploded during testing. This wreckage was displayed in a museum case for the edification of visitors. The message was crystal clear. Rockets can be deadly. Most of these rockets had exploded due to combustion instability during testing. The whole point of my Blue Flame rocket engine test program was to avoid this problem by having the Blue Flame engine "tuned up" by experienced professionals who understood combustion instability problems. We needed to make sure the rocket would not explode and kill the driver and crew.

Liquid bipropellant rocket engines release enormous power. The amount of thermal energy produced and emitted as exhaust could melt even the strongest metals, such as titanium or stainless steel, in a fraction of a second. At full thrust, The Blue Flame's engine would have been five times louder than an F-15 jet fighter plane. The sound produced by this type of rocket is frightening and almost indescribable. It sounds like a clap of thunder, a blood-curdling scream and the loudest mortar explosion you've ever heard twisted together to rip a hole in the air around you at 4-5,000 feet per second, causing a continuous sonic boom that rattles your teeth and shakes the ground beneath your feet as you run for cover.

The Blue Flame's driver could throttle the thrust from zero to one hundred percent. No rocket engine had yet been built with that capability. Al had been quick to point that out to me during my first conversation with him. Jim McCormick's design for The Blue Flame's hydraulic system was ingenious. The valves controlling this tricky hydraulic system were hooked up to a foot pedal similar to an accelerator pedal in a regular automobile. If the driver pushed the pedal down, the thrust increased. As he allowed the pedal to return to its original position, the thrust went down. This design was unique because traditional rockets fired at one "speed" until they ran out of fuel and burned out. The ability to throttle the rocket gave the driver control over the speed of the car.

The Blue Flame's rocket engine has a sophisticated combustion chamber specially designed to use two fuels: 90% hydrogen peroxide (HP) and liquefied natural gas (LNG). The common term, "natural gas" is really referring to methane in its liquid or gaseous state. The vast majority of "natural gas" is methane. Liquid methane is stored in special tanks at -265 degrees Fahrenheit. If liquefied methane gets much warmer than that, it automatically vaporizes into its gaseous state. Natural gas companies like to ship methane as a liquid because it takes up much less space than methane gas. AGA wanted to promote the use of liquefied natural gas into new markets, so it was important for The Blue Flame to use it as one of its fuels.

There were three stages to The Blue Flame's rocket engine. When properly fired, the rocket would advance through all three stages in two seconds, producing 22,000 pounds of thrust equaling 58,000 horsepower.

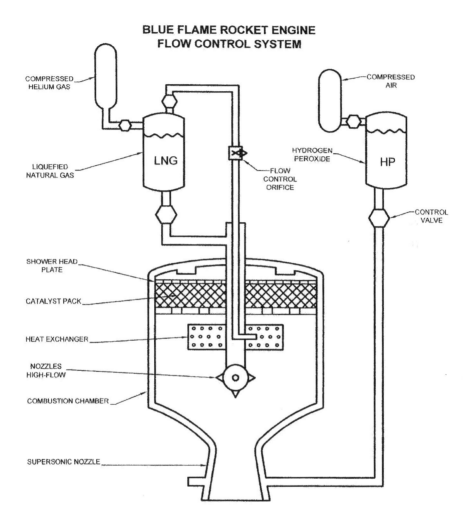

**BLUE FLAME ROCKET ENGINE
FLOW CONTROL SYSTEM**

COMPRESSED
HELIUM GAS

COMPRESSED
AIR

LIQUEFIED
NATURAL GAS

LNG

HYDROGEN
PEROXIDE

HP

FLOW
CONTROL
ORIFICE

CONTROL
VALVE

SHOWER HEAD
PLATE

CATALYST PACK

HEAT EXCHANGER

NOZZLES
HIGH-FLOW

COMBUSTION CHAMBER

SUPERSONIC NOZZLE

Sketch of The Blue Flame rocket propulsion system

BLUE FLAME NOZZLE INSERT
FLANGE MOUNTED TO SUPERSONIC EXHAUST
CONE FOR USE
WITH HYDROGEN PEROXIDE

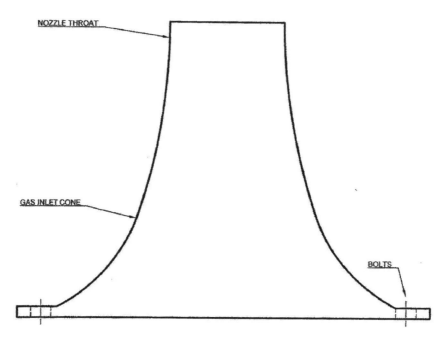

NOZZLE THROAT

GAS INLET CONE

BOLTS

MOUNTING FLANGE WITH $\frac{3}{8}$" BOLTS CIRCULAR SPACING

Sketch of the rocket nozzle insert for The Blue Flame rocket
(Ray Dausman 2012)

Inside The Blue Flame's combustion chamber was a series of parts designed to work together to fire this powerful rocket. There were four important circular parts with the same diameter stacked next to each other front-to-back inside the cylindrical combustion chamber. The first was a circular shower head plate, next to that was the pure silver and nickel catalyst pack, then the heat exchanger. The final crucial part was a circular plate with large spray nozzles downstream of the heat exchanger.

Stage One: The Blue Flame's driver opens the HP valve. The HP enters the combustion chamber and passes through the pure silver catalyst pack. The pure silver causes the HP to decompose and flash (split) into oxygen and water (steam). The oxygen and steam swirl around the combustion chamber and exit the rear of the car through the rocket exhaust nozzle at supersonic speed. This produces the first 11,000 pounds of thrust for The Blue Flame.

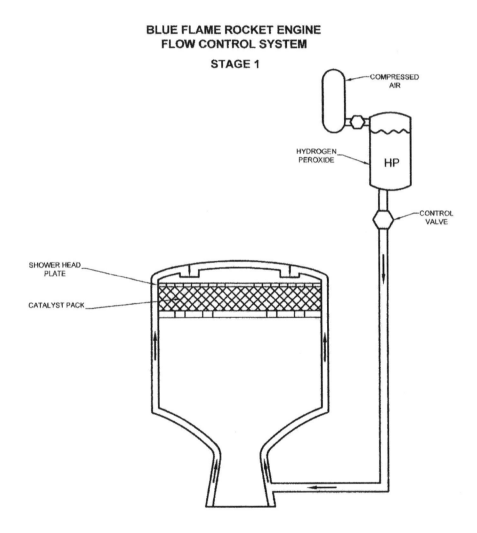

Sketch of stage one of The Blue Flame rocket (Ray Dausman 2012)

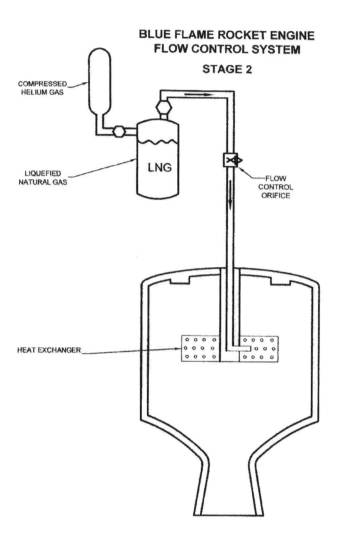

Sketch of stage two of The Blue Flame rocket (Ray Dausman 2012)

Stage Two: A bypass pipe takes the LNG through the center of the pure silver mesh catalyst pack cylinder into the heat exchanger. There are two valves for the LNG; one small and one large. The LNG needs to enter the heat exchanger at a precise rate controlled by a part called the flow control orifice. This part is simply a metal rod with a tiny hole drilled into it. This tiny hole sends LNG from the small valve into the heat exchanger at the calculated rate and pressure. If LNG is sent through the heat exchanger with too much or too little flow, it could result in combustion instability. Any combustion instability could cause an explosion in the heat exchanger, rendering it useless.

When the LNG reaches the heat exchanger it immediately turns to a gas and reaches a temperature of 1300 degrees Fahrenheit. The methane gas immediately exits the heat exchanger and combines with the oxygen flowing in the combustion chamber from stage one. The ignition point of methane is well under 1300 degrees, so when these two gases meet they burst into flame and raise the temperature in the combustion chamber to 4500 degrees. The flow control orifice has only let in a small amount of LNG, so this step does not produce much power. The purpose of stage two is to cause ignition and establish a stable flame inside the combustion chamber. If too much LNG is forced into the heat exchanger during this phase the system will become flooded with LNG. If that happens combustion in the engine could become unstable because the calculated ratio of LNG to oxygen is not correct.

The temperature inside the combustion chamber is now 4500 degrees Fahrenheit and a small blue flame starts to emerge from the rocket exhaust nozzle at the rear of the car.

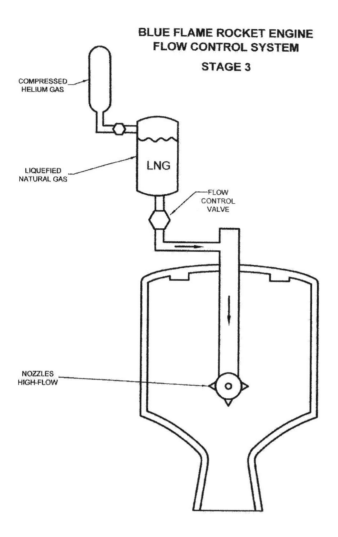

Sketch of stage three of The Blue Flame rocket (Ray Dausman 2012)

Stage Three: The large LNG valve opens. A much larger amount of LNG is routed around the heat exchanger and introduced to the combustion chamber as a liquid through large spray nozzles in back of the heat exchanger. This stage does not need the heat exchanger because there is already a fire burning at 4500 degrees Fahrenheit in the combustion chamber. The liquid methane automatically bursts into flame and generates up to an additional 11,000 pounds of thrust. The driver may open the large valve part of the way or all of the way. The additional thrust will depend on how far he opens it.

Stage three is much like tossing gasoline on a burning campfire. When the car is running at full power the exhaust jet is traveling at more than 4,000 feet per second. Poof! The rocket is burning at full power with a 20-30 foot red and blue exhaust flame trailing behind the car.

Two seconds. 22,000 pounds of thrust. 58,000 horsepower.

■　■　■

IGT was paying my salary until the end of December, 1969, so I continued to show up at Reaction Dynamics. I wrote letters to sponsors, answered the phone, but mostly I looked for a job. I had a wife and three kids to support. I needed to revise my resume and start over.

I went to the office on the day after Christmas. Dick and Pete were home with their families, so I thought I would visit the shop one last time. For a while I sat at my desk and rummaged through the drawers to salvage anything I considered my own. I plucked my collection of business cards from my Rolodex and left the plastic wheel empty and useless. I stuffed the cards into my winter coat pocket. The future might hold a new rocket building business for me if I played my cards right. Satisfied that I had not forgotten anything, I turned off the light and walked into the shop area.

A large chalkboard was fastened to the right wall and was covered with mathematical formulas and sketches of the rocket's hydraulic system. A large blue and white poster above the chalkboard boasted "The Natural Gas Industry's Blue Flame." A huge, rolling garage door with smeared, square windows took up most of the back wall and faced the alley behind 124th street. Trays of fluorescent bulbs hung above the cement floor and held the unfinished Flame in a cold, white light.

The car was pointed away from the office, so the rear of the car faced me as I took in the quiet. The Flame was half assembled and her gray metal skin almost blended in with the concrete floor. I could see the metal superstructure where the fuselage panels hadn't been fastened on yet, like a silver, cylindrical skeleton.

I paused and looked at the empty parking space for the X-1 prototype, which used to sleep next to The Flame like a red and white little sister. I wondered what would happen to the X-1 now that she was dismantled and posing as a snowmobile. Reaction Dynamics sold the X-1 after securing a sponsor for The Blue Flame. The new owner, Tony Fox, discarded the X-1's body and installed the rocket in a snowmobile he was planning to race across frozen lakes in Minnesota.

My eyes fell on a cardboard box of United "POP" Rivets. It was half full and urged, "Cut installation costs in half!" Yeah, right.

The rocket engine parts were on the floor. The valves, hoses, flow control orifices and combustion chamber were laying next to each other to the right of the car. This small pile of parts would surely crack the sound barrier and break the land speed record. I didn't want them to get dirty, so, except for the heavy combustion chamber, I put them on the workbench that lined the right side of the shop. I assumed Pete, Dick, or even Dean Dietrich would call me to help them assemble the engine since I was the only one who knew how the parts fit together. I gave the combustion chamber a reassuring pat. The metal felt cold and smooth. This chunk of stainless steel was what I had dreamed of building for so many years.

My eyes swept the room one last time. I took a deep breath and zipped my jacket up to my chin. I walked out of the door, clenching my jaw against the bitter December wind. I had to wonder. Would The Blue Flame perform the way I knew she could?

No one called me. They put the engine together themselves.

CHAPTER 22

MOVING ON AND SALT FLAT STRUGGLES

1970

I never went to the Bonneville Salt Flats to see The Blue Flame attempt to break the land speed record. I stayed in Wisconsin and looked for a new job. I had to put The Blue Flame behind me. My dream of owning my own business had failed and would have to wait until I was able to rebuild my goals and dreams. I needed to find a new focus.

After I left Reaction Dynamics, Inc., I tried to design a small rocket for use in schools to demonstrate the principles of rocket propulsion in a high school physics laboratory setting. The system would use 50% hydrogen peroxide as the propellant. I worked with Dr. Carl Uzgiris from IITRI to find new venture capital to finance the company, but we did not find the financial backing we needed. Phyllis tried to be patient, but after a while a certain amount of panic set in and we had several tense conversations about the status of my employment.

One February afternoon just before lunch I walked into the kitchen of our ranch home in Germantown, Wisconsin. I had been in the basement all morning working on some drawings for my high school rocket lab idea. Our home was bright and warm, thanks to Phyllis's attention to decorating details. Our kitchen had several windows, which were full of late winter sunshine and cozy yellow curtains she had ordered from Montgomery Wards. The room smelled of hazelnut coffee and snickerdoodle sugar cookies. Our three year old daughter Cathy was sitting at the kitchen table poking out fashionable outfits for her Daisy Darling paper doll. Her dark curly hair bobbed up and down and she grew more forceful with the flimsy evening gown she was trying to coax from the cardboard page. Cheryl, our seven year old, was sitting across from Cathy working intently on her Etch a Sketch. She was twisting the knobs and tilting the red plastic rectangle and hoping for a masterpiece to emerge. Our infant daughter, Sarah, wasn't in sight, so she must have been sleeping in her crib.

Phyllis was rummaging in the refrigerator. She stood up with an armload of bologna, cheese, lettuce and mustard before shutting the door with a swing of her hips.

"Ray, are you done in the basement?" she said.

"Yes, for now. What do we have for lunch?"

Phyllis ignored my question. "What are you working on downstairs?"

"I'm drafting some ideas Carl and I have for the new company," I said. "We need to have examples of designs to show when we meet with possible investors."

"Is Carl paying you to do this?" Phyllis asked. Her voice was getting a little higher and louder. She snatched a loaf of Wonder Bread from the bread drawer next to the sink and twirled its plastic bag to get it open.

I glanced at the kitchen table and watched our daughters playing for a few moments. They were oblivious, thankfully. Cheryl was hunched over the Etch a Sketch applying the finishing touches to her wobbly drawing of a cat's face. The whiskers on the left were much longer than those on the right, giving the cat a drunken and lopsided look. Cathy was folding the tabs of a mink hat over her doll's well-coiffed paper hair.

We didn't argue in front of our kids.

"No. No, he's not paying me. After lunch I'll look in the paper again and see if there are any new job openings."

Phyllis gave me a small smile. "Oh. Good. That's good. Do you want lettuce on your sandwich?"

We subscribed to the Milwaukee Journal and in those days the help-wanted section was full of jobs. It wasn't too difficult to find openings for research technicians. Each day I searched through the ads and circled the jobs that matched my qualifications. It was depressing because the jobs were entry level and not very high tech. They were just jobs, not dreams. I was going from "way up here where I wanted to be" at Reaction Dynamics to "way down here where I used to be" at Illinois Institute of Technology. I felt very discouraged that I had to start over.

The Blue Flame crew was finishing the car without me, and I felt that I needed to put that situation "in the closet," so to speak. I told myself that what had happened with Reaction Dynamics was a business decision; nothing more and nothing less. IGT had laid their cards on the table and forced a decision for the three officers of our small company. Pete and Dick took one option and I simply took the other. I didn't shed any tears or spiral into the depths of depression over the loss of the car or our company. It was what it was.

I managed to keep my regret and frustration in check for 30 years. But eventually that closet door burst open and I fell apart over my unfulfilled dream.

■ ■ ■

Throughout the late summer and early fall of 1970 I was anxious about the rocket motor. I was working as a research technician for Ewing Engineering in Milwaukee and actually liked my job. Initially it seemed like it would be entry-level and kind of repetitive, but as the months went on I realized the company was more interested in research and development than I thought. I was happily surprised to be assigned challenging projects and work with interesting people. But every day I would sit at my desk and listen to the radio, half expecting to hear that The Blue Flame rocket car had exploded at a drag strip near Union Grove, Wisconsin. I was worried that people from Reaction Dynamics or IGT would be killed.

We used Great Lakes Dragaway in 1966 to test the X-1 rocket engine by chaining the X-1 to a telephone pole on the drag strip and running the rocket engine without letting the car move forward. I suspected that this would be the only engine test the Blue Flame rocket engine would get because that was the only type of test Dick or Pete had witnessed in the past. The Blue Flame rocket needed much more than a telephone pole and amateur observers.

In September 1970, as I settled into my professional life at Ewing Engineering, Reaction Dynamics and crew drove across the country with the intent of setting the world record in a matter of days. The Blue Flame was perched proudly on a long and sturdy trailer as the Reaction Dynamics truck towed it toward Utah. The Bonneville Salt Flats are located just outside of Wendover, Utah, about 100 miles due west of Salt Lake City. The local Holiday Inn announced "Welcome Blue Flame Crew" on their roadside marquee.

It took the crew and Gary five weeks to set the record, with only hours to spare before the 1970 racing season was over. The car and the team were plagued with problems both minor and major during their weeks on the salt. The major road block was the rocket motor. It wasn't cooperating. The psychic at Lily Dale was accurate after all.

If you are relying on a rocket to get you a record, it is not the wisest thing to lose your rocket specialist. The rest of the crew did not know how to install let alone operate the rocket system. There were two people who understood and could have implemented the rocket propulsion correctly: Jim McCormick and me.

According to Pete, the crew initially attempted to fix the car right on the salt flats, but after a while they realized they had to try something else. The crew brought the car back to Wendover Field in town and set up shop in one of the hangars. They tried to get to the bottom of the engine problems and make enough adjustments in order to set the record.

My relatives in California sent me news clippings of the events in Utah, and the press in Milwaukee covered the story of The Blue Flame every few days, so I received frequent updates. There were reporters camped out at the salt flats and each morning they would ask the crew if today was the day Gary would break the record. I don't know how many of the news stories came from critical mistakes made by the crew, actual mechanical failures, bad luck, or bored reporters cooking up stories. It is also possible that the crew or sponsor embellished the stories for the reporters in order to divert attention from the fact that they didn't know how to make the rocket motor operate properly.

I collected the headlines:

"Parachute Stop Faulty; Flame's Trial Marred"
"Blue Flame Fails Again in Record Bid"
"No Brakes at 500 m.p.h.! Pilot Slides to Stop in Seven Miles"
"Blue Flame Gets Repairs"
"Lazy Blue Flame Still Misses Mark"
"Blue Flame's Chute Fails at 555 m.p.h."
"Flame Attempt Thwarted by Wind"
"Speed Bid Postponed"
"Blue Flame Repaired For Try At World Land Speed Record"
"Flame Hits 620, but Misses Record"

Why was The Blue Flame not setting the record? What was the trouble with the car? Among other things, the Los Angeles Times reported, "A malfunction in the catalyst pack that facilitates the burning of liquefied natural gas and hydrogen peroxide in the motor of The Blue Flame Rocket Car." In another articles The Times detailed the "wild ride" Gary Gabelich endured when a fire damaged the cords holding the car's parachutes in place. When Gary tried to stop, there were no chutes. The Blue

Flame was traveling over 550 mph at the time, so the slide took seven miles! The car ended up stuck in the salt, and it took hours for the crew to pull the car from the quicksand-like muddy bog. Gary joked afterward, "The Flame was covered with salt when it stopped. You'd have thought we were being sponsored by Morton the way it looked."

The crew created an aluminum shield to protect the nylon ropes from the car's exhaust. No one had attempted the world land speed record with such a powerful car before. The Blue Flame's crew were pioneers of a sort, and they had to keep coming up with backup plan after backup plan in order to get the systems to perform correctly. The Milwaukee Journal article "Leak Stops Rocket Car" reported, "A valve broke under the stress of repeated attempts at the world land speed record by The Blue Flame and stalled the racer Thursday on the very edge of success." Apparently this caused a hose to break loose, "spraying hydrogen peroxide over the 38 foot racer's sleek nose and sending up dark clouds of smoke."

Time was ticking and money was running out.

In "Record Ride on the Tip of an Arrow" published in *True* magazine in 1971 Gary Gabelich wrote about that last morning, October 23, 1970. He wrote, "I added it up: 5 weeks, 24 runs, the physical strain, three times shot across the salt without drag chutes, the explosion and the fire, the frustration of the turnarounds, the heat of the afternoon sun baking you inside your fire suit - it all came to zero. I hadn't set a record yet."

Gary tried to coax the car himself. While the crew fueled up The Flame, he walked around the car. In his 1971 narrative he described the sweet talk he murmured to her that day.

"Come on, baby, this is it. We gotta get it on. If we don't do it today we both go home losers. Don't let me down. Get it *on.*"

The Indianapolis Star reported that project manager, Dean Dietrich, "admitted that the crew was ready to scrub the speed attempt for this year if the record was not cracked this week."

I believe it all comes down to the sponsor's decision not to test the rocket at the Malta Test Station. Pete Farnsworth and a group of team members did test the rocket motor, but they tested it themselves at the

Great Lakes Dragaway in Union Grove, Wisconsin, a test that I believe was grossly inadequate.

According to newspaper coverage of the test, steel cables held The Blue Flame in place, tethering it to a concrete and steel post sunk 12 feet into the ground. The car underwent three days of testing at Great Lakes Dragaway and was able to produce 12,400 pounds of thrust. The news article states that by Friday of that week water vapor (steam) was the only exhaust emitted from the car. The steam exhaust knocked down plants growing 50 yards away. The headlines claimed that the tests were a success, but I knew that wasn't true.

If the engine were working properly for the duration of those tests, the reporter would have seen the telltale red and blue exhaust flame 20 to 30 feet long. At the time I believed the flow control orifice hadn't been installed correctly, and the tests blew out the heat exchanger for the rocket motor.

The flow control orifice let in a small stream of LNG to the combustion chamber during phase two of the rocket firing. This small stream established a flame. The third phase was supposed to be the large amount of LNG gushing through the four spray nozzles. If the flow control orifice wasn't installed correctly the LNG would come gushing through the heat exchanger with too much force and blow out the heat exchanger. Once blown, the heat exchanger would be useless and the last two ignition phases of the rocket would never occur.

You'd get steam. Lots of steam.

But there was no flame. During those tests, the motor was ruined.

■ ■ ■

One rainy afternoon in the middle of October, 1970, Gary Gabelich showed up at my door in Germantown, Wisconsin. I don't know if he came on his own accord, or if he was asked to visit me by the crew at

Bonneville. I didn't ask. Cheryl and Phyllis were ecstatic to see Gary since I think they both had a crush on him.

We settled ourselves on the couch in our living room. Through the window I could see the headlights of the commuters rushing home along Pilgrim Road and hear the uneven bursts of acceleration as cars tried to switch lanes and pass the slower cars in their way. Phyllis brought in two Miller High Life beers and a bowl of my favorite French Burnt Peanuts and set them on the coffee table in front of the couch.

Phyllis sat down in the gold upholstered easy chair across from the couch and said, "So nice to see you, Gary. What a surprise! Aren't you busy setting world records?"

Cheryl pranced into the room. Her dark, curly hair was in pigtails and she was practically dancing a jig in her red and white romper and white ankle socks. She chanted, "Gary! Gary! I have something for you!"

Gary turned towards Cheryl and smiled. She visibly melted a few inches under his gaze.

"Really? What do you have?" he asked.

Cheryl beamed. "Love beads. I made Love Beads for you! They will bring you good luck when you drive the rocket car."

She held out a string of tiny red, white and blue beads on an elastic string. The beads formed a tight circle of love and good luck for Cheryl's hero.

"You are a sweetheart!" said Gary. "I will be proud to wear love beads from my favorite girl when I drive the rocket car."

He reached out and took the necklace from Cheryl and placed it around his neck. Cheryl swayed back and forth with a loopy grin on her freckled face. I thought she was going to collapse and hit her head on the coffee table. Phyllis got up to escort Cheryl back to the kitchen and away from Gary's magnetic powers.

"Cheryl, why don't we finish your homework," she said. "I can read with you for a while so your father and Gary have a chance to talk." Gary and I sipped our beers and popped a few Burnt Peanuts. The peanuts had a hard candy coating over them that resulted in a satisfying sweet and salty crunch.

"So, I take it this visit is more than an update on the car. I've been following the news and I guess you guys have had a hard time so far."

Gary nodded and took a deep breath. His exhale was one long sigh. He started to say something, but stopped himself with another sip of beer. Gary set his can down on the coffee table and turned to me.

"Ray, we could use your help out there," he said. "The engine isn't working right and we've tried everything. The weather isn't going to hold much longer."

I looked out the window and squinted at the onrush of headlights. We should really get some better drapes, I thought, trying to distract myself. There was only one way I'd agree to help fix the rocket engine.

"I would come out there if we get ownership of the car again," I told him.

"That's probably not going to happen, though, Ray."

"I know," I nodded. "I know."

He left later that night and returned to the salt alone. I returned to my family, trying to put The Blue Flame out of my thoughts.

■ ■ ■

The team at the Bonneville Salt Flats was running out of time and good weather. The land speed season in Utah only lasts until the first rains hit the salt each October. Gary and the crew were scrambling and trying to force more power from The Flame.

The crew was beating the hell out of the rocket motor, trying to squeeze enough horsepower out of it to set the record. The rocket was damaged, and they didn't know how to fix it. They called Jim McCormick in Buffalo, and he advised the team to get a new catalyst pack made in Salt Lake City since the first one was contaminated when unburned LNG passed through the pack's silver mesh. The crew obtained a new catalyst pack, but the car still wouldn't run fast enough. It needed phase two and three of the rocket firing and they'd never get there without three crucial parts operating correctly: the catalyst pack, the flow control orifice and the heat exchanger. Their only choice was to keep sending Gary and the car across the salt and hope to squeak out just enough horsepower to capture the record.

The Federation International de l'Automobile (FIA) has jurisdiction over world land speed records and dictates the rules of a successful land speed record. The FIA requires that a land speed vehicle complete two runs over a measured mile. The vehicle passes through the measured mile in one direction and then a return run in the opposite direction must be made within 60 minutes. The average speed of the two runs would be the recorded speed for each land speed record attempt.

No one from Dean Dietrich's Blue Flame team anticipated that it would take so long to set the record. Fuel became an issue because Gary was making so many unsuccessful runs. The record was finally broken on the last available day of racing with the help of Dana Fuller, a photographer for The Guinness Book of World Records.

Dana was covering the record attempt and taking photos for Guinness Book for much of the five weeks The Blue Flame was out at the flats. He owned a truck with a powerful engine that had been modified so he could get around in rough terrain such as salt flats. Dana was using this truck at Bonneville as home and field studio. He had an idea.

Dana approached the crew and offered to use his truck to push The Blue Flame up to about 75 miles per hour, then drop back and drive to one side so Gary could start the engine without damaging Dana's truck. This strategy would provide a couple of seconds more of full power while passing through the measured mile. Dana thought the problem with setting the record after everything of a technical nature had been resolved could be lack of fuel. Dana's theory was that the car was running out of fuel and decelerating during the measured mile.

The crew thought it was worth a try.

■　■　■

The Broadcast-Milwaukee, WI: October 23, 1970

"Gary Gabelich is officially the fastest man on earth. He piloted The Blue Flame to 622.407 miles per hour, a new world land speed record, today along a one-mile course of the famous Bonneville Salt Flats. The Blue Flame rocket car destroyed the previous land speed record held by Craig Breedlove. Breedlove went just over 600 miles per hour in his Spirit of America car back in 1965…"

My head jerked up when it registered. I expected the same type of radio broadcast about The Blue Flame just missing the record or another engine problem plaguing the crew. Every day the WTMJ broadcasters would give a bleak update about The Blue Flame's quest for a land speed record so I expected more of the same today. Shocked, I slapped the switch on the drill press and didn't even wait for it to grind to a halt. I fished my handkerchief out of my pants pocket and my Ewing Engineering baseball cap from the nearby work bench. I swiped the sweat from my forehead and jammed the cap onto my head. I glanced around the workshop for someone to tell, then decided not to. Why bother. I left the radio playing as I pushed open the side door of the workshop and stepped into the bright October sunshine.

The door slammed behind me, drowning out my words. But I heard them and felt them as they erupted from the depths of my disbelief.

"What a waste!"

■　■　■

Dana Fuller's offer was accepted and a special push bar was fabricated on site and welded to the front bumper of the truck. Dana jumped in his truck and tried it out and it worked fine.

On October 23, 1970, Dana Fuller's truck pushed the Flame to give it a running start. The record was broken in the first two attempts. The speed for Gary's first run was 617.02 mph. The crew took 52 minutes to turn the car around, repack the parachutes and examine the car to make sure it was ready to return down the salt track. The speed of the second run was 627.287 mph, which earned the world land speed record for The Blue Flame with an average speed of 622.407 mph.

Dana Fuller saved the day. Without him, The Blue Flame would not have broken the record in 1970. It was a brilliant idea and very generous. Dana's truck could have been ruined in the process.

Gary remembered how it felt to set the record. In the 1971 *True* article he wrote, "Everyone was running around shooting pictures and asking how it felt and all I could say was 'Beautiful, just *beautiful*.'"

It started to snow within a matter of hours of the new world land speed record. Winter had arrived at the Bonneville Salt Flats, officially ending the 1970 racing season.

I believe the Blue Flame would have set a land speed record greater than 800 miles per hour if the rocket engine had been tested, tuned up at the Malta Test Station, then properly installed in the car with my LNG flow control orifices prior to going to Bonneville. It would only have taken two runs on a day with good weather.

The promotional videos published by the sponsor after the record was set must be of earlier, unsuccessful runs. I believe this because in all these years I haven't seen any videos with a pickup truck pushing The Blue Flame around.

The Blue Flame held the land speed record for 13 years even though it only used half of its power.

It is still the fastest American-built car ever made.

The Blue Flame and some of the crewmembers at the Bonneville Salt Flats near Wendover, Utah (Photo courtesy of the Peter and Leah Farnsworth Collection)

Gary Gabelich and The Blue Flame
(Photo courtesy of the Peter and Leah Farnsworth Collection)

The Blue Flame at the end of a high speed run. The parachute is out to slow it from over 600 miles per hour on the Bonneville Salt Flats (Photo courtesy of the Peter and Leah Farnsworth Collection)

The sun sets on the Salt Flats, The Blue Flame and its crew
(Photo courtesy of the Peter and Leah Farnsworth Collection)

CHAPTER 23

WORKBENCH CLUE AND MYSTERY SOLVED

1971

*The Blue Flame on display at McCormick Place in Chicago after setting
the world land speed record (Photo courtesy of Roger Dausman)*

The Blue Flame made a victory lap around The United States and part of Europe after setting a new land speed record. Articles in *Life*, *Paris Match*, Germany's *Stern Briefe* and Italy's *Aviorama* in-flight magazine proclaimed the glory of The Blue Flame. Europeans were especially enamored with Gary Gabelich and his rocket-powered car because The Blue Flame was the first car to travel 1,000 kilometers per hour (kmh). Automobile collectors became smitten with the idea of owning The Flame. IGT sold The Blue Flame, I have heard, to a Dutch oil executive for $10,000. That executive was a member of an exotic car collectors club that houses their personal collections at the Auto & Technik Museum in Sinsheim, Germany.

The Blue Flame returned from its promotional tour and was parked behind the IGT offices in Illinois. After The Blue Flame was sold, it was returned to Milwaukee for shipment to its new owner in Europe. Pete Farnsworth invited me to the Reaction Dynamics shop to look it over. Our relationship was still tense, so I appreciated his thoughtfulness.

When I arrived at the shop Pete was the only one there.

"Hi, Ray," he said, as we shook hands. "Go ahead and look her over. I need to get some of these tanks out so we can ship her to Amsterdam."

"How are things going, Pete?' I asked "How's Leah?"

"Good, good. She's same as always. What about your family?"

"Good, we're all good. We've got four kids now. Our son Paul was born in July."

"Congratulations. That's great, Ray."

"Let me know if you need a hand," I said. It was good to see my one-time business partner.

Pete smiled and nodded as he turned his attention to his task at hand. The new owner wanted all of the heavy tanks and hoses removed from the car so it would be easier and less expensive to ship to Europe. The rocket engine would go with the car, so this was my last chance to examine the damage to my rocket. The shop was quiet, except for the occasional cough or clank of a wrench.

I looked over the plumbing system that the record-setting car contained and I saw that it wasn't my design. This confirmed that the rocket motor had been installed incorrectly. I turned away, disgusted. My hunch was correct all along.

I looked around to see what had changed in the shop. Everything looked pretty much as it had been on my last day in December 1969. The same posters were on the wall and there were familiar boxes of parts stacked on the floor and resting on shelves along the wall next to the chalkboard. I could hear Pete pulling on one of the large fuel tanks and cursing, so I turned to offer him some help.

My eyes skipped over the workbench along the wall.

Suddenly, my heart leapt to my throat and I felt my stomach constrict as if I had been punched.

There it was.

The flow control orifice sat on the workbench, on the same workbench and in the same spot where I had placed it in December, 1969.

It was covered in dust.

They had left it out.

■　■　■

The Blue Flame never had a chance to reach its potential because no one installed the flow control orifice when they installed the rocket motor. This caused the LNG to enter the rocket combustion chamber with too much force during the Great Lakes Dragaway tests and blow out the heat exchanger. Once the heat exchanger was ruined the LNG could not be ignited in the combustion chamber.

Therefore, the second phase of the rocket ignition was never reached and the liquefied natural gas was not burned in the record setting run. LNG may have been in the tank and on board when the record was set, but it never burned as fuel. Even if they had piped in a small jet of LNG to the engine's combustion chamber to make some flame for the cameras, that would not have added significantly to the engine thrust.

I decided not to tell Pete. Nothing would be gained. By the time I found the dusty part on the workbench The Blue Flame's land speed record days were ancient history. Pete and I were not on great speaking terms, and I didn't want to make our relationship worse by telling him. It would have made him feel bad. He had been kind enough to invite me to see the rocket. It wouldn't have served any purpose to say anything. I'm sure he wasn't thrilled about packing up his beautiful Blue Flame and sending her over to Europe, so why make him feel worse? To this day, I still haven't told him.

At the time, the news of the mishandling of my rocket design really didn't get to me that much. I decided to move on and just try to put everything in perspective. I kept busy throughout the years and even managed to maintain a casual friendship with Dick since our wives had become such close friends. We got together from time to time with our kids for family dinners at each other's houses. Dick and I avoided talking about The Blue Flame or the collapse of Reaction Dynamics.

The Blue Flame's heat exchanger before it was installed into the car

The Blue Flame's damaged heat exchanger. A hole was blown through the heat exchanger during an inferior testing situation in Milwaukee before heading to the salt flats for the land speed record attempt. This damage ruined the rocket's chance of reaching its potential.

Close up of the damage to the heat exchanger

Another angle of the damaged heat exchanger
(Photos courtesy of the Ray Dausman Collection)

As predicted, Reaction Dynamics went bankrupt. Dick and Pete were able to secure a contract with Honda to design another land speed record vehicle called the "Honda Hawk" motorcycle. They decided to model the body and chassis after The Blue Flame design. However, The Blue Flame was a four-wheeled car with a tricycle style wheel design. There were two wheels spread out in the back and two wheels located close together at the front. The front wheels looked like one wheel because they were so close. This suspension design didn't translate well to a two-wheeled motorcycle chassis. The Honda Hawk kept falling over when it was trying to set the land speed record at the Bonneville Salt Flats. The motorcycle never set a land speed record. It is my understanding that Reaction Dynamics wasn't able to secure any more major projects and therefore went bankrupt.

Leah and Pete Farnsworth bought the Reaction Dynamics assets, artifacts and property at auction during the bankruptcy proceedings. I think Pete and Leah showed how much they cared about The Blue Flame by buying the property and keeping it in their personal collection all these years. It would have been a shame to have everything scattered all over the place.

The school rocket idea with Dr. Carl Uzgiris from IITRI didn't pan out at all. It got to the point that it was obvious the new company wasn't going to work. I decided at that point to drop the idea and focus on my work at Ewing Engineering.

I admit, there were times when I would think about The Blue Flame with what I can best describe as longing and melancholy. Once in a while I would allow myself to ponder and play the "What if..." game. What if the sponsor had been reasonable and not demanded ownership of the car? What if they had installed the rocket correctly? Where would I be then?

Forty years after The Blue Flame's historic runs at Bonneville Salt Flats I was on the telephone with Dick Keller. We were talking about a possible reunion for The Blue Flame crew. During our conversation about the past he said to me that people will always say, "We woulda, shoulda, coulda done something different."

I was for saying "shoulda" in 1969!

Over the years, if I was busy, I wouldn't even think about The Blue Flame. But if I had any amount of time on my hands I would get to wondering. Thoughts of The Blue Flame would creep in if I were waiting for a flight at the airport or driving around trying to find a hotel on a business trip. Or if I wasn't too happy about the current project I was on, I'd stop and wonder what it would be like if I had my own company again. Times like that, The Flame would enter my thoughts.

This wondering over the years wasn't too painful. It produced a small ache and highlighted an empty spot I had in my heart.

It was when I saw the car again that I really felt the regret and frustration I had kept locked up for so long.

CHAPTER 24

The Lake and its Legacy

Me, about age 7, at The Lake

The Lake is my church, I think. I have traveled all over the world, but in my mind the best place to be is Lake Manitou in Rochester, Indiana. The Lake is my serenity when I am anxious or worried. It is my peace when I am troubled and an extension of my joy when I am happy. The Lake is where I have always felt free to think and feel what I wanted to because the waves and sunsets encourage my creativity and flow of ideas. If I need an answer, I stare at The Lake. If I need reassurance, I head out in my fishing boat to be closer to the rhythm of The Lake because it is the place I feel closest to my parents. I can feel their presence and guiding hand. I let my gaze relax, turn my chin to the breeze across the water and contemplate. The Lake calms me and brings me back to the core that is my true self. Answers are available when I ask The Lake, and decisions become simple with the clarifying cadence of the waves, wind and boat motors passing by.

My family owned a house on Lake Manitou since I was a very small boy. They bought it with a couple of Mother's siblings and shared both the happiness and responsibility of owning a second home. After a while my parents bought out the other owners and our family took over the whole thing. We spent the majority of our summers at The Lake when I was a kid, and I believe I'm a better person because of it. I think every kid should have a place to go and just daydream, roam, sit around and, maybe most of all, search out their own adventure.

(In the boat) My cousin Carl Bloomer, Jr. is in the front seat. I am on the left in the middle seat and my sister Marilyn is sitting on my left. My Aunt Margaret is sitting in the back seat. My sister Nola is the sitting on the hill behind the boat. (On the pier) My Aunt Louise is holding on to Carl Jr. The woman in the middle is Mother, and she is holding my sister Marilyn. My Uncle Carl Sr. is standing behind Mother.

Rochester, Indiana, is a small town in Fulton County, located in the "Michiana Area," according to the evening news desk as they sternly dole out the current events of Northern Indiana and Southern Michigan each night. The town was an early white settlement that sprouted around a grist mill set up by the federal government to fulfill their end of a treaty with the Potawatomi Nation. The grist mill ground corn for the Potawatomi people and provided a prime spot for a trading post, blacksmith shop and eventually a city called Rochester. Officials installed a dam on Rain Creek which provided power for the mill and created a 775 acre lake they dubbed "Manitou," which is Potawatomi for "good spirit" and "bad spirit." The Potawatomi people believed the lake contained a monster fish or serpent which is still referred to today as the "Manitou Monster." When the ice expands each winter with loud "booms," the old timers say it's the Manitou Monster trying to break through the ice. No wonder The Lake has always been good for my imagination.

There used to be fancy hotels on The Lake like the Fairview and Colonial Hotel. Crowds of people would take the train from Chicago or Indianapolis to relax in the sun by day and dance away the nights. Big bands and big names such as Glen Miller, Cab Calloway, Duke Ellington, Louis Armstrong and Claude Thornhill would perform on the weekends where it wasn't unusual to have two to three thousand people attending each night.

The Rochester News Sentinel ran the Colonial Hotel Weekly Calendar of Events in the late 40s that encouraged people to join in the "Dancing Under the Stars" and take advantage of the "Bathing! Boating! Fishing!" The larger hotels had open air dance floors with bandstands at one end where live music and dancing was promised "every night of the week!" Smaller venues such as the Lakeview Hotel claimed they had the "finest bar on the lake" and urged readers to make their dinner reservations for chicken, steaks, frogs legs and fish – just phone 708!

My sister Nola worked as a lifeguard at the Colonial Hotel when she was a teenager. There was a three-story diving platform set up in the lake, where the kids would show off their best dives to the delighted squeals of the people watching from the water below or from the beach in front of the hotel. There were several other private resorts to rent cabins and boats. The lake was a busy place and Rochester was a thriving small city. Overstreet's Resort had a large area for picnicking, boat rentals and shops that sold soft drinks, cold cuts and other groceries for those that lounged around or rented the cottages.

Mother would bring us down to The Lake for the summer and Dad would join us on the weekends. He would take the train from Chicago and Mother would go "into town" to pick him up every Friday. Us kids never went into town except to attend Mass every Sunday. We caught glimpses of the action from the car windows as we commuted from Harvey, Illinois, to The Lake.

The downtown streets of Rochester were lined with independent grocery stores, barber shops, drug stores, bakeries, furniture stores, hardware stores and restaurants. There was the fancy three-story Arlington Hotel on Main Street, a Boston Store, and one of my personal favorites, The Modern Dairy Bar, which sold Sealtest ice cream and specialized in curb service. One could "Get Good Goods" at the Maytag Grove Hardware store and "Buy Today or Have One Put in Lay-Away" at M. Wile and Sons Department Store because it was "Worth Your While to Shop at Wiles."

Mother brought as many supplies as she could from our house in Harvey. She would have to venture into town each week to pick up rolls and bread from Stewart's Finer Pastries and stock up on milk, eggs, Swiss steak and rump roast at Berkway Super Market on 9th and Wabash.

My summer days at The Lake followed a strict schedule:

Get up and eat breakfast.

Mess around in the yard and down by the shoreline.

Come inside, "Wash your hands!" Eat lunch.

Get on my bike, find some other kids hanging around the lake and mess around.

Come inside. "Wipe your feet!" Eat dinner.

Go fishing.

Release the fish so I wouldn't have to clean them.

Come inside. "Brush your teeth!" Go to bed.

Adhering to this "rigorous" routine allowed me plenty of time to think through ideas and explore the lake and surrounding swamps and bogs. I loved to scare up adventure and new summertime schemes. Besides my filial duties of washing my hands, wiping my feet, brushing my teeth and occasionally mowing the lawn, I could fill my hours as I saw fit. Some afternoons I just sat on a chair and looked at the lake, picking my nose. This nose picking regimen looked unproductive to certain adults, but it was the best time for me to call up questions and riddles I had been puzzling over and see if I could get some answers. If I looked at the lake long enough, the answers and ideas could just pop into my head if I had allowed the question to mull around in there until they were fully baked.

The Lake was always my place to connect with relatives. Mother's sisters would visit from Indianapolis and I spent so many happy days and nights playing with my cousins and cooking up fun things to do each day. We would forage around the shores for frogs and turtles, ride our bikes, go fishing, share family meals, splash in the water and swim to our hearts' content. The Lake reminds me of family.

When my father was nearing his mid nineties he decided he wanted to die at The Lake. Not right away, of course, but he insisted that he spend his last days there. He didn't want to just sit around some nursing home or be shuffled between his children's homes in an effort to look after him. So all six kids had a meeting and decided what we should do with him. Dad still had an apartment in Evergreen Park, Illinois, near Nola, but he informed us that he wanted to live at the lake "from now on." He was so independent and spry that we had to start keeping an eye on him because one day we found out he was up on the roof trying to get leaves out of the gutters. We decided to hire full time care to live with him at the lake house during the week, and we would all take turns staying at the lake house with him on the weekends.

Every six weeks Phyllis and I would drive down to Rochester from Wisconsin and spend time with Dad. During warm months he would sit in his metal patio chair on the lawn facing the lake. Sometimes he would sit in his metal patio chair in the driveway facing the lake. When feeling energetic he would putter around his garage and arrange his tools and organize his work bench. During the colder months we would watch Purdue games on television, play cards and read books.

It was interesting to see Dad just contemplating his world as it shrunk down to just his metal patio chair by The Lake. Dad was a good fisherman, so he was good at waiting and watching, mulling and thinking. He taught me the art of fishing and digging up the patience to appear to do nothing when that was the right thing to do. He didn't pick his nose while he was sitting in his chair, but I could see full well where I got the ability to just ponder.

My father at the lake. His love for The Lake has spanned four generations so far.

When I was growing up I never saw Dad sit still except when he was fishing. He was always tinkering with something. Dad had his knee replaced when he was in his late eighties and had to endure a stint of rehab, which he considered nothing short of a prison sentence. I went to visit him at the rehab hospital and he showed me where he placed a thick, impatient "X" through each day to mark his time in rehab until Medicare ran out and he was sent home.

Mother was good at giving instructions. I visited her in the hospital right before she passed away in 1990 at the age of 85. My daughter, Sarah, Dad and I were standing next to her bed and we were talking quietly. Mother had been in the hospital for a series of strokes and heart problems off and on over the past few years. This time she had a DNR "Do Not Resuscitate" order on file, so she didn't want to be forced back if she started to pass on. Dad left the room after a while, shuffling awkwardly on his new knee. Mother looked at me and said simply, "Take care of him."

We did. The weekends where Phyllis and I drove down to Indiana for our rotation of "Dad Watch" contained the most consecutive hours I ever spent with Dad. He was usually working when I was a kid, so I didn't spend too much time with him except when we were fishing, looking at arrowheads or when he let me "help" him with a household project. The hours were filled with quiet companionship and a sense of calmness that only The Lake could bring.

Dad died at The Lake. He was 94 and a half. I was happy for him that he was able to go out on his terms and in the place he loved so much. In true Hoosier fashion he chose to do so on a football Saturday while Purdue was winning. I guess he decided it was wise to go out on a high note, as they say.

Phyllis and I now live full time at The Lake. When my parents died they left the lake house to all six of their children. Three of us wanted to keep it, so we bought out my other siblings. For many years three couples owned the house together and negotiated a rotation that allowed for all three families to occupy the house on their allotted weeks. Phyllis and I bought a house near Rochester on the Tippecanoe River after I retired and we sold our house in Wisconsin. That was the beginning of the end of joint homeownership. After that, the lake house situation seemed to go downhill and there wasn't room for me to visit my own house to fish when it was "someone else's week" so lines were drawn and feelings were hurt. One night my sister Dorothy tried to chase me off of my own property with shrill screams and accusations of ruining "her week" because I showed up out of the blue. I had simply walked down to the pier and took my fishing boat out for my usual dusk fishing trip. We all tolerated each other for a few more years before selling the house. The new owners tore it down and built a huge replacement that sits like a huge brown eyesore on that side of the lake. It is actually a beautiful house, but it will never be the same perfect house we had for so many years. They kept Dad's garage, though. His work bench lives on!

Phyllis and I bought a house ourselves on a different shore of the lake and live there year round. I go fishing whenever I can. Our kids come down to visit during the summer and the fun continues for us at Lake Manitou. I have found that the house didn't matter as much as The Lake itself.

Family picture from 1973. From left to right: Me with Sarah on my lap, Cathy, Phyllis with Paul on her lap, and Cheryl.

Fun and fishing at The Lake continue to this day. My grandson Paul Jr. and I show off our catch of the day.

CHAPTER 25

Invitation and Fishing Contemplations

2010

Email forwarded to me from Dean Dietrich
From: "Richard Keller"
To: "Dean Dietrich"
Sent: Thursday, July 29, 2010
Subject: THE BLUE FLAME REUNION AGENDA – PLEASE RESPOND

Blue Flame Reunion Agenda
Thursday, Sept. 16
5:00 PM get together at Montego Bay Hotel
Friday, Sept. 17
10:00 AM departure from hotel to Salt Flats
Watch activities on Flats, renew old friendships and make new ones.
3:00 PM return to Hotel
5:00 Cocktail hour (cash bar)
6:00 PM Dinner

7:00 PM Program (Dean Dietrich MC)
I plan on having a roving Open Mike for all who wish to tell their story of the last 40 years and how the Blue Flame may have played a role. I hope all of you will participate.
Adjourn when we are done.
Saturday Depart

Please RSVP with names of attendees and guests to Dean Dietrich ASAP

I read the email a few times and then exited my account to check the lottery numbers online. I sat at my desk for several minutes, just staring at the lottery website and wondering how I would fit into the reunion or even if I wanted to try.

"Are we rich yet?" Phyllis asked as she walked through the office on the way to our bedroom. She was carrying an armload of sheets fresh from the dryer.

I smiled and started digging in my wallet for my lottery ticket. I always used the Quick Pick option since insisting on your own lottery numbers seems counterproductive to me. Why do so much work when Quick Picks have the same chance of winning? I glanced at my ticket and compared the numbers to the screen with the usual results. I ripped up the ticket.

"Not yet," I told Phyllis on her next trip through the office on her way to the kitchen to pour a cup of coffee. I could smell it from the office, so it must be done. It was three almost 3:30 so we were on our second round of caffeine for the day.

"One of these days," said Phyllis.

"Yup," I agreed.

I didn't say anything about the reunion to Phyllis yet. I wanted to think about it for a while. Later that night I collected my Styrofoam container of worms from the refrigerator in the garage, my orange Dang! Root Beer hat and my fishing pole. I checked the gas tank in the pontoon boat. When I was all set, I walked back into the house.

"I'm going fishing. Did you want to come along?" I asked Phyllis. She was sitting on the couch in front of the window facing the lake, reading a novel.

"I've got book club tomorrow, so I'd better stay in and finish this. We've had so much company lately I haven't had as much time to read as I usually do," she answered, holding up her copy of *The Help* by Kathryn Stockett.

It's true about the company. This summer our kids have traveled to Indiana more than usual. I think it's because our daughter Sarah told everybody they needed to keep an eye on us and not leave us alone for too long. In March I had a tumor removed from one of my salivary glands. That tumor turned out to be benign, but when the surgeon was in there he saw a lymph node that was "suspicious" so he took it out and biopsied the mass.

Secondary Squamous Cell Carcinoma was found in the suspicious lymph node. This meant that the cancer drained into the lymph node from somewhere else—the primary cancer site. I had several tests and scans done, but the doctors could not locate the primary source. I decided to take my doctor's recommendation that I go through a course of chemo and radiation this summer as a preventative measure to give me a greater chance that all of the cancer was gone.

The first time Sarah saw me after I started chemo she made a bee-line back to Wisconsin and informed our other two daughters and son that they needed to spend a lot of time at The Lake to keep us company. I believe the words she used were, "Get your ass down there! Don't believe Mom and Dad when they say everything is fine!"

I think it was the hair. I had really thick white hair forever and the sight of me with very little of it left let sent Sarah into a tailspin; squawking to her siblings that they needed to be on red alert. Our kids have been down to see us multiple times, and so have Phyllis's siblings and a few friends, so we haven't had our usual "alone time" to just read and fish.

The summer was almost over, and I have just recently finished my treatment. Most of my hair is gone, I have lost thirty pounds and my taste is shot. I lost ten of those pounds right before I found out about the cancer because Phyllis and I were on our "Poor Man's Weight Watchers Diet" where we just bought a lot of Lean Cuisine frozen meals and cut down on my beloved Dairy Queen runs. If I see an ice cream stand I feel compelled to stop, what can I say? I don't have a paper route anymore, but I have retirement savings to spend, so I feel like I deserve a treat now and then, maybe every day. Why not?

The sun was low in the sky when I backed the pontoon boat out of our parking spot next to our pier. One of the restrictions I have is that I can't be in the direct sun. During the day I stay in the shade or stay inside. My fishing trips need to be after the sun starts to set, which is okay since that is the best time to fish. All summer I've had to avoid the sun, which is harder than one might think. A friend from church volunteered to mow our lawn a couple of times and I have to wait until night time to water our flowers. Good thing I felt so tired that I didn't always feel like leaving the house.

Early in my treatment I had an allergic reaction to the chemo the doctors were pumping into me and that put me in the hospital for a week! My white blood count went down to literally nothing, (0.7) to be exact, so if I got an infection during that time I was a goner. I was in isolation for several days. All summer I have been avoiding crowds— even church because I don't want to risk getting an infection when my immune system is low.

The night was warm with just a hint of a breeze as I drove the boat past the orange bobbing buoys guarding the No Wake Zone. I have several family members that own houses on Lake Manitou, and I checked them out as I made my way to one of my favorite fishing spots. My sister Nola's house was across from Honeymoon Island on a windy point that jutted into the lake a bit. Around the corner from there I saw my nephew Roger's three story modern house with a basketball hoop planted in the water and shiny new boats parked at the pier. Nola's daughter Karen and son Bobby also owned homes at The Lake, but they were across the road from the lake side, so I couldn't see them on my cruise tonight.

Reunion. Hmm.

I killed the boat engine when I arrived at my fishing spot. Clear across the lake from my house, it was an area of the lake that contained a thick marsh with turtles, the occasional blue heron and swarms of dark, quick birds that swooped over the tall grasses continuously with loud rustles and shrieks in amazingly tight formations.

Reunion.

Hmm. My fingers baited my hook using the memory of motion after all these years of fishing. I looked hard into the marsh grasses, and hoped that clarification would come before I headed back home.

So. Actually there was no decision to be made. There was no way I could venture out to the Bonneville Salt Flats and stand around in the sun all day. My doctors haven't cleared me to be in the sun yet. Secondly, Phyllis and I had tickets for an Alaskan cruise for September 9-19, so we were going to be out of town anyway. Earlier this year I had been told a reunion was going to be taking place, but that was shortly after I found out about the cancer and of course everything was "wait and see" since that point. Phyllis and I went ahead and scheduled the cruise once we found out I would probably have enough time to recover from chemo and radiation by mid September.

The reunion invitation was forcing me to take this monkey on my back called "The Blue Flame" and put it in perspective with the rest of my life, if I could. That was my true challenge on my fishing trip tonight. I cast my line toward the cattails and reeds of the lake marsh, expertly plopping my bobbered line and hooked worm inches from a cluster of lily pads. Maybe I could snag the Manitou Monster and let that distract me from the even more intimidating task at hand. Perspective, forgiveness, regret and hope swirled around my boat and in my head.

I have seen The Blue Flame since it was relocated to Germany. Twice, actually. Both times it was a very intense and emotional experience. I am not known for showing a lot of emotion, and when I saw the Flame for the first time since it left the United States I was speechless. I felt a huge amount of anger, pride, longing, sadness and melancholy all at once that smacked me right in the forehead when I turned the corner in the museum and saw her resting on the elevated platform in her foreign home. Why is it in Germany? Great question. I wish I had a great answer. My plan for the car after setting the land speed record was to donate it to the Smithsonian Museum in Washington, D. C.

The Blue Flame sat outside of the IGT offices in Illinois after the land speed record was set. IGT refused to do anything with it besides parade it around the country for several months to show off its accomplishment. The car could have easily been repaired and tuned up to set another land speed record, this time closer to the 1,000 mph it was designed to reach. IGT had no interest in pursuing the potential of the car, however, and just left it in a back lot to rot and rust. It was almost as if they didn't want anyone to know it was there. Couldn't they have put it in their lobby at the very least? Why put it out of sight? They owned the fastest car in the world and they left it outside like a neglected and useless pile of junk metal.

In 1999 I made a trip to see The Blue Flame at the Auto & Technik Museum in Sinsheim, Germany. I was with my daughter Sarah, her husband, Paul, and Phyllis. I was surprised by my reaction. I had an immediate emotional jolt of recognition like seeing an old friend or loved one. I began to tear up and could not speak without choking up. I had to try and hide this because it was such a strong feeling and I was stunned by it. It was unexpected.

*My 1999 visit to see The Blue Flame at the Auto Technik museum
in Sinsheim, Germany*

Sarah asked me what I thought, and the museum staff wanted to know what I thought, but all I could do was walk away to gather myself before facing their questions.

"Dad? So how do you feel?" asked Sarah. I wish she hadn't.

"I…it is emotional," I answered. It was all I could say. Waves of sadness and melancholy took my breath away and I had to stop walking around the display area because I was afraid I would stumble and fall. My head felt flushed and my heart was beating in my throat. The corners of my eyes burned and slippery tears refused to stay down despite my desperate effort to squelch them. I was losing it. My facial muscles betrayed me and crumpled into a hot grimace wet with a half choked sob. I grabbed the bridge of my nose and covered my grief with a cough and quick escape to the men's room. If I tripped on my way I guess that was better than breaking down in front of everyone.

I spent a few moments in the restroom, trying to pull myself together. The only thing that helped me regain composure was to focus on good memories instead of my anger, regret and incredulity of seeing The Flame in such a foreign place. I think I was literally recoiling from reality for a minute because I was so shaken up.

I thought about the joy in designing the rocket and the amazing people I worked with during the Blue Flame project. I thought about my family and life that I had built with Phyllis. I was successful. I was happy. I had a lot to be proud of and a lot to be thankful for. There was no reason to dwell on the past. Nothing could be gained from it and I certainly didn't want to talk about it with anyone, so I managed to emerge from the restroom and join my family in the museum.

Thankfully, no one commented on my disappearance. Please, no more questions about how I feel about this visit.

Sarah walked around to the other side of the car and examined the life-sized dummy dressed up as Gary Gabelich standing next to the car. The fake Gary was all decked out in a Reaction Dynamics jacket, hat and long, gray pants. He had a weird, dopey smile that Gary certainly wouldn't have worn. Gary's smile was always quick and warm, oozing with confidence.

I was very proud of The Blue Flame and having a part in its creation. It looked like such a beautiful machine. It embodied the fulfillment of a dream and I swelled with pride to see it sitting there in such a prominent place.

Thankfully, Sarah stopped asking me questions. Phyllis knew better than to ask me to elaborate on what I was feeling at that moment. I had to stand and look at it for a long time until the emotions settled down. For some reason I couldn't handle the sadness I felt as The Blue Flame sat there where it did not belong. It belonged in the United States, not here.

A few years later I had much of the exact same reaction when I viewed it the second time. I still feel it now as I write this document. It is a feeling like viewing a body of a young person at a funeral home that had died too young and was not going to be able to fulfill his life ambitions.

I did not reply to the 40th Anniversary Reunion invitation.

CHAPTER 26

WEIGHING IT ALL AND MISTAKES WERE MADE

2010

The night was getting dark, and I hadn't caught anything yet, so I reeled in my line and removed the worm from the useless hook. I tossed the worm into the water for a free meal to the clever fish that had evaded me tonight.

The Blue Flame project was, for a while, a dream come true for me. I always hoped that somehow I would be able to design and build a large liquid propellant rocket and put it to use in some meaningful way. For at least one year, I was involved in that exact dream. I also dreamed of having my own business. That also seemed to be happening. Although I had two business partners, I was hoping for the best outcome, but it was not to be. Why?

I was never interested in racing. I was interested in rocket engines. I had mentioned that fact to my colleagues a number of times during the X-1 project. I was never going to be a land speed record guy. I certainly didn't want to drive the cars. I was in it for the rockets and nothing more. In my mind the land speed record was supposed to put our business on the map as a high tech company with the ability to design and deliver rocket-powered vehicles for the private and public sector.

Dick Keller, Pete Farnsworth and I all thought we wanted to have a business, but as it turned out I was the only one that seemed to be committed to that goal. Pete and Dick had made setting a world land speed record their greatest priority. Their fiduciary responsibility to Reaction Dynamics Inc. was of second priority. Hence, their decision to go to work for IGT and lose the Blue Flame. Land speed won out over developing a business.

At that time, none of us had any business experience and our financial investment in the Blue Flame was zero. We spent the sponsor's money on our own area of responsibility for the project. I submitted the bills, but each of us decided what to spend for our part of getting the car finished. We split up the responsibilities for the tasks required for developing the Flame. Hindsight tells me we each should have had more extensive involvement in the entire project. This would have made us a stronger partnership, and avoided the blame game later on when IGT took over the project and The Blue Flame (barely) set the record.

Reaction Dynamics did not have a business plan other than hoping that if we were successful with The Blue Flame, we could secure another high-tech project and go forward with more great projects. It was not a well thought-out plan. We had no experience in making budgets and meeting business deadlines. Pete, Dick and I were very young. I was only 26 years old when we formed Reaction Dynamics. When I left the company in 1969, I was 30 years old.

Above all, we failed to realize that the sponsor was only interested in the advertising big picture for the AGA and their deadline was 1970 for setting the speed record. 1970 was the end of the line for AGA and The Blue Flame. After that, the car might as well have vanished off the face of the Earth. It almost did. It's in Germany, after all.

We made every mistake in the book, with predictable results.

From my fishing boat I added up the facts, my emotions and the perspective that only decades can bring. I considered The Blue Flame project an abject failure and a dream unfulfilled.

CHAPTER 27

WATER SPEED AND MIXED LIQUOR

Gary Gabelich and I went back and forth for a while with the idea of designing a rocket-powered boat for him, since he wanted to hold the land speed record and water speed record simultaneously.

■ ■ ■

Dear Gary,

Hope everything is coming along fine for you these days. We missed seeing you on your last visit to Milwaukee, but our schedules just didn't match very well at that time.

I have an idea on a high-speed boat that you may be interested in. It would be rocket-powered but nothing like we have ever discussed before. It is probably unlike anything anybody has ever discussed before. It will break any speed record you want to break. In my opinion it is a completely novel idea and a great departure from "conventional" rocket boat ideas. This boat will be the ultimate in safety and reliability. IT WILL BE THE CHEAPEST WAY TO GO. The principle working fuel will be lake water which need not be carried on board the boat during the run. The engine operation is noiseless.

Of course I am still interested in drag cars, etc. etc.

Cheryl has your love beads and pictures and says thanks again. She shows them to everyone she meets. You sure made a hit with her. Next time you are in town drop in and see us.

Sincerely,
Ray

■ ■ ■

1047 Pine Avenue – Long Beach, California 90813

R. DAUSMAN
W156 N19919 PILGRIM ROAD
GERMANTOWN, WISCONSIN 53022

DEAR RAY,

PLEASE FORGIVE MY NOT WRITING SOONER. I LEFT FOR THE USAC VIETNAM HANDSHAKE TOUR NOVEMBER 28TH, AND AS YOU KNOW WAS BUSY UP TO THAT TIME. I AM VERY INTERESTED IN GETTING TOGETHER WITH YOU ON THE BOAT PROJECT; AND IF YOU'RE STILL INTERESTED IN YOU AND I RUNNING THE PROGRAM OURSELVES, I FEEL MY CONTACTS ARE STRONG ENOUGH TO OBTAIN COMPLETE FUNDING FOR A PROJECT OF THIS NATURE. I WILL BE TRAVELING EAST SOON AND WILL CALL YOU FROM CHICAGO AND SPEND THE TIME WE NEED WITH YOU. TILL THE VISIT, KEEP THE LOVE BEADS POLISHED.

SINCERELY,
GARY GABELICH

■ ■ ■

Unfortunately, it never happened. Gary couldn't find anyone to give him the money for his water speed idea. It would have been an interesting project, and I was disappointed we weren't able to see it through.

Meanwhile, I was still working at Ewing Engineering Company. Ewing was all about new product development testing and development for industry and any ideas the founder and president of the company, Lloyd Ewing, came up with. Most of the product development had to do with sewer piping or sewage treatment schemes.

I learned a great deal about corporate research and development and how to do a lot with the least amount of financial input to gain the greatest value for your dollar in product. This was the other extreme to IITRI, where usually the financial expenditure was taxpayer money from government funding. I spent nine years at Ewing, mostly involved with sewage treatment projects for Water Pollution Control Corp., Ewing Engineering's best customer and a company in which Ewing was a major stockholder.

I became expert in measuring the efficiency of submerged air diffusion equipment in sewage plants all over the country. Most sewage treatment plants process the waste products that enter their facility by maintaining a balance of waste products, dissolved oxygen and microorganisms in their tanks. The microorganisms are those found naturally in soil and water The oxygen in the waste water treatment tank keeps the microorganisms alive and the waste products serve as food for the microorganisms. The sewage treatment industry calls this potent cocktail "mixed liquor."

The mixed liquor is kept in a constant "Jacuzzi" type motion with a diffusion system. A large air compressor in a separate building forces air through pipes with holes in them. The holes produce bubbles as the air is forced through the pipes. As the bubbles rise to the top of the tank, oxygen in the bubbles dissolves into the fluid in the tank. The sewage treatment plant needs to keep the diffused oxygen level above a critical level to make sure the waste products are processed correctly.

In 1970 we moved to an old farmhouse on an operating dairy farm in Jackson, Wisconsin. We owned the house, but a local farmer owned the barn, the cows and the alfalfa fields. Shortly after moving in and doing some redecorating, Phyllis and I decided to find information on when the house was built. I went to the courthouse and did some research and found that the house was probably built about 1843. An addition was added to the original home in about 1890. The separate fieldstone summer kitchen was built in 1880.

My research revealed that the original house was built by David Fellbaum, who was an immigrant from the Kingdom of Prussia, which is now part of Poland. Phyllis and I found that finding historical data on local buildings was almost impossible, since records of building construction were not required until modern times.

I decided to do some genealogical research on the original owners of our house, the Fellbaums. I searched through the records of several churches and in so doing I got very interested in local history. I discovered there was no historical society in our community that provided an organized archive of historical information about the Town of Jackson.

Phyllis and I took matters into our own hands and decided to try and start one. I asked the Wisconsin State Historical Society how to do this and they explained a procedure that would enable us to start a society for the Town of Jackson that would also be affiliated with the Wisconsin State Historical Society. I attended the next meeting of the Jackson Town Board. I suggested that the town consider allowing a group of local residents to use an abandoned Lutheran Church on property that the town owned, as a historical museum, if this group incorporated as The Jackson Historical Society. After due consideration over several months where we worked out the details, the town agreed.

Our group formed a board of directors and incorporated in 1975 with me as the president. We moved our monthly meetings into the church and our first major project was to gather information and publish *The History of Jackson from 1843 to 1976*. This publication was intended to be a community service project and celebrate the nation's bicentennial. We also hoped to attract members into the society.

The book was very well received and our society grew quickly. We acquired a huge collection of all types of old pictures, books, genealogical information, farming and local industry artifacts of all types and sizes, and developed a computerized reference library. We restored the old church school, the church cemetery and moved and restored a nearby pioneer log home to the museum site. By the time I retired from the board in 1996 we had over 100 members and The Annual Jackson Historical Society Raspberry Festival was a local tradition and successful fundraising event.

In 1979 I left Ewing Engineering and went to work for Water Pollution Control Corp. I continued to do the same work for WPCC until 1986, when I formed R. J. Dausman Technical Services, Inc.

I was finally in business for myself and had complete control and responsibly for the company. I could now make use of the lessons learned the hard way at Reaction Dynamics during the Blue Flame project. I was now an expert in something and could try to make it on my own, at age 47. I knew that if I worked hard and did things right, I could hope to make life and security for my family much brighter.

R. J. Dausman Technical Services was an independent testing firm conducting oxygen transfer testing of wastewater treatment plants for industry and municipalities nationwide. The sewage treatment equipment company would hire me to test their equipment at sewage treatment plants around the country.

I would walk in to the treatment plant and ask to see the mixed liquor. The next thing I would do was turn off the compressor. After waiting for a brief time I would turn the diffusion system back on and record how long it took for the equipment to return the mixed liquor to the proper oxygenation levels. I would submit a report to the local municipality in which the plant operated. If the sewage treatment system didn't perform correctly the equipment company had to make repairs or adjustments to their equipment at the treatment plant.

Fortunately, it was successful and I retired at age 65 from the testing activity. My firm was considered the best in the business for all those years. I traveled to practically every state in the nation as well as several Canadian provinces and worked with dozens of companies during my water pollution testing career.

My boyhood interest in archaeology, stemming from my hobby of collecting arrowheads, led me to volunteer as a member of Archaeological Rescue (AR). AR was run by the Milwaukee County Museum and was active in excavating sites of archaeological or historical importance prior to their destruction for other uses of the land. The government mandates that a site study be conducted if an important historical site is about to be demolished. The Archaeological Rescue teams would have a short time to swoop in and salvage the artifacts for further study. It's sort of like grabbing important items out of a house that is about to be demolished or burned down by the local fire department for a training exercise.

Phyllis and I joined in 1988 and got hands-on experience helping with various excavations around the Milwaukee area. We also helped in the museum archaeology laboratory where we learned the post excavation work of archaeologists. Phyllis and I were involved in a two day study of a location near Oshkosh, Wisconsin. The site was smack dab in the middle of a very heavily traveled location both in prehistoric and historic times. A wastewater treatment lagoon was going to be installed near Lake Butte de Morts, outside Oshkosh, and AR was called in to do a survey.

The area around Lake Winnebago and surrounding lakes has been inhabited for thousands of years. Native Americans, traders, trappers and modern families have been drawn to this location due to the abundance of inland lakes and its proximity to Lake Michigan. During the course of our two day study we salvaged prehistoric artifacts such as arrowheads and fragments of clay pots that were clearly thousands of years old. We discovered archaeological elements such as evidence of a shelter, fire pits and refuse pits. Phyllis and I also found artifacts from the 1600s. This area of the state has layers upon layers of artifacts since it has always been heavily traveled. Our AR team brought the artifacts to the Milwaukee Public Museum for further study.

As part of the lab work, I learned how to do soil flotation analysis. I invented a Flote-Tech machine. The machine is a great help to archaeologists when sorting through piles and piles of soil, searching for tiny artifacts. Flote-Techs allow archaeologists to pour in buckets of soil laden with small artifacts such as pottery shards and bones. The Flote-Tech uses aeration and my unique design to simply separate the soil from the artifacts, flush the soil out of the machine and allow the artifacts to end up on a screen at the top of the machine.

My experience in sewage treatment enabled me to design and build a better method of flotation, which resulted in the Model A and Model B Flote-Tech Flotation machines. We went into the business of making and selling the machines to archaeologists both nationally and internationally in 1990. There are Flote-Tech machines collecting soil samples for historical analysis at high profile sites such as Mount Vernon, Monticello, Jamestown and Colonial Williamsburg. The University of Bournemouth in England has used their Flote-Tech machine to help categorize and process soil samples from Stonehenge.

We are still in the business of selling Flote-Tech machines. Although we no longer do excavations, we do go to archaeological conventions and meet many people in the archaeological profession, most who are now our customers.

*I am demonstrating an early model of my Flote-Tech machine,
which is used in archaeological digs.*

■ ■ ■

The Kids, Our Best Invention

Our Family at our 50th Wedding Anniversary party on June 9, 2012. From left to right (front row) Our granddaughter Emma, daughter-in-law Lisa, grandson Ben and Paul Jr., (second row) granddaughter Kelsey, grandson Connor, granddaughter Haleigh, daughters Cheryl and Cathy, me, Phyllis, son-in-law Paul, daughter Sarah, granddaughters Liz and Val, (back row) grandson John, sons-in-law Dave and Tom, granddaughter Lauren, son Paul and granddaughter Stephanie.

Cheryl is married to Dave and has three daughters and one step-son. She is very caring and dedicated to her profession and to family and friends. Cheryl is a cardiac rehab nurse. It seems like she is always on a quest to help someone. Cheryl is a world-class caregiver and has put herself in situations to help total strangers if she thinks it is the right thing to do. She has helped alleviate the pain and suffering of thousands of her fellow human beings. Her approach to life reminds me of something I read in the Bible. Jesus said, "What you do unto these the least of my brothers, you do unto me". What more can I say!

Over the years Cheryl has been a Life Flight air ambulance transport nurse for pediatrics, ski patrol member, emergency room nurse, neonatal intensive care nurse, seeing-eye dog trainer, foster parent and has volunteered for a medical mission in Haiti. She is not afraid to try something new. Cheryl gets unusual or scary (to other people) ideas on how to make a difference in this world and she never hesitates to try.

She is always inventing, in a way. If she sees something is wrong or someone has a problem she is always quick to try and fix it and doesn't give up until she does.

When Cheryl's friends call her and ask for help they know she will figure out what to do. Cheryl almost always knows someone connected to the issue at hand. "Oh, I know a doctor at work whose sister has gone through that for years! I will call her and call you back," she'll say. It's uncanny. Cheryl has been told by friends that her mindset is unique because she just has the confidence to put herself on the line if she believes it is the right thing to do. She is most proud of the fact that her twenty-something daughters tell her they want to be a mother like her when they have a family of their own.

Catherine (Cathy) is so friendly and fun to be with; a great one to talk to. She is a hard worker, and has found her niche in the health-care industry. Cathy is a MRI Technologist and has several certifications in her field. She is married to Tom and they have three children, two daughters and one son. Catherine is the best mother on earth! She has combined her artistic skills and imagination and set an example that her children are using as a model to turn themselves into very successful people in adulthood. Catherine has been extremely involved in her children's lives and has spent countless hours volunteering, driving carpools and organizing outings and trips to enrich her family life. Over the years she has sacrificed her social life by arranging her work schedule to maximize the amount of time she could spend with her children. For several years she and her husband worked opposite shifts so one of them would always be home with their kids.

Cathy is very creative and used to work in the interior design industry before she got married. Her home is always decorated extremely well and she is confident in her design style and choices. Cathy decided to go back to school and pursue a second career in the medical field once she had kids. She just decided that she needed a different career, so she figured out how to make it happen and never looked back. She loves to travel with her family, read and stay active. Cathy is probably our most nurturing, warm and easy-going child. It is hard to rattle Cathy and her laid-back confidence. She just smiles, sighs and fixes whatever needs fixing. Cathy is most proud of her kids.

Sarah is a public school teacher. She is married to Paul and they have a son named Paul. That's a lot of Pauls since her brother is named the same. Sarah has renamed him "Brother Paul" to keep things straight, but it sort of sounds like he has become a monk.

Sarah is very passionate about her career and is determined to make a difference in the lives of her students. She is an excellent motivator for her students. Sarah has excelled as an educator and educational leader in the field of gifted and talented students. She is a gifted writer and instills the joy of reading into her child Paul and all her students. Sarah has a disciplined and loving approach to parenthood while still being very playful.

While Cheryl doesn't hesitate to help the world, Sarah goes out of the way to help the people in her life that are important to her. She has a wide circle of friends. Sarah shows the important people in her life that she cares by making a point to spend time with them and make them feel important. She is creative, and an excellent problem-solver. If Sarah starts a project, she will see it through. Not too long ago she replaced her kitchen faucet just to see if she could figure it out and she did. Her mindset is "If plan A doesn't work, just cooks up several plan Bs and gives those a try." Sarah detests routine and would rather be off doing something she's never tried before. Sarah is most proud of her son and strong friendships she has nurtured throughout the years.

Our son Paul is CEO of his own consulting company. He is married to Lisa and they have three children, two daughters and one son. Paul, with his technical creativity and business acumen, has created a top notch business firm that will go world-wide soon. As a wonderful, hands-on father, Paul did whatever it took to succeed for himself and his family. He is fun to be around and has a unique sense of humor.

Paul's company focuses on information technology and product development strategy. He works with companies of all sizes from small start ups to large corporations. Paul's expertise is to take a business idea and turn it into business intelligence. He finds solutions with technology to bring the original business idea to fruition in a way that actually works. Paul is extremely determined, confident and can be stubborn with what he thinks is right. These traits have helped him be very successful in his field.

Paul planned to be a success with computers ever since he was an elementary school student. When Paul was about 11 years old he started using his 300 band modem on our family Atari 800 XL computer to access online bulletin boards to exchange programming and gaming files with his new online "friends." This was in the early 1980s, way before the Internet was a household name. Paul created a fake "grade changing" program that was supposedly connected to Kennedy Middle School's grading system. His best friend was disappointed when his report card came home with his real grades instead of the fake grades he thought Paul's program allowed him to achieve.

The FBI contacted us after Paul started to access online bulletin boards to gain information on cracking the codes at nationwide long distance carriers. The programs circulating around these online primitive bulletin boards generated random numbers until the code was cracked and voila! Free long distance. The FBI convinced Paul that free long distance wasn't worth it. In high school Paul created a very early IM/Chat program and won awards for his programming skills. He is most proud of being an entrepreneur. Paul is proud that he can take the risk with an idea and turn it into something that makes money and employs people.

CHAPTER 28

FORTY YEARS AND FIRST TIME EARS

2010

HOW TIME FLIES

PLEASE JOIN US IN CELEBRATING
THE 40TH ANNIVERSARY
OF
"THE BLUE FLAME"
BREAKING THE LAND SPEED
RECORD
Date: October 23, 2010
Place: Silver Spring Country Club
Menomonee Falls, Wisconsin
Please send payment and response
To: Pete and Leah Farnsworth

■ ■ ■

Oh boy. Pete had called me to let me know the reunion was in the works before he sent me this invitation in the mail. Phyllis and I were still debating if we should go. It didn't occur to me that someone would force my hand.

Landspeed Louise told my daughter Sarah about the reunion. Louise Ann Noeth (Landspeed Louise) is a freelance writer, photographer and graphic artist that also happens to be an expert on land speed vehicles. She wrote an illustrated history book entitled *The Bonneville Salt Flats* which chronicled the quest for speed over the last century. Louise is currently working on a photo history of The Blue Flame project. Louise and Sarah found each other during their research and have exchanged information over the last few years.

Louise seems to know everyone there is to know in the land speed world and has spent decades around the salt flats and pits surrounding speed demons. She was friends with or associated with all the famous names in speed such as Craig Breedlove, Don Garlits, Art Arfons, and yes, Gary Gabelich. She has been a racer herself for years and has test driven numerous cars and trucks. Landspeed Louise would have driven The Blue Flame herself "in a second!" -- if she had been given the chance. Louise describes herself as "most happy when the speedometer is humming along in excess of 100 mph ... top down, music up, radar detector at full sensitivity."

One night in September, 2010 Sarah called me. Her son five year old son Paul spoke to me first.

"So. Whatcha doing, Graaaaandpa?" Paul asked.

"Oh, just watching TV with Grandma."

"Did you go fishing today? Did you see The Grumpus?" Paul often asked multiple questions in a row without giving me a chance to reply. The Grumpus is an imaginary monster. I told Paul that The Grumpus lives in my basement and isn't nice to little boys that mess around when they're not supposed to. It was a private joke between us and he often asked about the whereabouts or welfare of The Grumpus.

"No, no fishing today. The Grumpus is down in the basement. I heard him knock over the litter box a few minutes ago."

Paul giggled and said, "Goodnight, Grandpa. Here's Mommy."

"Hi, Dad. So. I know about the reunion. Are you guys going?" Sarah was not one to beat around the bush.

I played dumb to buy some time. "What reunion?"

"The Blue Flame. The 40th! Are you going to come up for it? Louise told me all about it. They're going to play a recording of the land speed record in real time exactly 40 years after the record was set. I guess they have a tape of Gary while he was driving." Sarah said.

"Your mother and I are talking about it. It's possible."

It didn't occur to me that she would take matters into her own hands, although it should have. She has always been independent and strong-willed. It's almost like she didn't even hear me. Sarah tends to make announcements about what she will do or won't do and it's not easy to change her mind. I guess she reminds me of my mother that way. Her determination makes her stubborn.

"Well, I'm going. I think I should be there for the book and record what happens. Louise said I could call Pete and get an invitation."

That's that. We are going.

"Well I imagine Mother and I will be there," I said.

"Good. Because I'm going to call Cheryl, Cathy and Paul and tell them that they should come too."

A few weeks later I stood outside the main banquet room at The Silver Spring Country Club. "Blue Flame 40th Anniversary" was spelled out in little white letters on a sign by the open doorway. I wondered if anyone would know who I was. When I worked on The Blue Flame I pretty much kept to myself and either stayed in the office or spent time in Buffalo with Jim McCormick consulting on the propulsion system. Would there be people here today that held a grudge against me for refusing to stay with the project? I didn't know how many people knew why I left Reaction Dynamics. I had always wondered if there was animosity towards me. Did they know I had wanted to keep the car in the United States and wasn't happy that Reaction Dynamics lost control of our car? Would I get the cold shoulder?

"I see him. Dad! We're in here." My daughter Cheryl was standing in the doorway, smiling. "We're all here," she said. She opened the door wider and waved me inside. I held the door open for Phyllis and followed her in.

The room had ten circular tables for eight set with fancy dishes and linen napkins. Bright yellow flowers poked out of glass vases on each tabletop. Large windows opposite the door gave us a beautiful view of the golf course and mid-autumn foliage. Large folding tables with Blue Flame memorabilia lined the perimeter of this large room. Several people were perusing The Blue Flame exhibit tables with drinks in hand. I could see my oldest granddaughter, Stephanie, snapping pictures of The Blue Flame comic book at one table and my daughter Cathy was flipping through a photo album at a table nearby. A vintage videotape of Gary Gabelich and The Blue Flame's record run was playing in a loop on a small TV set up on the very last table in the corner.

Phyllis and I were a little late, so we didn't have time to look at the displays. Landspeed Louise was crossing the fancy carpet in our direction. She is a dynamic and outspoken person. Louise has a deep, commanding voice, curly blond hair and a confident grin that she uses to attract and gain attention from her audience no matter how small or big.

"Ray! You're here. No time like the present. Your family is set up at the table in front with me. Sarah is already here. Go ahead and take a seat," said Louise.

"Good to see you, Louise," I said.

"Phyllis! Your whole gang is here. Good showing! How was the drive from Indiana?" asked Louise.

"Fine. The traffic wasn't bad at all. We took a wrong turn in some construction when we got off of 94, though. We thought we would be early and here we are late," said Phyllis.

"Ah. That's okay. This crowd will gab all day about the good old days at the drag strip. It will take a while to settle them down in time to play the first tape."

"The tape of Gary?" I asked.

"That's the one! Pete is going to play both tapes in real time as it was 40 years ago. He'll play the first run, then wait the actual turnaround time it took to get ready for the second run and then he'll play the world record run exactly 40 years after the record was set. Good stuff, Ray. I'm glad you're here." Louise grinned, patted my shoulder and walked up to the podium to check the sound system. At the very front of the room was a long table covered with white linen and flounced with a ruffled table skirt. The only thing on the table was a CD player/clock radio. Louise checked to make sure it was plugged in and popped the top to make sure a CD was loaded and ready to go.

I saw Pete and Leah Farnsworth talking to a few people near a podium they had set up at the front of the room. They were dressed in matching outfits. Pete and Leah were wearing navy blue button down shirts with a large blue and white "Blue Flame Land Speed Record Team" patch sandwiched between bright yellow capital letters that spelled out "Reaction" on top and "Dynamics" on the bottom. A circular blue and yellow "Reaction Dynamics" patch was sewn on the front of their shirt on the left side and their first names were embroidered in yellow letters on the right. Pete had shoulder patches sewn on his shirt as well. One was an American flag patch and the other was a racing symbol. They were both wearing blue jeans. I'd say they hadn't changed much over the years. Pete still had carefully combed brown hair, intense eyes and a square jaw. Leah still had her pretty smile, quick energy and warm enthusiasm. They lived nearby in Menomonee Falls, Wisconsin, which is about twenty minutes northwest of Milwaukee. They moved to the area decades ago to raise their three kids in a safe neighborhood with lots of space and good schools.

As I waited for Pete and Leah to finish their conversation I glanced over and noticed that there was a cake table set up to the right of the podium. I nudged Phyllis and pointed toward the table. Pete and Leah had arranged for two elaborately decorated cakes to mark this important event. Why two? I looked closer. They were rectangular cakes that fed probably close to 50 people each. The top of each was decorated with a large frosting photo of The Blue Flame in the center. Blue icing was piped around the edge of each cake. I studied the cake further and discovered that the message was different. One cake read, "40th Anniversary 622.407 mile ~ Land Speed Record" and the other had "40th Anniversary 630.888 kilo ~ Land Speed Record." Pete and Leah were very thorough to cover both bases! The Blue Flame held the land speed record for the kilometer until 1997. I took a picture of each cake and turned back to see if Pete was free to talk and he was.

I walked up to Pete as he was setting his drink down on the table to mark his spot. Leah was standing next to him.

"Hi, Pete," I said, "Hi, Leah."

Pete turned around. "Ray. Glad you could make it."

"Hi Ray, hi Phyllis," said Leah. She was welcoming and warm as usual.

We spent a few moments on small talk and Pete reintroduced me to his children who were joining them at the table. The only one I remember was his oldest son, Eddie. Nods and smiles all around. When I asked Pete if Dick Keller had decided to attend, Pete snorted and gave me a sideways look.

"Nope. Dick won't be here. He has a friend's birthday party today, I guess," he said.

We exchanged raised eyebrows and meaningful, "Hmphs."

Phyllis pulled on my arm and pointed to a table nearby. Sarah was waving and pointing to two empty seats next to her. Our children were all sitting at the table with nametags proclaiming their first name and "Ray Dausman's daughter" or in Paul's case "Ray Dausman's son." All three of our daughters have brown, shoulder-length hair. Cheryl and Cathy are about the same height and Sarah is several inches taller. Our son is the tallest of all and he has straight brown hair peppered with gray at his temples. Paul wears glasses and has a dry, sardonic wit and confident, sometimes dismissive demeanor. All of our children are intelligent, successful and have a self-deprecating sense of humor. Phyllis and I raised them to be independent, confident and not to take themselves too seriously. That way they don't get too disappointed if things don't work out. They can just pick themselves up and try again.

It was great to have all four of them at this 40th Anniversary event. All four are married, but the spouses were all home watching their kids.

We told Pete and Leah we would catch up later and started to take our seats. On the way we bumped into a couple of people that really made an impression on me.

Pete's oldest son, Art, stopped me. He was a small boy at the time of The Blue Flame. Art spent as much time as he could with his dad at Reaction Dynamics while Pete built the car, so I got to know him fairly well. One afternoon I took him fishing at Phantom Lake in Mukwonago, Wisconsin and gave him tips on casting and baiting a hook. I shook his hand and smiled.

"Ray! So good to see you. I'm Art. Pete's son?" he said.

"Oh, hi, Art. Do you remember my wife, Phyllis? How are you? Boy, it's been a long time, hasn't it?" I said.

"Yes. A long time. You know, Ray, I'm so glad you are here. I just have always looked up to you and I remember that you used to talk to me when I was at the shop," said Art.

"Ah, thanks. You were really such a great kid and I liked taking you fishing that one time."

"I don't know, yeah. That's was really great. I guess I just…I just really respect you---you know, with leaving the project and all. I can respect your decision. I respect you for what you did," he said.

"Thanks, Art. That means a lot, it really does. Thanks." I was really glad he told me that. It made me feel more at ease because it didn't appear there were hard feelings about how things with The Blue Flame turned out.

Gerard Brennan also approached me as I made my way across the room to my seat. He had helped Pete build The Blue Flame and had been there from the beginning of the project through the days on the salt flats. Gerard was even named "alternate driver" for The Blue Flame in case something happened to Gary Gabelich. Gerard told me much the same thing that Art did. Gerard let me know that he respected the fact that I left Reaction Dynamics and didn't participate in the land speed record attempt. I told him why I wanted to keep control of The Blue Flame and have Reaction Dynamics stay in business.

"I know, Ray. I can understand that. There weren't any bad feelings because of you leaving. I respect you for it," he said.

Those two interactions surprised me because I had no idea how The Blue Flame crew felt about me when I left or if they had spent 40 years thinking I was a colossal jerk. The fact that Art and Gerard went out of their way to let me know they respected me made me feel like I belonged in the room and that my part in the project had been recognized all along, even though I wasn't a part of the action. This lifted a weight from my shoulders which has lurked in my mind over the years. I continued on my way across the banquet room with a lighter step.

Phyllis and I finally sat down and joined our family. It made me feel very proud that they took the time to be there. My son's wife had just recently had their third child, Lauren. She had been born at 29 weeks, so he was spending his days and nights in the Neonatal Intensive Care Unit for the past several weeks. Yet he had made a point to be there for me.

There were 65 people at this event, most of who didn't work on the rocket engine with me. Several people such as Jim McCormick and a few from the shop that I knew had passed away, so there weren't too many people that I recognized. A very nice buffet lunch was served and the crowd took some time to talk quietly at their table while waiting for the program to begin.

Pete and Leah were kind enough to make sure I had a chance to address the crowd. I took the microphone and looked around the room. All eyes were on me, and I finally had a chance to clear the air a little bit. I took a deep breath.

"Most of you guys probably didn't know who I was or whatever. Be that as it may, all I can say is that it was a great pleasure working with Pete and Dick and everybody involved. The Blue Flame project was one of those things where you get one chance in your whole life to do something."

Everyone was still paying attention. My eyes fell on the X-1 rocket engine on one of the display tables in the back of the room. Pete and Leah had arranged to track down the rocket and buy it back for their collection of Reaction Dynamics artifacts. I looked at Phyllis, who was smiling and nodding. This encouraged me to keep going. I scanned the rest of the room and decided to say what needed to be said even though I just realized it needed saying.

"I wasn't a racer. I just was not into racing. It took a while I think for everybody to figure that out because I didn't really come out and say it all the time. Even though I wasn't a racer it turned out to be something important to me. I got a chance to build a rocket engine—a big rocket engine and that's something that I had wanted to do since I was a little kid. That was my prime motivation in the project---to be able to build that rocket engine. So. Fortunately I was successful in being able to do that and one thing led to another and here we all sit."

The audience applauded and I felt a huge weight lifted off of my shoulders. I interpreted this reaction in a positive light. They accepted my perspective and valued my part of the project. I took my seat next to Phyllis and grinned at her.

"Nice job, Ray. You're right. You aren't a racer," she said with a laugh.

"Great job, Dad," said Sarah.

"Wow, Grandpa," said Stephanie. She was tall, blond and smiling from ear to ear. Stephanie is a very caring and warm person. I was proud to have her here.

■　■　■

Pete and Leah played the tape of Gary Gabelich's first run for the land speed record on October 23, 1970. Pete laid the microphone on the table directly in front of the clock radio and we listened to Gary's commentary as he sped across the salt flats in search of the world record once again. The audio was difficult to understand. What Gary was communicating to the crew was muffled for the most part but at the very end you can make out a distinctive line.

"Six fifty!" Gary said.

The recording continued with a loud whine and sound of The Blue Flame slowing down and preparing for its wide turn on the salt. The car had to return through the same measured mile within one hour to meet the requirements of an official world record. Pete picked up the microphone and said, "When he said 650, that was one minute past 40 years ago when he actually made the run. I'm sorry that the audio is not that good but that's what we have. In 46 minutes we'll play the second run."

In the meantime, Pete and I took questions from the crowd. Someone asked for more information on the van pushing The Blue Flame to give it a head start. Pete explained.

"What was so important about Dana Fuller's van that he pushed us with was that his was the only vehicle available to us to get us up to a speed that would make a difference. We had 20 seconds of burn time in the propulsion system and then we were out of fuel. We had to make the best use of that burn time and we tried to add it on to the top end by pushing him up to a certain speed."

During the question and answer period I told the audience the story of testing our 25 pound rocket in the Blue Island alley and how they were looking at, "The first guy to ever get baptized with hydrogen peroxide."

Landspeed Louise got a good laugh from the crowd when she stood up and added from the floor, "I have an addendum to that! Now you'll remember that Craig Breedlove prior to the world record being set by The Blue Flame parked his car in the water and he said at that time, what was the word? For my next trick I will set myself on fire? See? He took his cue from Ray."

At the 40ᵗʰ anniversary of The Blue Flame's land speed record run. From left to right Pete Farnsworth, Leah Farnsworth, Phyllis, me and Landspeed Louise Noeth

The cakes were served and we spent the rest of the 46 minute wait time socializing at our table. Paul filled us in on the latest news about his daughter and how she was gaining weight and warding off infections in the hospital's NICU. Sarah was flipping through the pictures on her digital camera and erasing old images in order to make room for more photos. Phyllis had a cold, so she was quietly blowing her nose from time to time. I thought it would be interesting, but not really a big deal to listen to the second run that hurtled The Blue Flame into the history books.

I was wrong. It was a very big deal.

■ ■ ■

Pete walked over to the clock radio, hit play and placed the microphone in front of the speaker once again. We all stared at this small cream colored clock radio with its blue blinking lights: 12:00…12:00…12:00…12:00. The sound rushed down at us from the ceiling speakers as if Gary himself was being channeled from the Great Race Course in the Sky.

At first all we could hear was his breathing. In and out. In and out. In and out through his oxygen mask. He sounds like Darth Vader. His respiration is by far the loudest sound, even louder than the high intensity whining and whooshing sound that is the air rushing past The Blue Flame as Dana Fuller's van pushes it down the course, approaching the measured mile. Dana Fuller pulls the van off to the side of The Blue Flame when he is done pushing Gary and this is Gary's signal that it is safe to start the rocket engine. There is also a crewmember standing to the side of the track who waves a flag at Gary when the coast is clear to fire the rocket.

What we were hearing on the recording was what Gary heard through his headset that day. The sound of the air flying past the car and the wheels rumbling down the salt combined in a relentless high-pitched whine. The Plexiglas windshield shook and salt was whipped up, spattering itself in a frenzy against the blue and silver aluminum stressed body work.

Most of us continued to stare at the clock radio, totally transfixed by the sound. I glanced around and saw that Pete and Leah were quietly eating their piece of cake. They must have heard this recording countless times. But a large part of the audience had their eyes closed, many with their heads slightly bowed, as if they were in church. It felt like church. It felt like a moment full of awe that I had never witnessed before. But somehow it did feel familiar.

Breathing in and out. In and out. In and out. In and out.

Gary's voice interrupts. "Okay, I'm getting ready to turn everything on."

Breathing in and out in and out: kwooooahhh…puhhhh… kwooooaahhh…puhhh kwoooahhh puhhh kwoooahhh puhhh.

A crewmember. "Okay, Gary. I see him waving the flag."

Gary. "We're going, baby. Right about now."

The sound on the tape changes immediately. The roar and rumble deepens and expands into a deep grumble that is groaning. Burning. Searing. Hot and piercing, the sound nails me to my chair and grabs me by the throat. I can't move. I can't blink my eyes, I can't turn my head. My stomach is being stuffed into my Adam's apple and tears spring from my eyes. My rocket. I am listening to my rocket.

After all of these years I am finally a witness. I am glad to be here. The emotion that shocked me into paralysis turns quickly to intense pride and happiness. It's like watching someone you love do something great. I know why this feeling is familiar. I have felt this way when I walked each of my daughters down the aisle, when I watched my son graduate from college and when I met my newborn grandchildren. I am bursting with this new excitement and smacked squarely in the forehead with pride and near ecstasy because I know how this recording ends.

Breathing in and out: kwooooahhhhh puhhh kwooahhhhh puhhh

Gary's voice breaks through. He is rattling off his speed. "150.........200.....250."

We can't hear breathing sounds anymore. Gary is holding his breath. His voice is getting harder to hear above the sound of the burning rocket and outside air tumbling by his cockpit.

"300…350…450!..Five!...550…Six!...650!"

The rocket has stopped burning and the high pitched whine is the only thing we can hear. Then Gary's voice once more. "We did it! Yeah!"

Pete stopped the recording. The audience broke into applause. There were a few cheers and one or two whistles. He turned slowly to face the crowd. Pete said something next that meant a lot to me.

"40 years ago to the minute we set the land speed record and all of you…WE did it!" said Pete. "It was very important in our lives and hopefully it's been peripherally important in your lives too."

Leah clapped enthusiastically and beamed in Pete's direction. Everything fell into place. Their uniforms. The reunion. The fact that they had reclaimed the X-1 rocket engine. The photo albums and artifacts that they had kept in pristine condition for 40 years. Pete gave Leah a huge smile and a nod that honored their love of this special car that has been in their hearts and in their family for all these years. Pete and Leah have been the caretakers of The Blue Flame. In a way the car belongs more to them than anyone else. The car may be housed in a fancy museum in Germany, but it will forever be Pete and Leah's car.

The rocket may be mine, but in the end that is just a small part of what was accomplished. I realized that I did belong in this room. My rocket may not have been installed correctly or functioning properly at the time of the land speed record run, but it was a part of the success of the car.

■　■　■

Phyllis and I drove back to Indiana the following day. The billboards on Highway 80 flashed by and I was relieved that the traffic was moderate and relatively truck-free. My thoughts drift to my part in the whole Blue Flame experience. All these years I've considered it a failure. My rocket was ruined before the record runs, so I had written it off before breaking down the levels of success and deciding if what I did was enough. I decided to make a list of pros and cons while I navigated my way back to Indiana.

I had designed the engine to go 1,000 mph. It didn't succeed. Had my design been implemented it would still hold the land speed record today. The Blue Flame left the country and is on display in a foreign country. A stranger owns it. Does that really mean it is a total failure, though? That might just be the price of invention. Can I demand that my invention work perfectly? If it doesn't, does that mean it was worth nothing? The Blue Flame is still the fastest American-built vehicle, after all, so does that mean as inventor I have to readjust my thinking?

If I look at The Blue Flame experience a different way I see all the positives. It did hold the world land speed record for the mile for 14 years. It held the world land speed record for the kilometer for 27 years. The Blue Flame was the first land speed vehicle to go 1,000 kilometers per hour. My rocket design was the first propulsion system that used a throttleable rocket engine to set a world land speed record. I left the project, but I left with my integrity intact. I stood my ground and didn't compromise my principles to fire a rocket without testing it properly.

I did form my own business and I had a long and interesting career in water pollution control. I learned from the mistakes we made during The Blue Flame project at Reaction Dynamics and made my business a success. I followed my inventive nature and started a second business selling my archaeology invention, the Flote-Tech, around the world.

I wish The Blue Flame was back in the United States. But I can still try to make that happen, can't I? Maybe instead of wishing I should start investigating the possibilities of getting the car back. I would love to donate it to the Smithsonian Institute.

Most importantly, I'm proud of my family. Phyllis and I have a strong marriage which has lasted fifty years and counting. My children have inherited my creativity, inventive nature and willingness to try new things. I believe each of my children has learned from me that it is okay to take risks. Change is good. Believe in yourself and stick to your principles because they are worth something. What's even more satisfying is that my grandchildren are learning the same lessons and starting their lives with the mindset that anything is possible if they are willing to look past their fears and just go for it.

I tally up the pros and cons that I have just compiled. The sum of my contemplation is clear. The Blue Flame was a success. Pete was right. All of us together did something important and its effects are permanent on my soul. It shaped me as a person and as a father. I tried to encourage my children to find their talents and strive to go after their goals. I think the fact that my dream wasn't entirely realized made me push my children harder to be bold, try harder, believe in the impossible and don't let fear stop you when you believe you can do something great.

I'm at a turning point here. Was it worth it? Did I succeed? What is my bottom line? Which would I rather have? My current life or something imaginary had The Blue Flame gone 1,000 mph? What's it going to be? Come on, what is the verdict?

The last thing I want to lose is my family and the life I have built with Phyllis. The very last thing. I'd rather have my family than any land speed record. A switch is flipped and the rest of The Blue Flame baggage flies out the window. Why haven't I seen it before? When it comes down to it, there's nothing I'd rather have than what I have right now.

"Ray. Let's go through South Bend and try that new Italian restaurant. It got a really positive write up in the paper." said Phyllis.

I'm a little startled because I was lost in thought. I look over at my wife. She is smiling beside me. I feel happy that I'm driving down the road with my best friend. We've been on this road literally and figuratively for a long and interesting journey so far. I tilt my head and raise my eyebrows before I answer.

"Okay," I said. "Why not?"

You never know unless you give it a try.

My favorite root beer stand. I went back to Kankakee, IL with Sarah and Phyllis in 2004 and had to stop for a hot dog and cold drink.

EPILOGUE

By Sarah Kasprowicz

June 2010

"Wowwwwww!" Paul Junior said, as only five year olds can. His blue eyes are wide and his mouth is open in a fascinated and stupefied grin.

We've been at The Lake for several days. My dad and I have been pouring over his boxes of Blue Flame records for the umpteenth time and my son has been having a blast exploring and playing at The Lake as we all have, growing up. This is the last stint at research for us, because we are nearing the end of this memoir and we are making sure we've covered all of the details. Paul has been fishing, playing, riding his bike, swimming and eating lots of ice cream, so I think The Lake has just moved up in his distinction as HIS favorite place in the world. Happens to all of us.

"What do you have there?" I ask him.

I just want to see what he will say. I, of course, know exactly what it is.

In Paul's hands is a miniature Blue Flame car. He holds it up to the light for a better look. The car is made out of plastic and sports all of the decals of the day. The white plastic has started to yellow, and the blue parts and stickers look a little faded now. Paulie has unearthed what he probably thinks is an ancient Hot Wheels car. It was in a box with old slides, photos and videos, including a short 8mm film containing the footage of the 25 lb rocket motor test done in the Blue Island alley.

"Why does Grandpa have a jet?" he asked.

"It's a rocket!" I say quickly. Good grief. A jet? I hope my dad didn't hear that. He's all the way across the house, checking his email or lottery numbers or something, so the coast is clear. My mom is at the Rochester Farmer's Market picking up Indiana corn on the cob for dinner.

"Mommy, why does Grandpa have a rocket in this box? Can I have it?" Paul asks, waving the car back and forth in front of him as if it were flying.

"Grandpa built that rocket, Paul. The car is called The Blue Flame and Grandpa built it. What do you think?" I ask.

My son stops waving the car and looks at me. His curly brown hair, dose of freckles and laughing blue eyes are the spitting image of none other than Grandpa when he was a small boy.

"I think you should put it in your book you're writing with Grandpa. That's what I think," he says.

■   ■   ■

September 2010

"Mommy, I know what I want to bring for Show and Share tomorrow in 5K," Paul Junior announces this morning.

"Really? Do you still want to bring your toy soldier? I think that is a good idea," I tell him.

"No, that's not what I want to bring. I want to bring the coolest thing we have," he tells me.

"I told you that you can't fit your hockey net in the Mystery Box for Show and Share. How about something else?" I say. Oh brother. I do not have time for this rebuttal.

"No. I want to bring Grandpa's jet."

"It's a rocket!"

"I want to bring Grandpa's rocket. Can I bring it? Will he let me?" says my son.

"Yes, Paul, Grandpa will be proud if you show and share his rocket car."

■ ■ ■

So. Show and share we have.

Thanks, Dad.

I love you, and I'm proud of you.

~Sarah

Sarah and Paul Jr. at The Lake in 2010

Acknowledgements

Thank you, "LandSpeed" Louise Noeth, for your brilliance, creativity, sense of humor and energy. Your feedback and advice have been instrumental and so appreciated. Thank you for coming up with the title and subtitle for this book and informing me that my ideas were too weak. I appreciate a straight shooter more than anything. Your belief that this story should be told has helped it become a reality.

■ ■ ■

In my opinion Pete and Leah Farnsworth have been the "parents" of The Blue Flame since the October day she broke the world record. Thank you, Pete and Leah, for organizing the 40th Anniversary Celebration in Wisconsin and for taking care of The Flame all these years.

The best ideas are the result of giving yourself a chance to stop and wonder about it all.

Author's Note

This memoir is the result of over 14 years of digging, researching and questioning. I spent weeks transcribing taped interviews and questioning my dad over and over again to bring forth memories. I consulted public news archives and libraries. I visited my dad's boyhood home in Kankakee, Illinois, and followed him around town to his favorite root beer stand and fishing spot on the riverbank. In a sense I had to become my dad in order to write in his voice. Fortunately, my dad kept meticulous records. I spent countless hours poring over boxes of yellowed file folders containing reams of musty graph paper filled with math equations, photos of dragsters, piles of business cards bound together with a rubber band, and correspondence that detailed The Blue Flame story as told by the rocket designer.

Memoirs are narrative nonfiction and quite separate from biography. Since I was not alive when most of this story unfolded, I had to take liberties with certain aspects such as who said what to whom. The conversations in this book are not direct quotes, however, they reflect the essence and tone of what happened according to my father's best recollection. The sequence of events is accurate according to newspaper and magazine articles, as well as my father's records, memories and reflections about his life.

8505558R00169

Made in the USA
San Bernardino, CA
12 February 2014